AF291390

15 MINUTE ART
PEN & INK

ANNA TROMOP

Quadrille, Penguin Random House UK, One Embassy Gardens,
8 Viaduct Gardens, London SW11 7BW

Quadrille Publishing Limited is part of the Penguin Random
House group of companies whose addresses can be found at
global.penguinrandomhouse.com

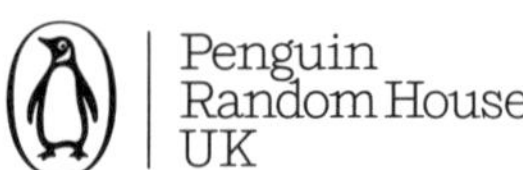

Design and layout © Quadrille 2025
Text and illustrations © Anna Tromop 2025

Published by Quadrille in 2025

www.penguin.co.uk

A CIP catalogue record for this book is available
from the British Library

ISBN 9781837834761

10 9 8 7 6 5 4 3 2 1

Managing Director: Sarah Lavelle
Editorial Director: Harriet Butt
Series Commissioning Editor: Kate Burkett
Editor: Sofie Shearman
Design Manager: Katherine Case
Design and Art Direction: Double Slice Studio
(Amelia Leuzzi & Bonnie Eichelberger)
Illustration: Anna Tromop
Senior Production Controller: Martina Georgieva

Colour reproduction by F1

Printed in China by C&C Offset Printing Co., Ltd.

The authorised representative in the EEA is Penguin Random
House Ireland, Morrison Chambers, 32 Nassau Street, Dublin
D02 YH68.

15 Minute Art

Pen & Ink

ANNA TROMOP

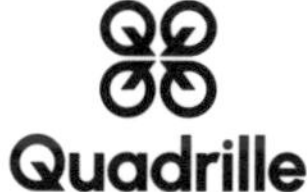
Quadrille

Hello and *Welcome*

My name is Anna Tromop and I'm an illustrator and artist from Norway. I've always been obsessed with drawing. My favourite things to draw as a young child were buses, hammerhead sharks and trolls. Although the subject matter has changed quite a bit since I was in kindergarten, my love for drawing has not.

I think my initial excitement for pen and ink came from looking at artwork from fairytales, fantasy books and magic- and medieval-looking manuscripts. I would spend hours rewriting chapters from *Harry Potter* with a quill to practise my calligraphy, which might have been slightly obsessive, but it did give me great nib control! My love of stories and natural history is still central in most of my work. Nature is a subject I keep circling back to, and it felt like a perfect fit for this book, which is structured around a camping trip through the woods.

I moved to the UK to do a degree in illustration, and enjoyed it so much that I went on to do a postgraduate degree in children's book illustration. Now I run my own business illustrating for packaging, publishing, events and more. I have an online shop and sell my work at craft markets. There is so much joy to be found in making something; I love the meditative aspect of drawing and painting, and can get absolutely lost in my work. I have always been very focused when it comes to tiny details, but please know that there is no right or wrong way to draw. In this book I will teach you how I do it. Feel free to retain the parts you like, and leave the bits you don't. Nothing is ever perfect, so have fun and keep going. Practice makes improvement.

Tools and *Materials*

Ink is an incredibly popular medium with a long history, dating all the way back to Ancient Egypt and China circa 2500 BCE. Although I've worked with a variety of media over the years, there is something about ink that keeps pulling me back in. Its appeal might be the simplicity of pen and ink and black and white, or that ink has a rich heritage to draw inspiration from.

This book focuses on pen and ink and the textures you can make using only them. You don't need much to start. You'll need a bottle of ink and a nib pen (or just a fine liner drawing pen), paper and some tissue or scrap paper to get started. If you want to begin with a sketch, a pencil and eraser are also necessary. I recommend familiarising yourself with these before branching out and trying new materials. I've listed my favourite tools, materials and brands to give you a starting point, but there are lots of great alternatives. Don't be afraid to ask at your local art store; the staff are usually incredibly helpful and knowledgeable.

Playing with new art materials is one of my favourite ways to keep things interesting and get out of a rut if I am stuck. I encourage you to keep playing and trying new things. There is a plethora of ink-related materials on the market, including coloured and metallic inks, Chinese ink sticks, marbling inks, liquid charcoal (this boggled my mind the first time I tried it and is great fun!) and many more. Try different drawing tools if you want to have a play or loosen up your drawings – use sponges, old toothbrushes, moss, grass or sticks. Anything can be a tool.

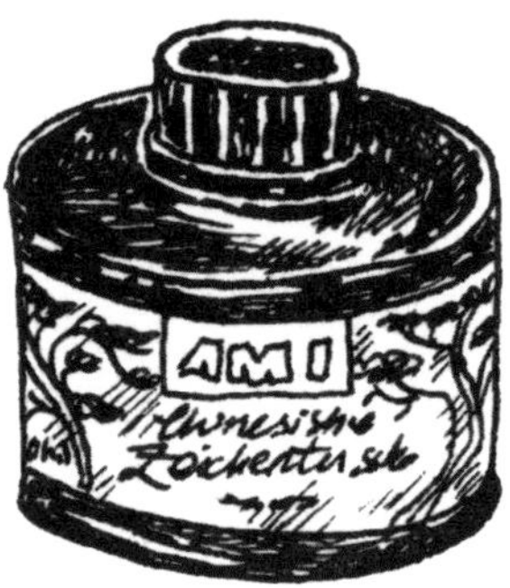

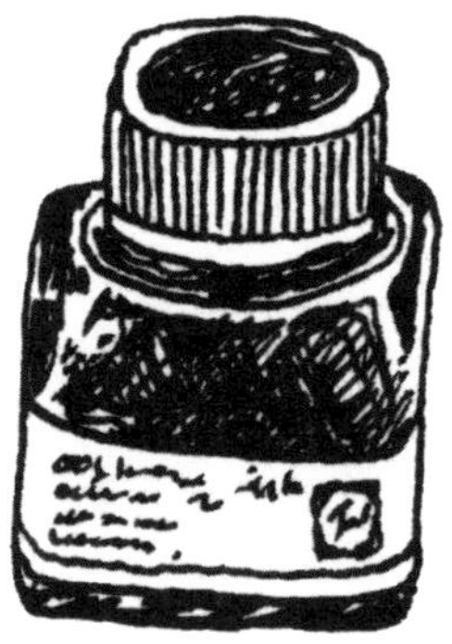

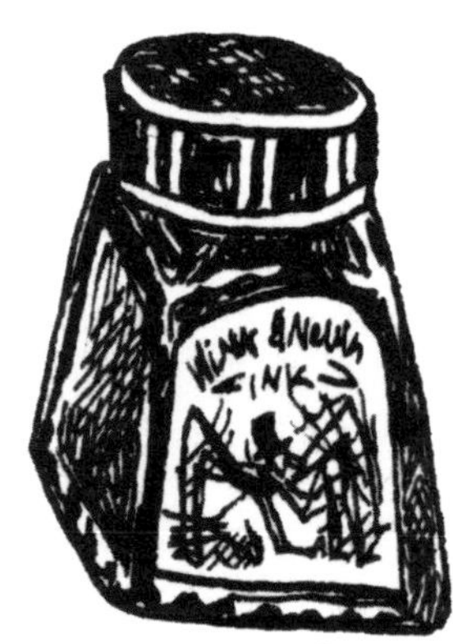

INK

I used Winsor & Newton Black Indian Ink for all the drawings in this book. There are so many brands and types of ink out there, but if you are looking for a solid black, 'Indian ink' is a good place to start. I have a big 250ml (8oz) bottle I bought probably 10 years ago and it's still going strong – just remember to put the lid on properly after you've used it, or it'll dry out.

If you happen to get some ink on a table, the floor or, in my case, smeared inside my scanner (oops!), the best advice is to clean it up right away. If you don't notice a spill until later, a bit of white spirit or nail polish remover will take you a long way in most cases. Just be aware that once ink dries (maybe don't use it with your best paintbrushes) it won't rewet.

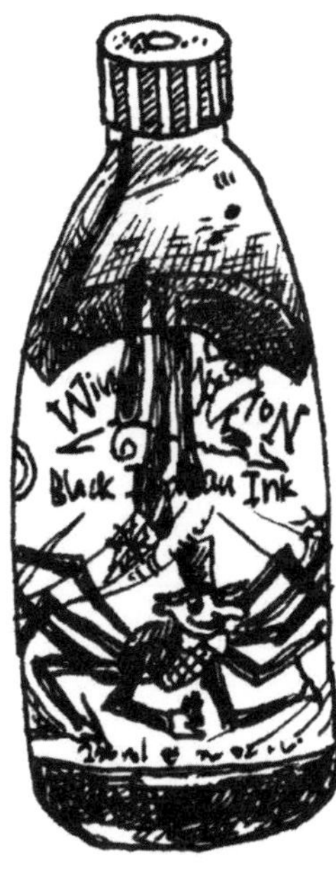

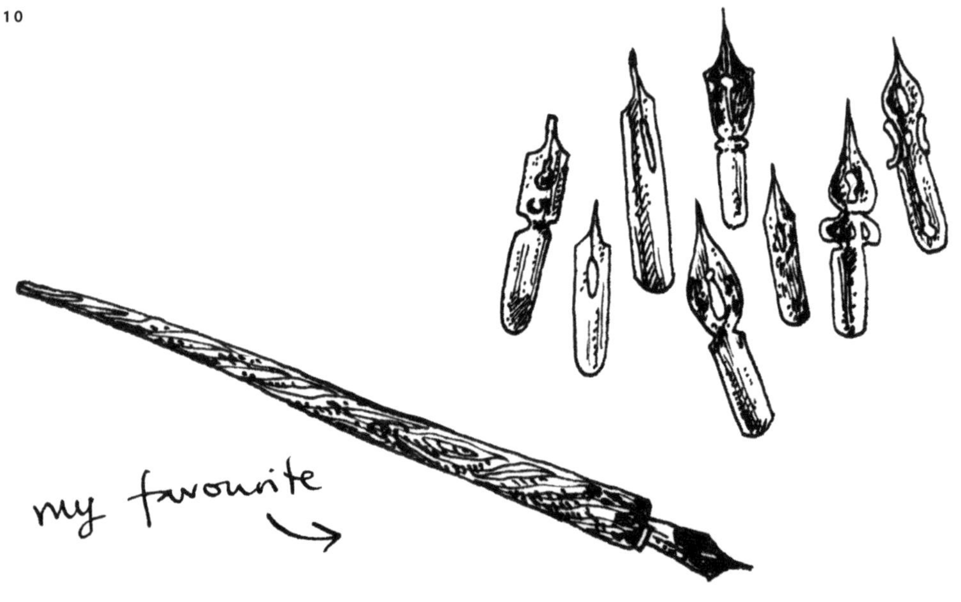

NIBS AND HANDLE

Most of the nibs I own are old and were very cheap. You never really know what kind of line a nib makes until you've tested it, and there is also no way of knowing your preference until you've tried more than one. I have a little collection I've picked up in various art stores and second-hand shops over the years, and most of them cost a few pennies each. My favourites are the small, straight ones. Any art store that sells nibs will also have handles, and your handle doesn't need to be fancy.

When dipping your nib in ink, dip it to about the halfway point (almost covering the little split down the middle). Less pressure will give you a finer line, while more pressure will open the split more and give you a thicker line. How thin and thick the line can be will depend on the type and size of your nib.

If you take care of your nibs properly they will last you a very long time. Have a bit of tissue paper to hand to wipe your nib on if you dip it too far into the ink, and remove it from your handle to clean and dry it properly once you've finished drawing.

DRAWING PENS

You might prefer to use drawing pens instead of nibs and ink throughout this book. They are easier to transport, potentially make less of a mess and are easier to control. I used fineliner pens a lot when I was a teenager, and they are great for putting in your pockets and drawing on the go. I have since shifted to pen and ink because I like the line quality better – I prefer when you can see the imperfections in my drawings, and the line is less uniform. Using pens is quicker, but I find (and this is my personal preference, it does not have to be yours!) that the image can come out a bit flat.

I still use drawing pens, but usually only in my sketchbook and when I'm drawing outside. There are lots to choose from! When it comes to fineliners, in my opinion, Microns are superior. They are waterproof and come in lots of different sizes, which you can get individually or as a set. I also love the Pilot G-TEC-C4, which is a rollerball pen that I always reach for, but sadly it is not waterproof. If you want something with a bit more variety in the line width, you can go for a brush pen.

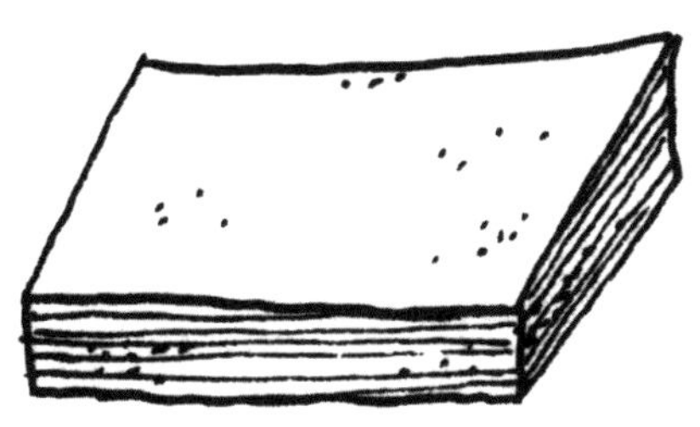

PAPER

Most types of paper will be fine for pen and ink drawing. I wouldn't use anything under 120gsm, but I have used everything from cartridge paper, watercolour paper, mixed media paper and tracing paper (which looks cool, but takes forever to dry) to old maps. If you don't have any paper lying around that you want to use, I'd recommend cartridge paper or any less-textured watercolour or mixed media paper. Experiment with rougher and smoother surfaces to figure out what you like.

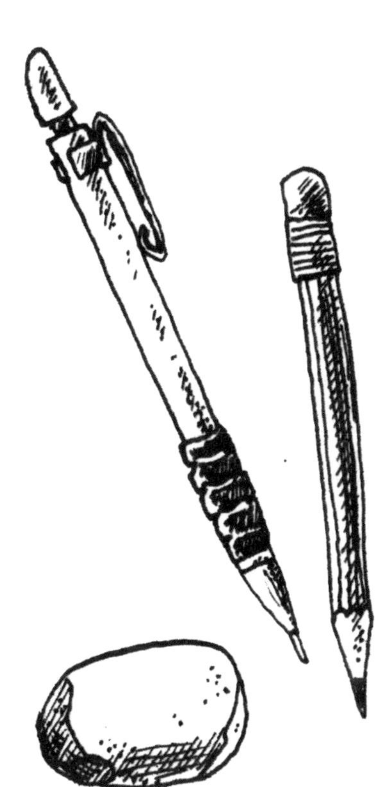

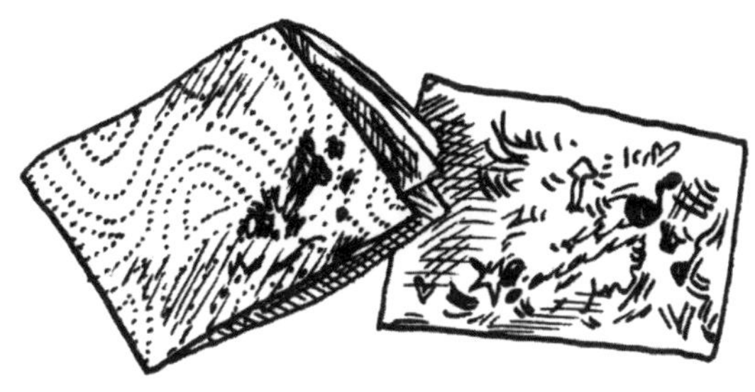

PAPER TOWELS AND SCRAP PAPER

A small piece of scrap paper is incredibly useful for testing your nib on after you've dipped it in ink, and for pushing off excess ink. I also always have tissue paper or kitchen roll to hand for wiping ink off my nib whenever I've accidentally used too much, or need a quick clean between drawings.

PENCIL AND ERASER

You'll need a pencil for sketching, and an eraser to rub out your sketch once the ink is completely dry. I like using a mechanical pencil so I don't have to sharpen it. If you are in doubt whether your ink is dry or not, always wait a bit longer. I've been too impatient countless times, and now I always wait till the next day to avoid the frustration of ruining a finished drawing.

Techniques and tone

Throughout this book we will be using a range of techniques and mark-making using pen and ink, and I want to give you an overview before we get started. When using black ink and line, you don't really have any greyscale to work with, but by layering marks you can give the illusion of tone and the gradual change from light to dark. Try squinting, or looking at the image from a distance, to see what I mean! There are more techniques and ways of achieving tone than those listed below, but they are the most fundamental, and the ones we will be using.

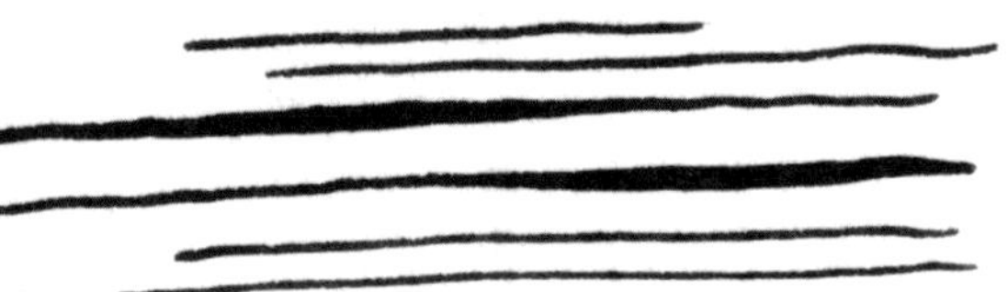

LINE

Line is probably the quickest and easiest way to describe a shape. I like to start my drawings with line, and fill in texture and shade later to take the drawing from two to three dimensions. Unlike a marker or felt tip pen, a nib pen makes it possible to play with the thickness of the line by changing the pressure you are putting on the nib. Practise your pen control by making straight and curvy lines, and see what happens when you change the pressure without lifting the nib from the paper.

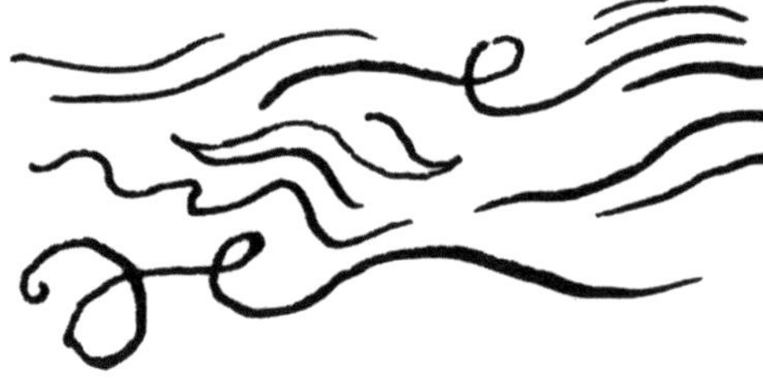

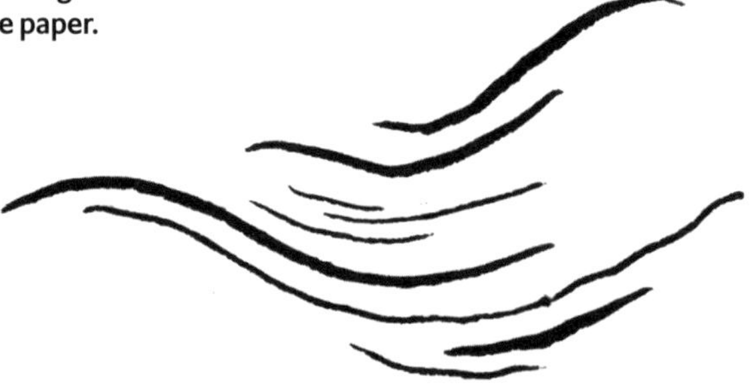

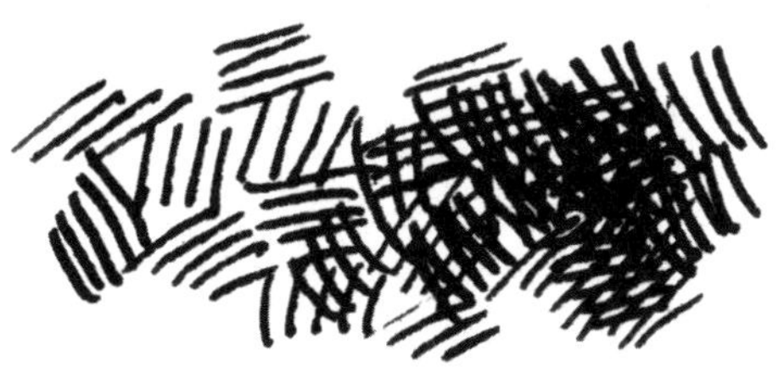

CROSSHATCHING

Crosshatching is a traditional way of shading. It is a way to trick the eye into thinking you are seeing greyscale, when there is only solid black or white. You draw short lines, parallel to each other, with varying white space between them, to make different shades of grey. After you've drawn the first set of lines, add another set on top at a different angle. You can also curve your lines to give your object shape.

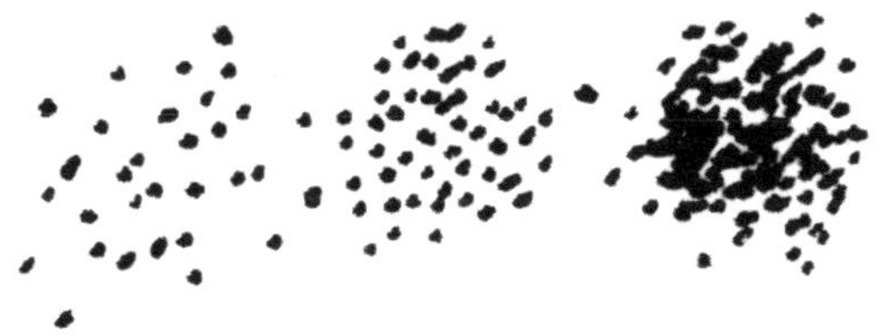

POINTILLISM

Pointillism is painting small dots, or stippling, in order to shade an object. If the dots are close together the area will look darker, and if they are further apart it will look lighter. It is by far the most time-consuming of these shading techniques, but it is also my favourite.

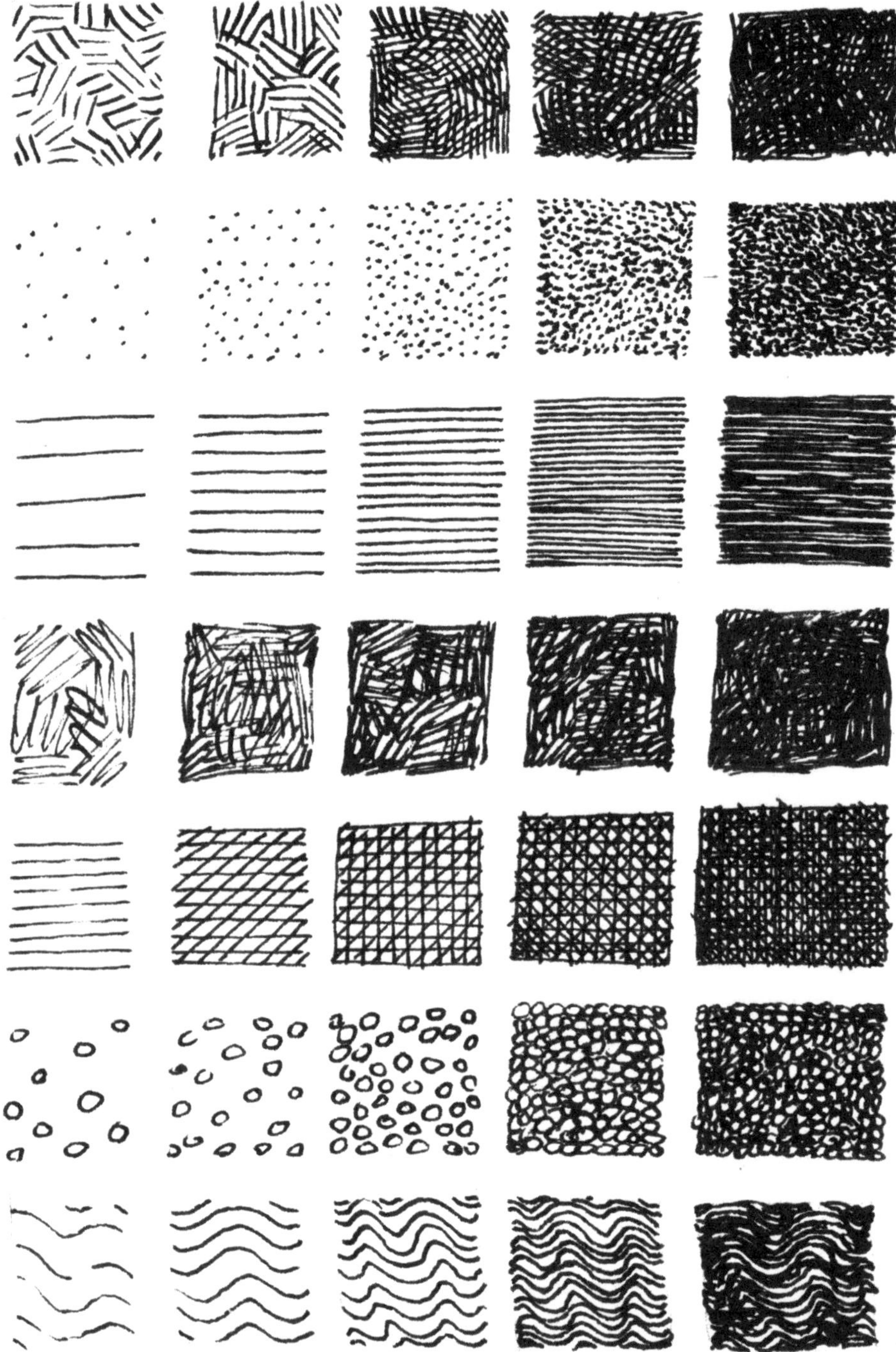

OTHER WAYS TO ACHIEVE TONE

There are really no limits except your imagination when it comes to creating tone. Ink is an incredibly versatile medium with a long history. Experiment with texture and mark-making, and maybe you will discover some fun new techniques!

Why not try out some mark-making in the space below?

Sketching

Making something out of nothing is always a bit like magic. Every drawing I make starts off with a sketch, and usually more than one before I am happy with my plan. Nobody cares if your sketch is a bit messy. Sketching is a tool, and it doesn't have to be perfect. I usually start off lightly with a pencil, and once I am confident in my placement I'll go over my final lines with more pressure. I like to trace my sketch onto my drawing paper because it is less messy and easier to erase the sketch later, but sketching and inking on the same paper is also fine.

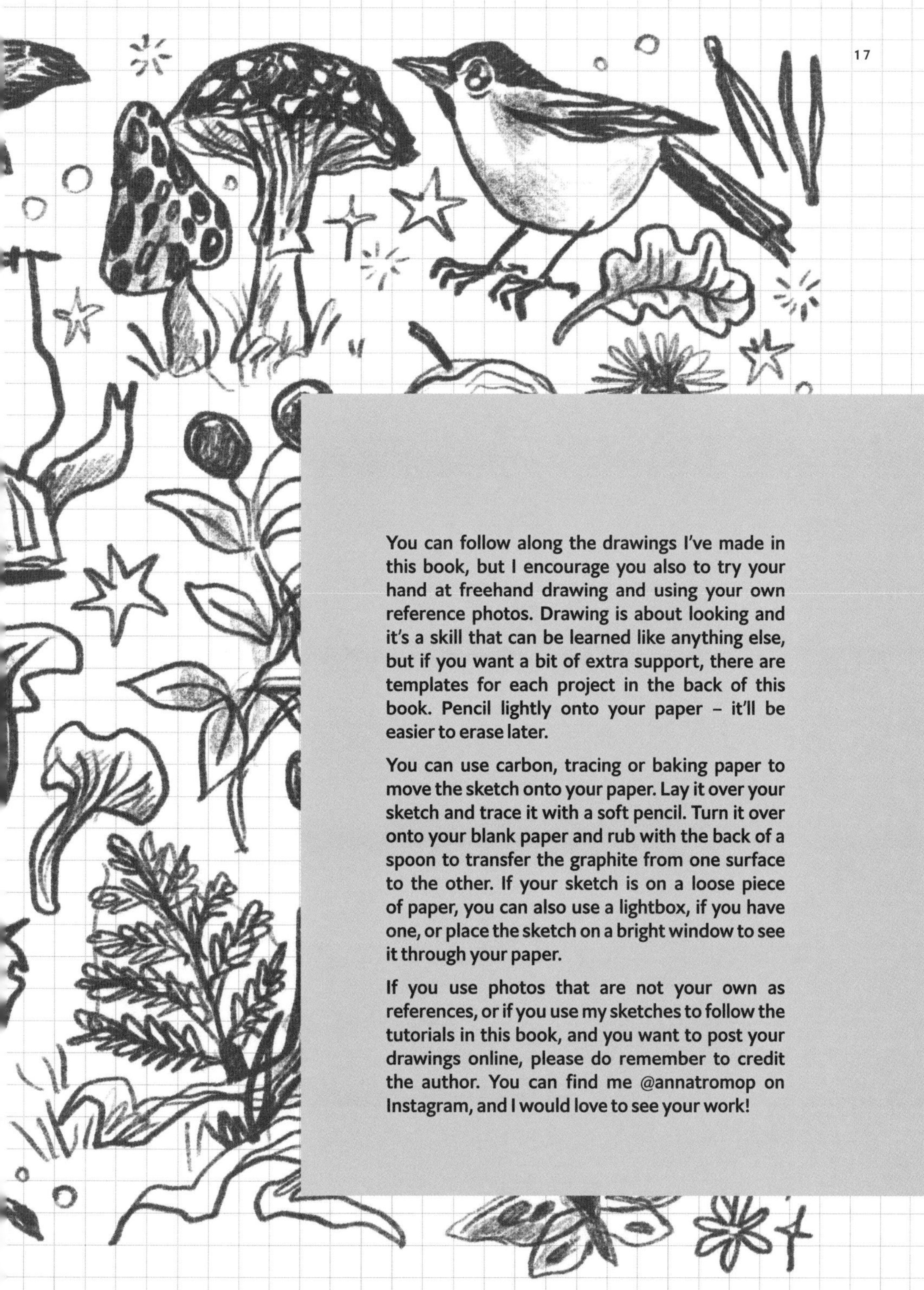

You can follow along the drawings I've made in this book, but I encourage you also to try your hand at freehand drawing and using your own reference photos. Drawing is about looking and it's a skill that can be learned like anything else, but if you want a bit of extra support, there are templates for each project in the back of this book. Pencil lightly onto your paper – it'll be easier to erase later.

You can use carbon, tracing or baking paper to move the sketch onto your paper. Lay it over your sketch and trace it with a soft pencil. Turn it over onto your blank paper and rub with the back of a spoon to transfer the graphite from one surface to the other. If your sketch is on a loose piece of paper, you can also use a lightbox, if you have one, or place the sketch on a bright window to see it through your paper.

If you use photos that are not your own as references, or if you use my sketches to follow the tutorials in this book, and you want to post your drawings online, please do remember to credit the author. You can find me @annatromop on Instagram, and I would love to see your work!

Project 01

Thistle

I love a good thistle.
This resilient and spiky
plant is beautifully
decorative.

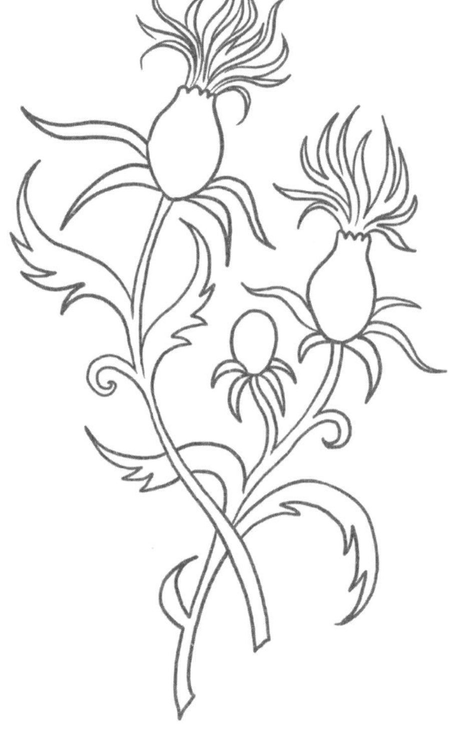

STEP 1

Sketch the shape of the thistles using flowing lines for the stalks, leaves and flowers and round shapes for the bulbs, or trace the outline on page 228.

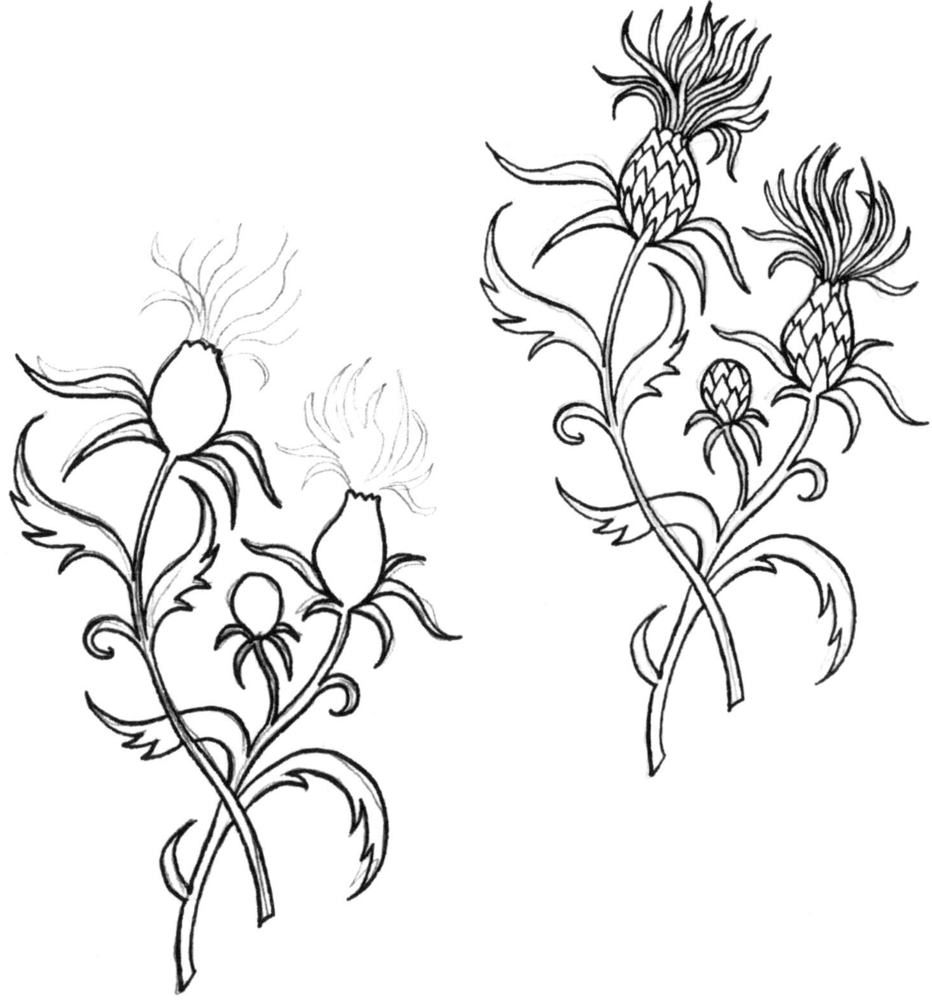

STEP 2

Ink the outline of the stalks, leaves and bulbs.

STEP 3

Add a triangle pattern to the bulbs, starting with a row at the bottom and working your way up inside the shape. Add the flowers to the top by drawing double lines connected by a sharp point. They can overlap and flow in different directions, and be as long or short as you'd like.

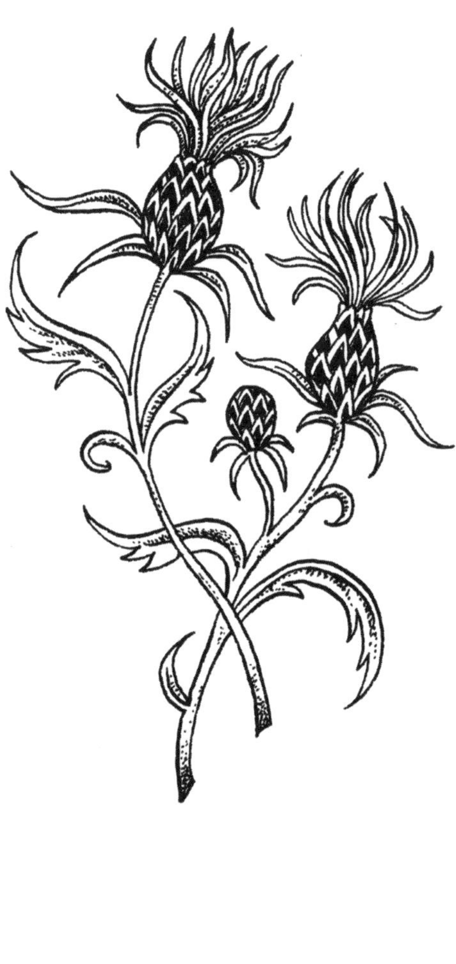

STEP 5

Use dots along the leaves, tops and stems to add a little shade. Once the ink is completely dry, rub out your pencil lines.

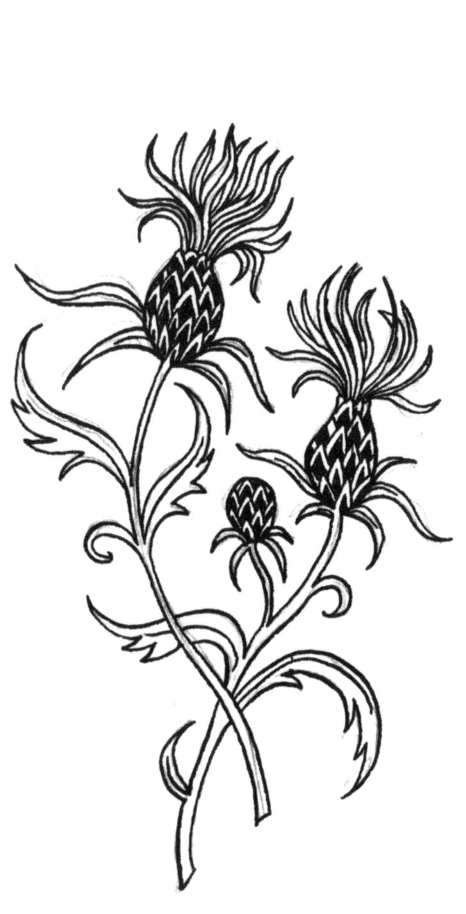

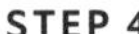

STEP 4

Inside each of the triangles on the bulbs, draw a smaller triangle inside, then fill them in black. Add a centre line detail to all the leaves.

Project 02

Acorns

&
Leaves

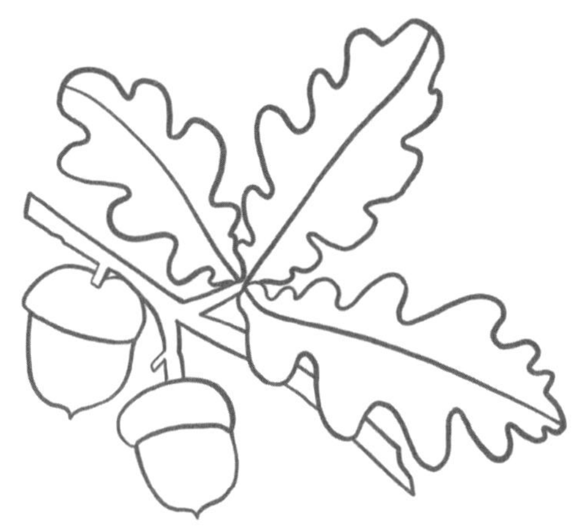

Here we are going to draw acorns and leaves. In Norse mythology, acorns were thought to protect against lightning, after Thor (the god of war) sought shelter underneath a giant oak tree during a violent storm.

STEP 1

Draw the shape of a branch with three leaves, each with rounded edges, and two acorns in their cups, or trace the outline on page 228.

STEP 2

Ink the outline of your sketch but do not ink the centre line of the leaves. Feel free to play with the pressure you put on your nib to get a variation in line thickness.

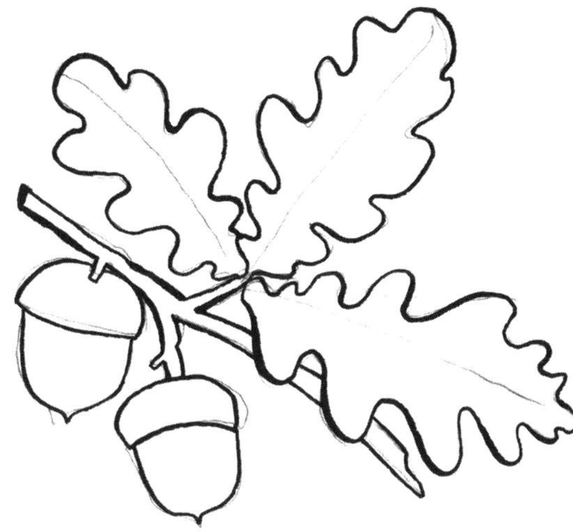

STEP 3

Draw small half circles to 'tile' the acorn cups. Using slightly wavy lines, draw a grid of veins on the leaves, running down the middle and branching outwards. The inside of these double lines will stay white. If you find this difficult to draw freehand, sketch it in pencil first.

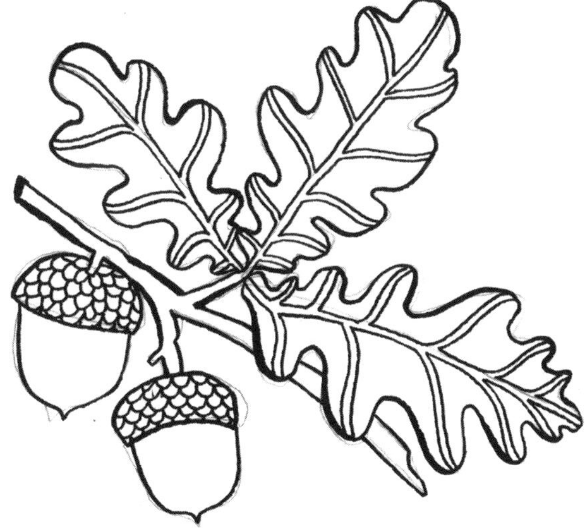

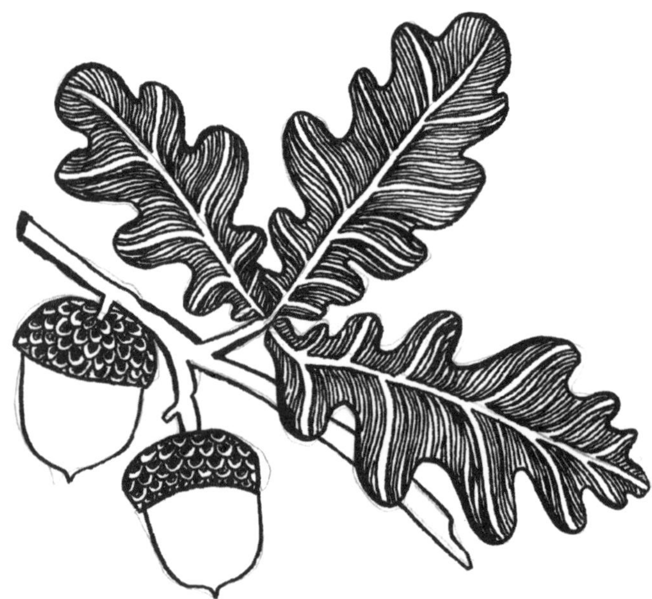

STEP 4

Inside each half circle on the acorn cups, draw an inner half circle, then fill them all in. Use thin lines running up and outwards to add texture to the leaves.

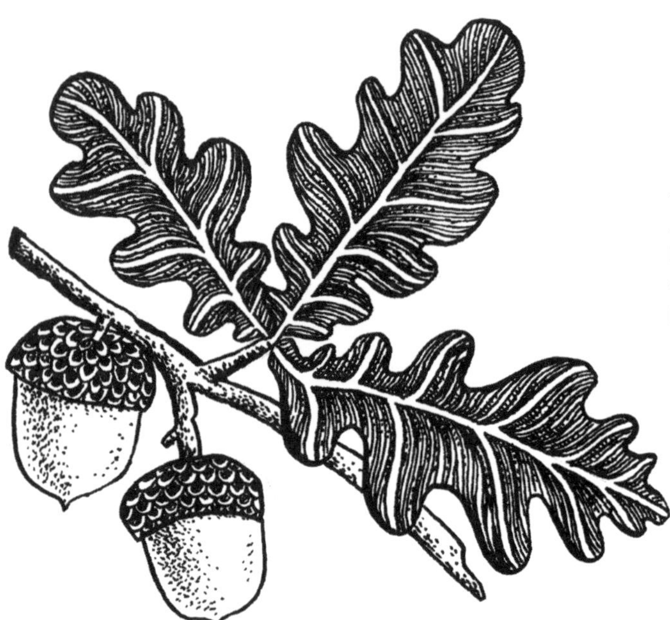

STEP 5

Use dots to add shade to one side of the acorns and the underside of the branch. Once the ink is completely dry, rub out your pencil lines.

Project 03

Fly agaric

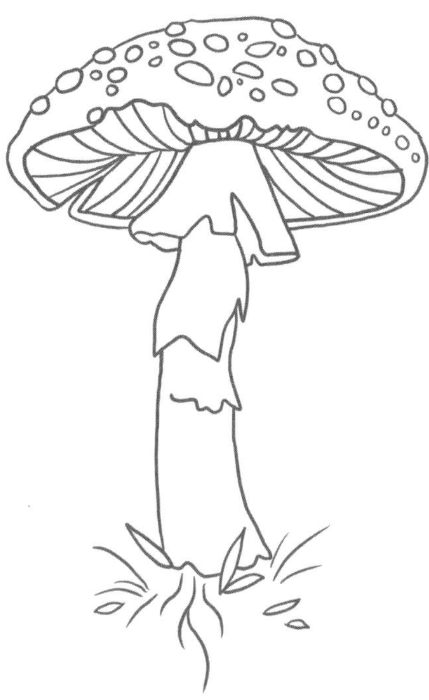

Fly agaric is probably one of the most iconic toadstools and the easiest to recognise. We're going to practise crosshatching on the cap. This would also be a great project to try out different coloured inks.

STEP 1

Sketch the stalk and cap of the toadstool, and some grass for context. Add the iconic white spots on the cap, or trace the outline on page 228. I've varied the size and shape of the spots to add visual interest and for realism.

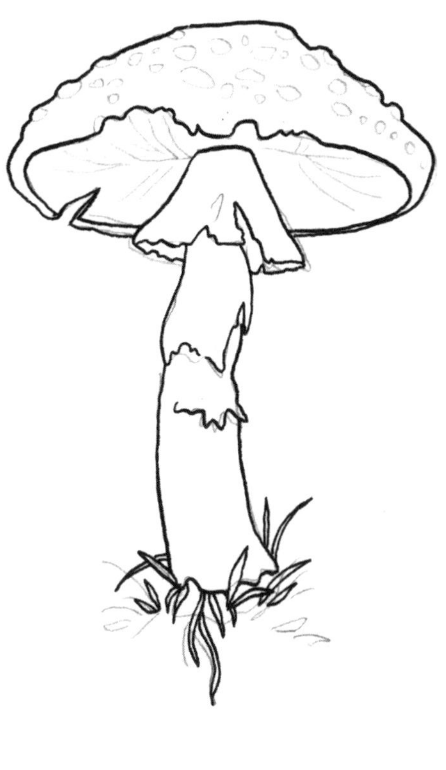

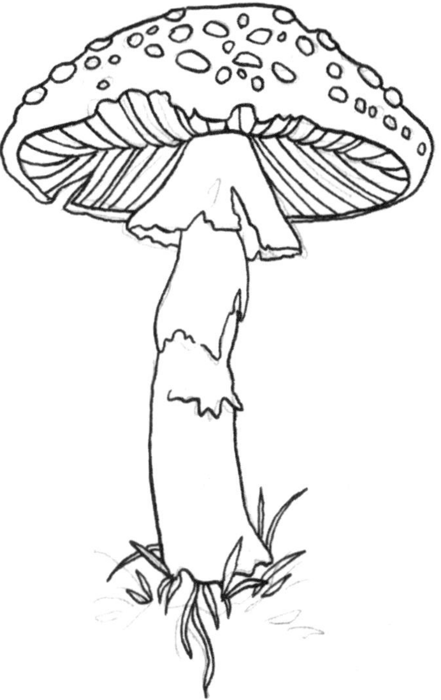

STEP 2

Ink the outline of the toadstool and add a little grass or roots to the base of the stalk to ground it.

STEP 3

Add the gills inside the cap by starting with a 'U' shape in the centre, at the top. Build upon this shape by drawing lines (half a 'U' if you like) repeatedly until you've made it round the underside of the cap. Ink the outline of the spots on top of the cap. Making the patterns a bit uneven will add to the realism.

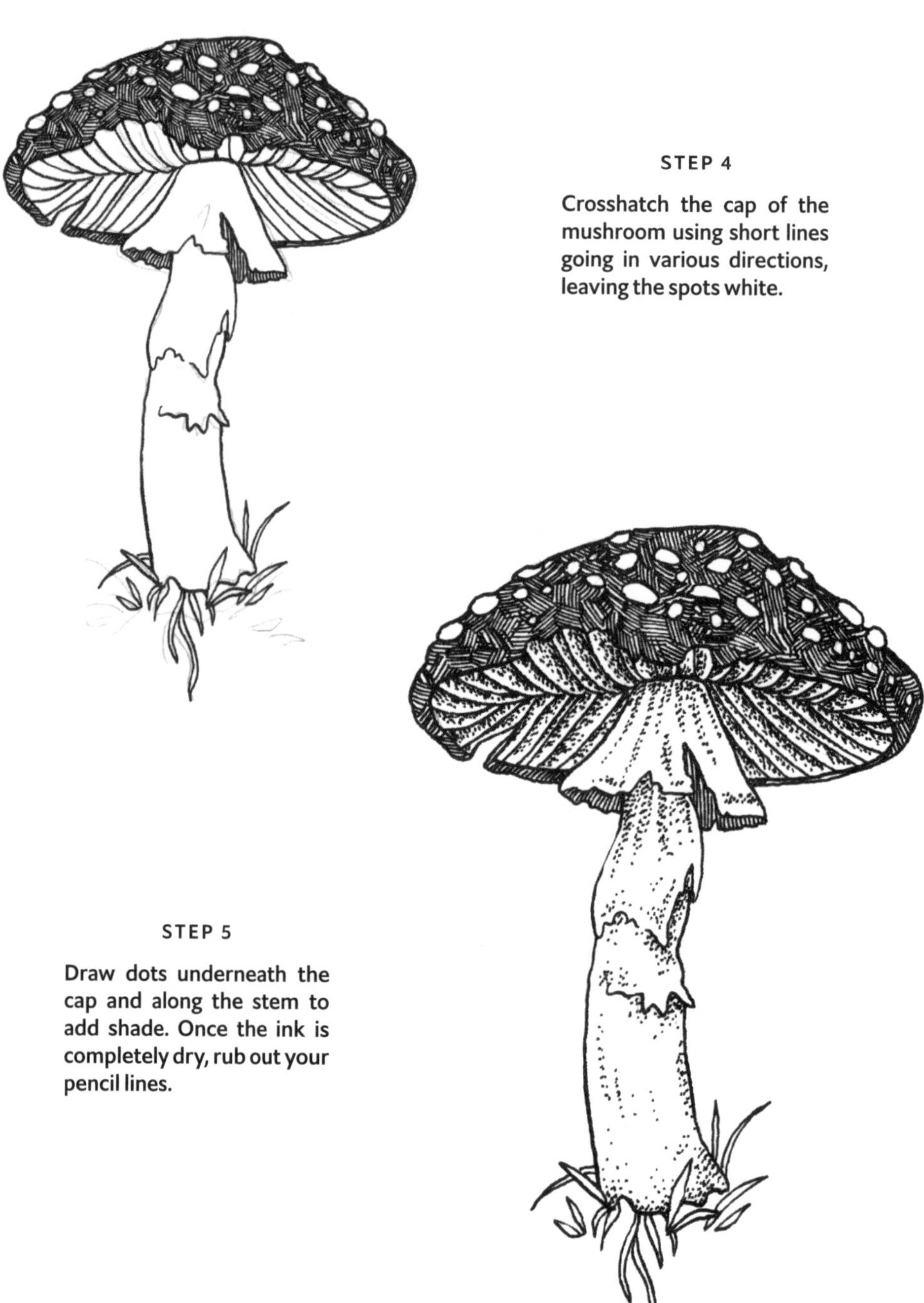

STEP 4

Crosshatch the cap of the mushroom using short lines going in various directions, leaving the spots white.

STEP 5

Draw dots underneath the cap and along the stem to add shade. Once the ink is completely dry, rub out your pencil lines.

Project 04

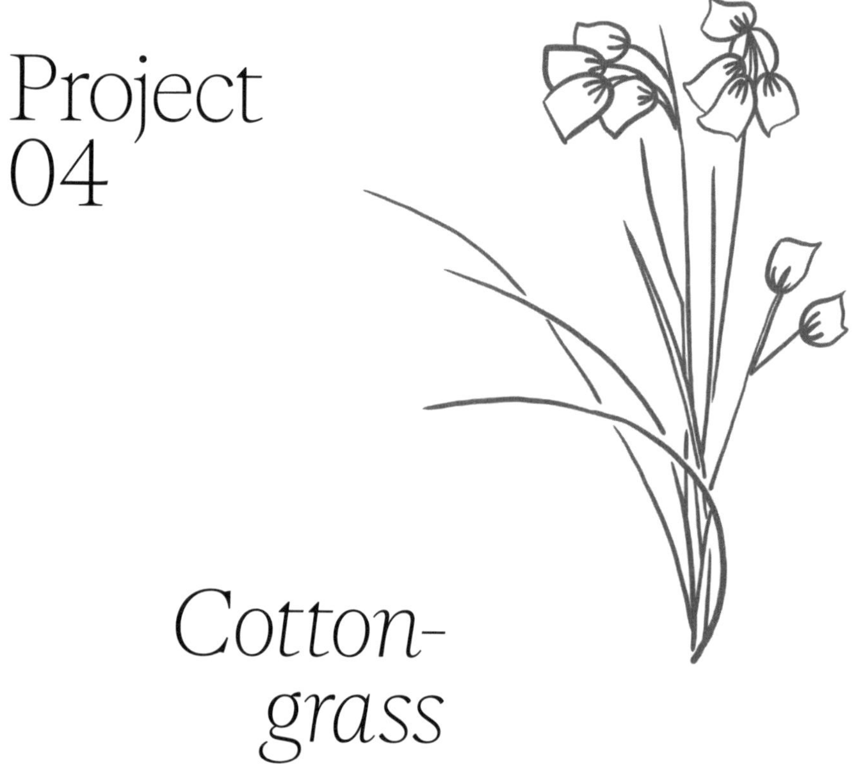

Cotton-grass

How magical is a field full of cotton-grass contrasting with the heather in autumn? You can experiment with texture thanks to the smooth stems and fluffy cotton balls.

STEP 1

Sketch out the shape of your cotton-grass with fluffy heads and long stems and leaves. Alternatively, trace the outline on page 228.

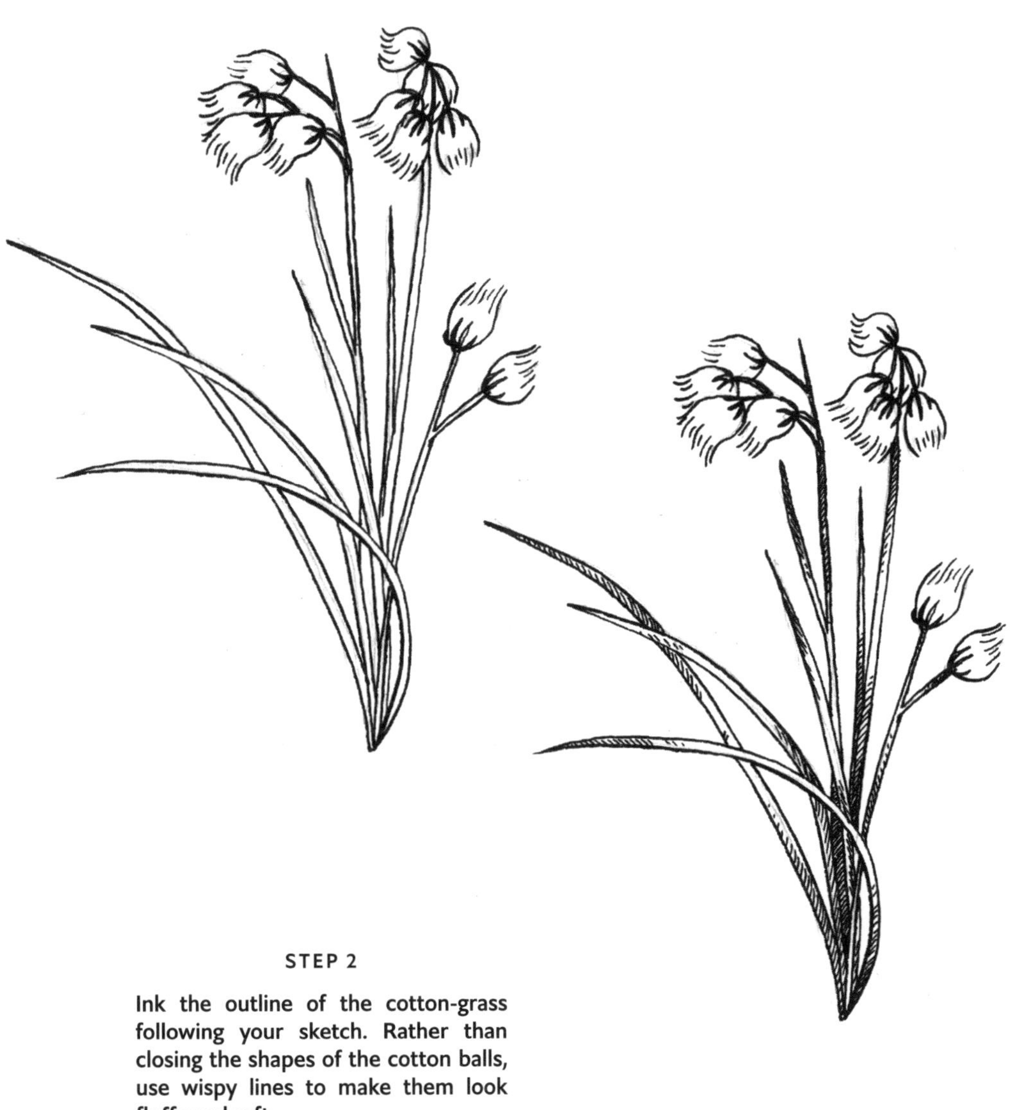

STEP 2

Ink the outline of the cotton-grass following your sketch. Rather than closing the shapes of the cotton balls, use wispy lines to make them look fluffy and soft.

STEP 3

Use small diagonal lines to shade the top and bottom of the stems.

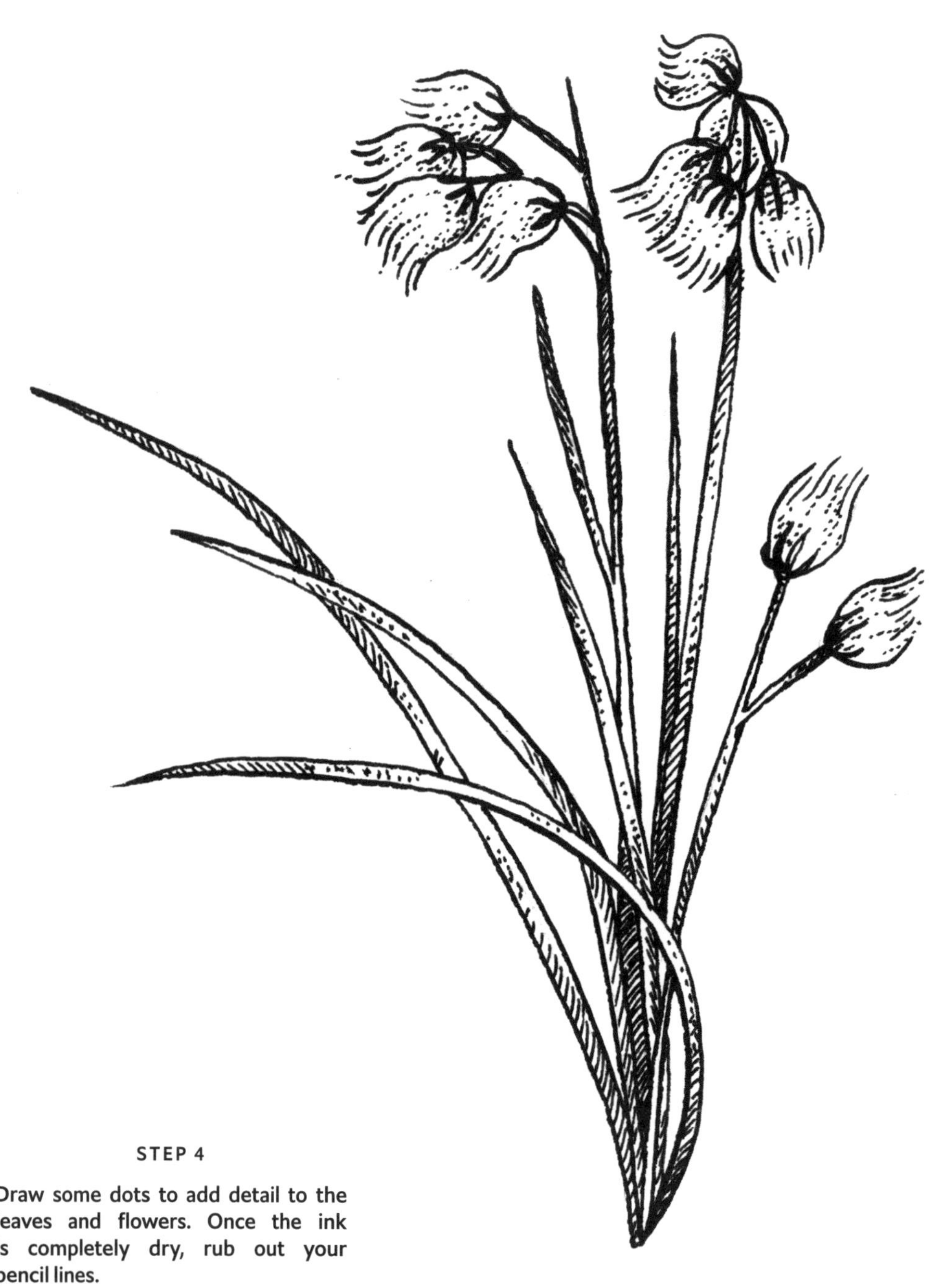

STEP 4

Draw some dots to add detail to the leaves and flowers. Once the ink is completely dry, rub out your pencil lines.

Project 05

Fern

Often overlooked, ferns are some of the oldest plants on Earth. I love drawing the symmetry and repetition of their fronds.

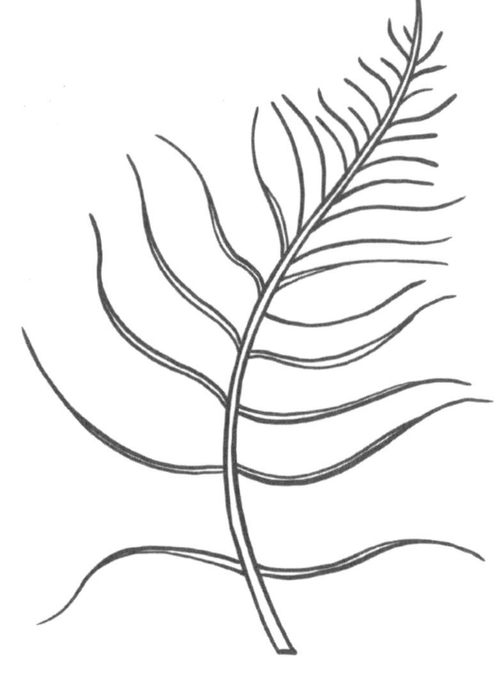

STEP 1

Sketch the fern using long, flowing lines or trace the outline on page 229.

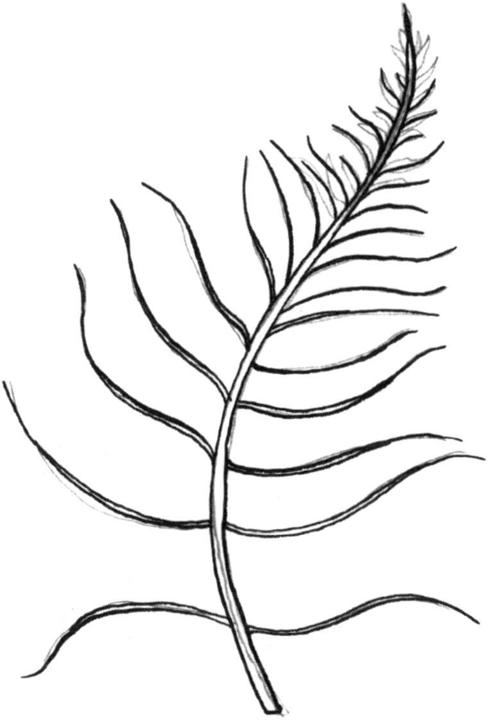

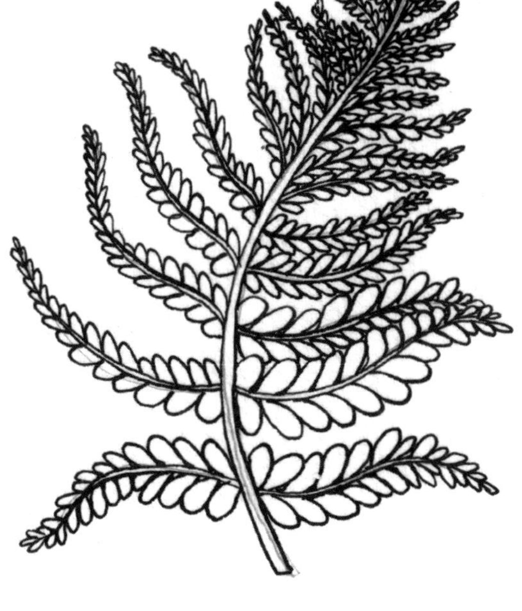

STEP 2

Ink the skeleton of the plant, using double lines on the thickest parts (the bottom of the stem and the bottom half of its 'branches'), and single lines towards the top, where it is thinner.

STEP 3

A fern frond is a single leaf made of tiny leaflets. They are biggest along the bottom and nearest the stem and get gradually smaller. Following the line of each of the 'branches', draw small rounded leaf shapes (almost like the shape of a tear drop) until each 'branch' is filled.

STEP 4

Wherever there is room, add a midline to each leaflet. Towards the bottom of the stem, where the leaflets are larger, add little ribs to the midlines. Add detail to the stem with a few dots at the top, bottom and in the middle. Once the ink is completely dry, rub out your pencil lines.

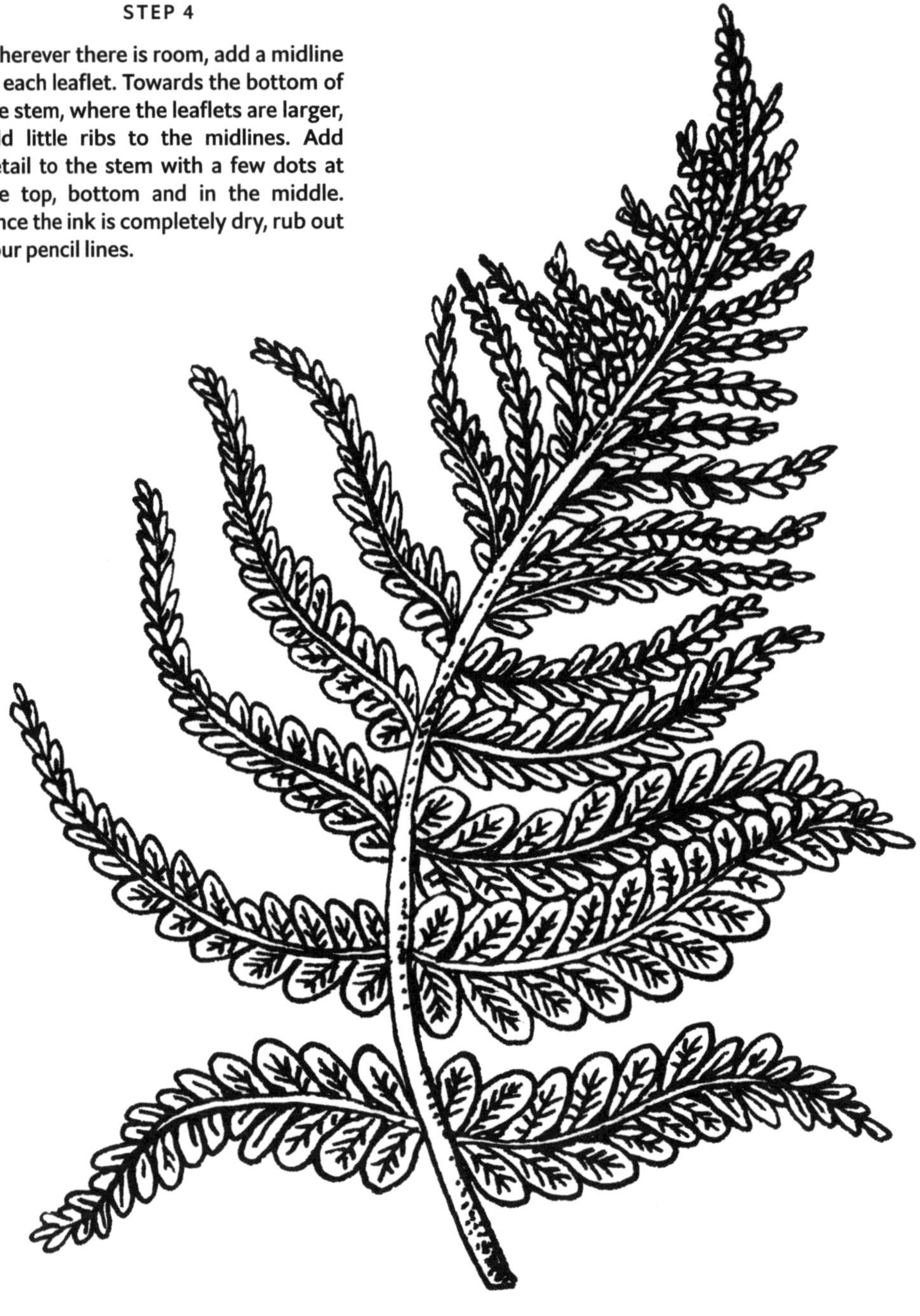

Project 06

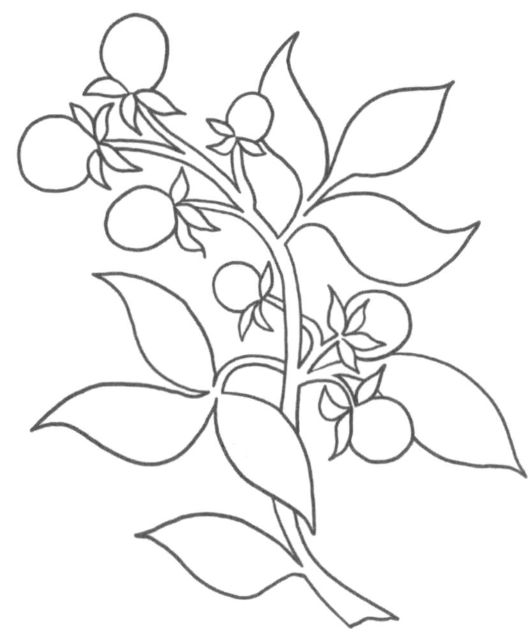

Blackberries

Blackberries are much sweeter than lingonberries, quicker to pick than bilberries and are amazing in a crumble! They're fun to draw, too – uneven shapes are not only good but preferable, as nothing in nature is uniform.

STEP 1

Sketch the shape of the blackberry branch, along with basic leaves and circles for the blackberries, or trace the outline on page 229. Don't worry about details, as you only need the placement of the berries and leaves for now.

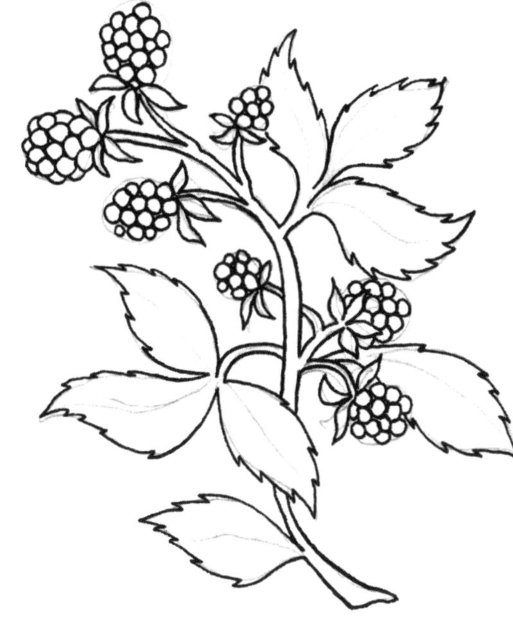

STEP 2

To ink the outline, fill the blackberry shapes with small, uneven circles. Add jagged edges and small spikes to the outline of each of the leaves (a bit like a zigzag).

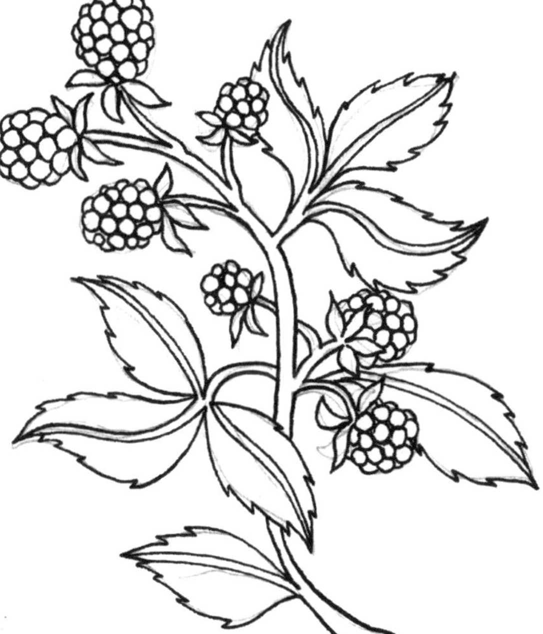

STEP 3

Draw small half circles along the edges of the blackberries to complete their shape. Add two lines down the middle of each leaf for the stem.

STEP 4

Add parallel lines to the leaves to darken them and add texture.

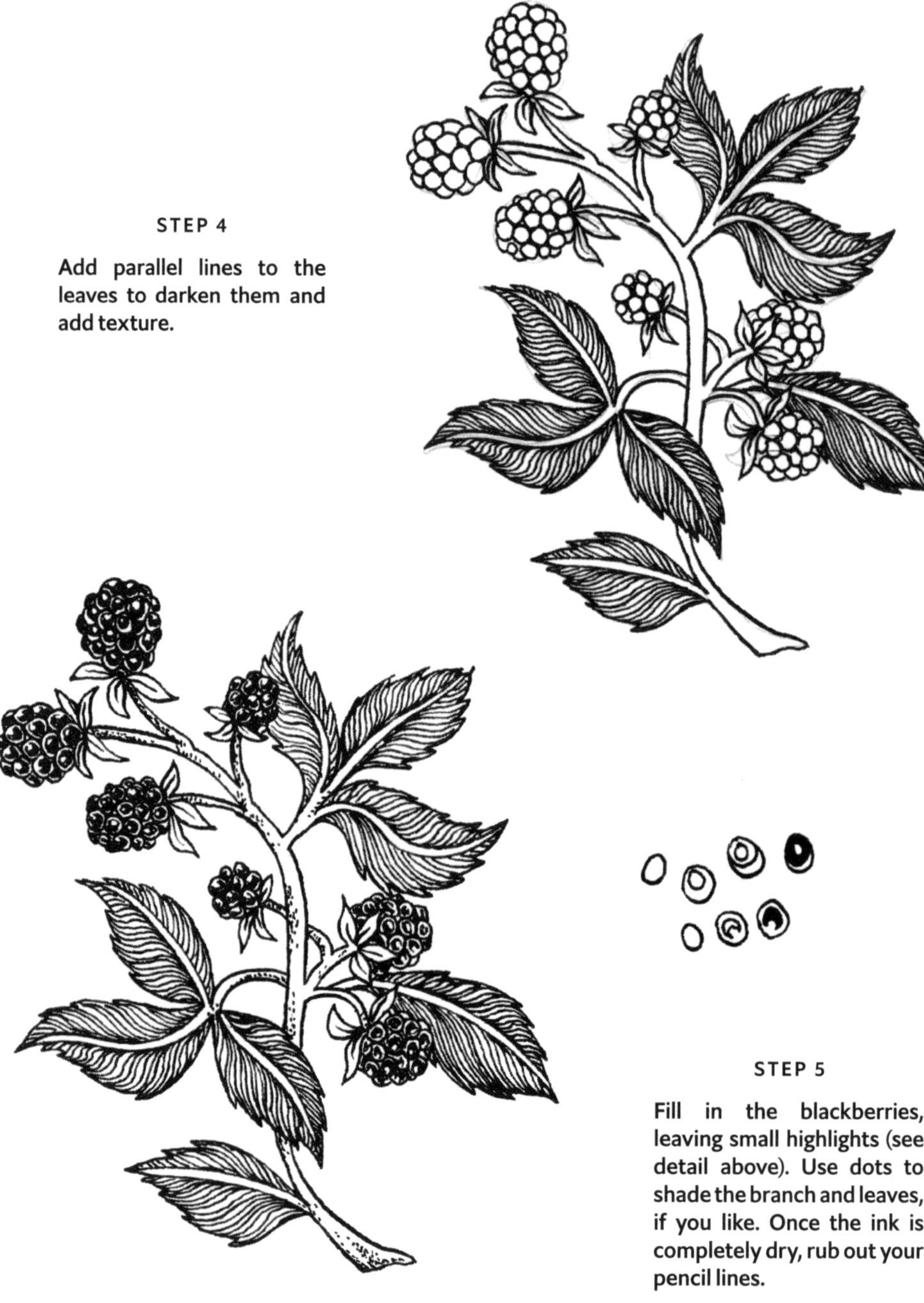

STEP 5

Fill in the blackberries, leaving small highlights (see detail above). Use dots to shade the branch and leaves, if you like. Once the ink is completely dry, rub out your pencil lines.

Project 07

Shaggy ink cap

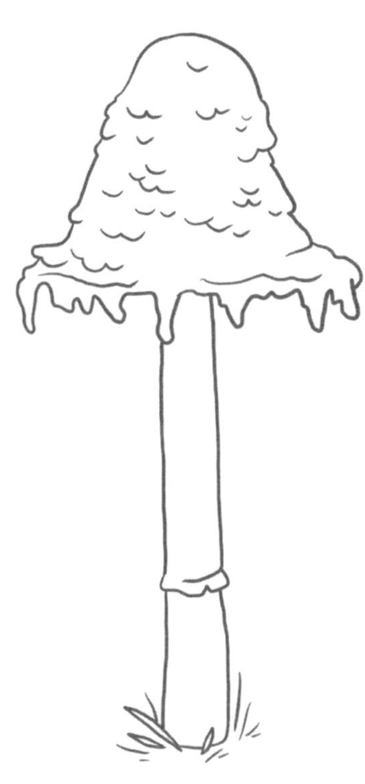

This fantastical mushroom looks like something straight out of a witch's tale. You can make this as realistic or as magical as you like.

STEP 1

Sketch the outline of the mushroom and the iconic dripping edge of the cap, plus a little grass for context. Alternatively, trace the outline on page 229.

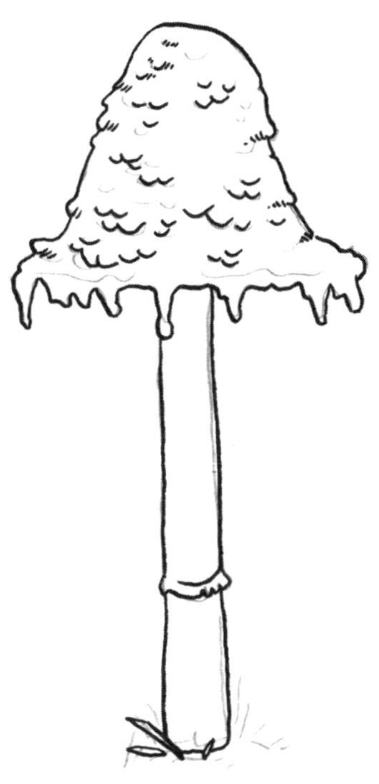

STEP 2

Following your sketch, ink the outline of the mushroom, as well as small 'scales' on the mushroom cap and a few blades of grass to ground it.

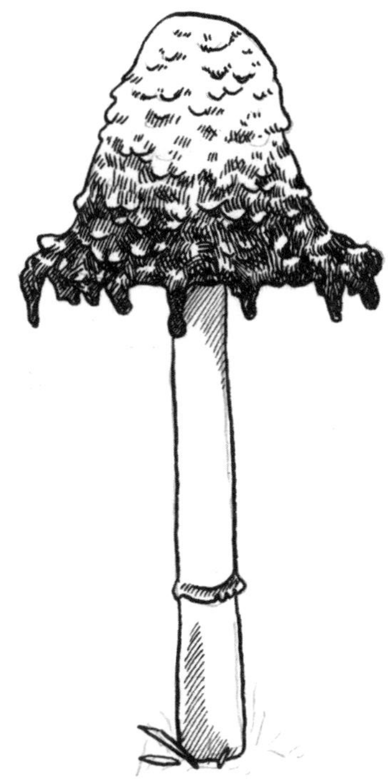

STEP 3

Shade the mushroom's cap using small strokes, giving them more space towards the top and overlaying them gradually more towards the bottom to add graduated crosshatching. Leave small white highlights on your 'scales'. Lastly, use diagonal lines to shade underneath the cap and at the bottom of the stalk.

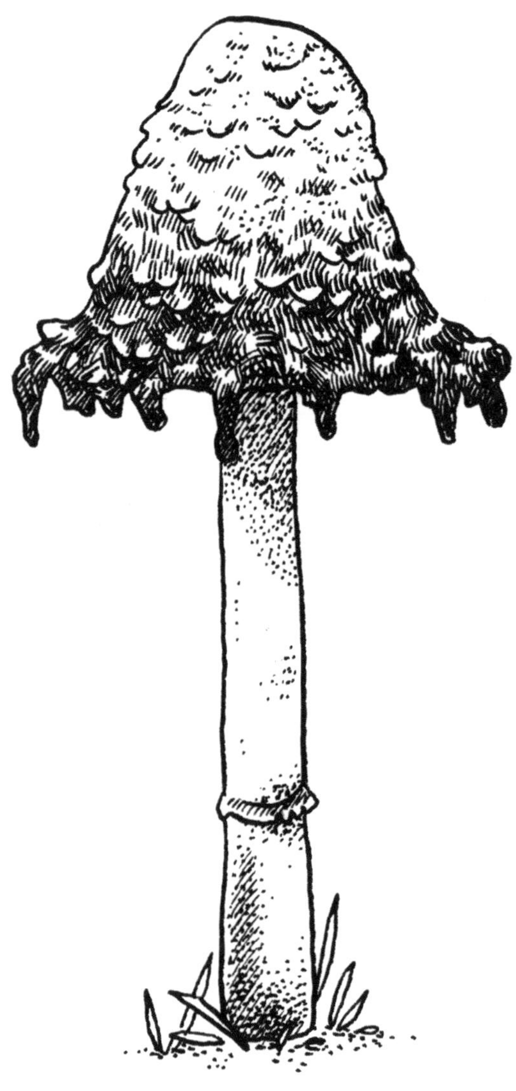

STEP 4

Add a couple more blades of grass to the base. Use dots to further shade the cap and stem, and add a few dots on the ground. Once the ink is completely dry, erase your pencil lines.

Project 08

Snowdrops

Nothing signals the approach of spring more than snowdrops poking their heads out of the snow or grass. We will add just a bit of shading to their little white heads.

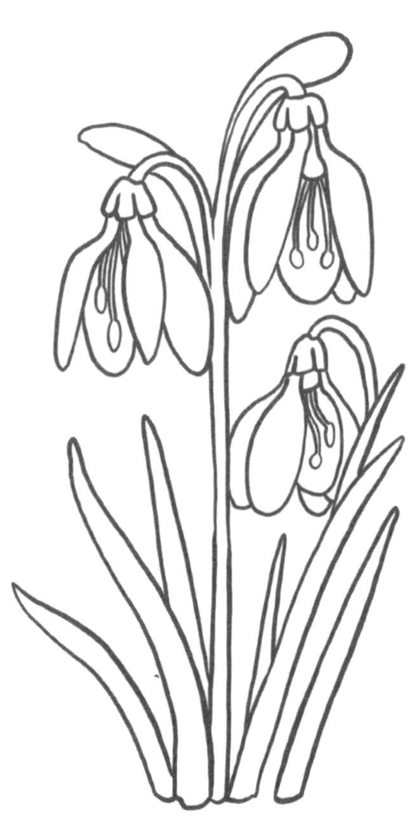

STEP 1

Sketch the outline of the flowers and stems using loose shapes, and double lines ending with a circle for the stamens, or trace the outline on page 229.

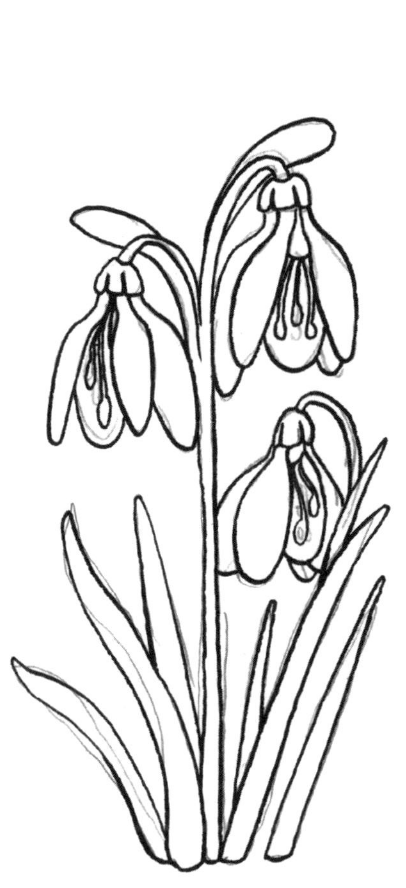

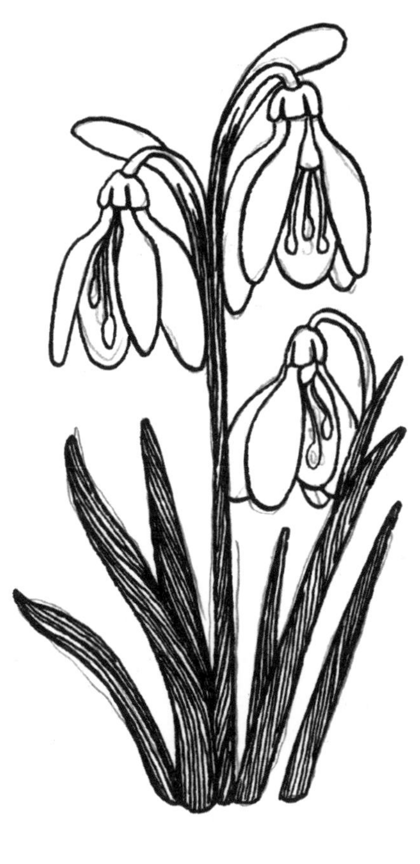

STEP 3

Use diagonal lines to shade in the leaves, leaving the flower stems white.

STEP 2

Using your sketch as a guide, ink the outline.

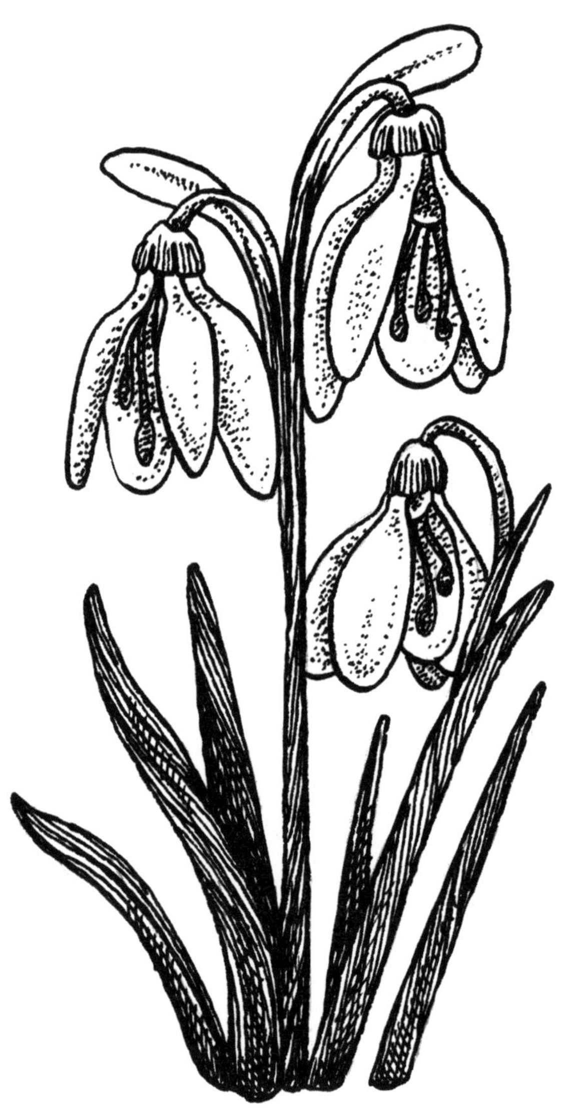

STEP 4

Add more shading to the bottom of all the leaves by drawing diagonal lines in a different direction to the ones in the previous step. As the flowers are white, we want minimal shading – use a few dots to give the stamens and the edges of the petals texture and shape. Once the ink is completely dry, erase your pencil lines.

Project 09

Clover

I have memories of countless hours spent very close to the ground on the field next to my primary school in search of four-leaf clovers. I've included one here – if you can't find what you're looking for, why not draw it?

STEP 1

Sketch the outline of the clover using circles for the rough outline of the flowers, a mixture of ovals and pointed shapes for the leaves and long, flowing lines for the stems, or trace the outline on page 230.

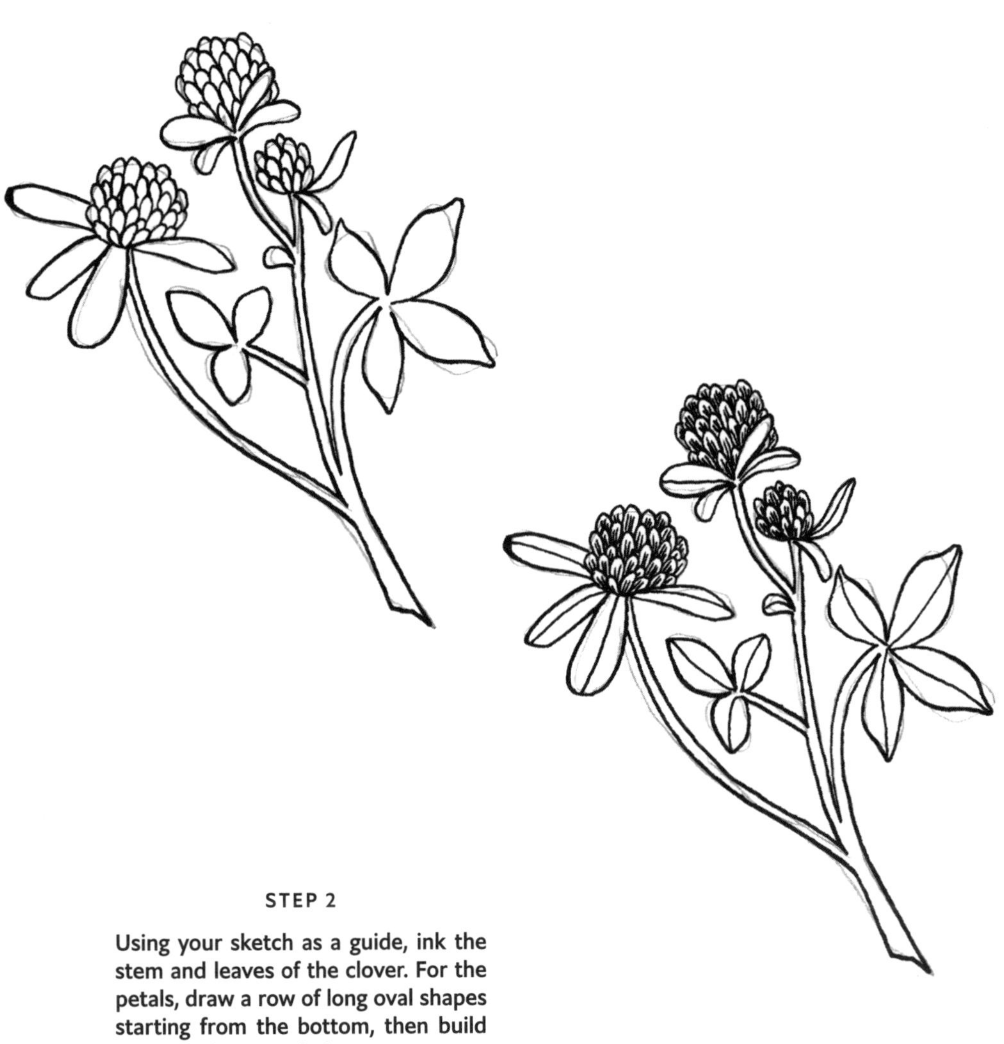

STEP 2

Using your sketch as a guide, ink the stem and leaves of the clover. For the petals, draw a row of long oval shapes starting from the bottom, then build them until you reach the tops.

STEP 3

Shade the petals using little lines pointing upwards from the bottom of each oval shape. Add a centre line to the leaves.

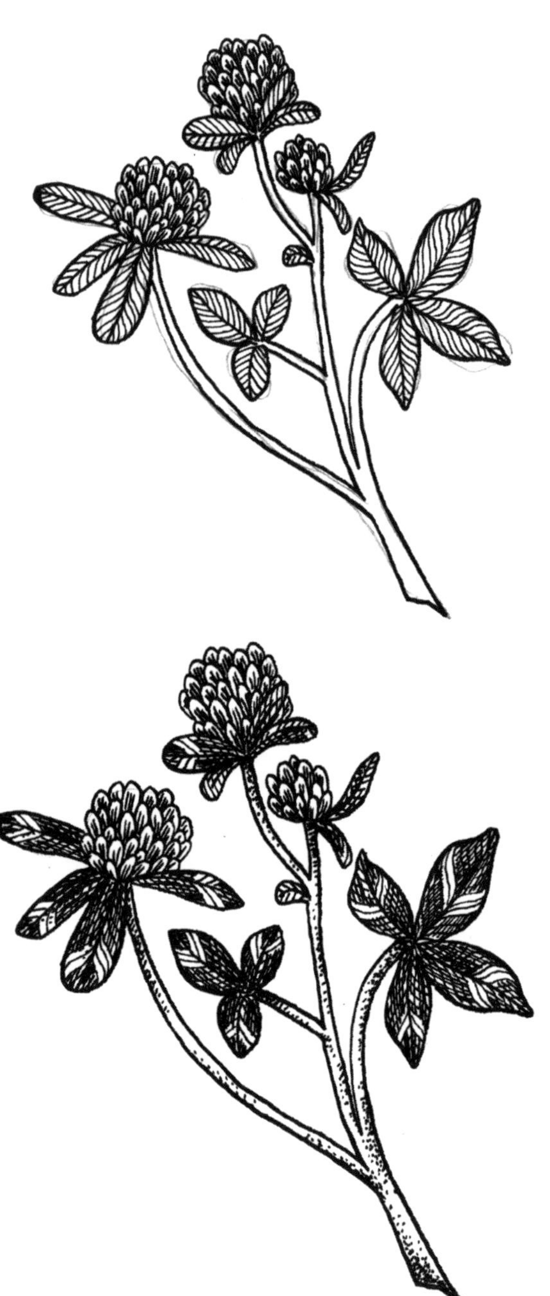

STEP 4

Draw veins on the leaves with lines radiating from the midline. I like to curve them a little to give the leaves the impression of volume, but straight is also fine – the stylistic choice is up to you.

STEP 5

Give the clover leaves their characteristic pattern by leaving a light section close to the top of each leaf, then adding lines in a different direction to shade the darker parts. Draw a few dots for shading and texture on the leaves and stem to bring it all together. Once the ink is completely dry, erase your pencil lines.

Project 10

Chanterelles

As you may have noticed,
I love drawing mushrooms!
Chanterelles are commonly
known in Norway as 'the
gold of the forest', and are
one of the most sought-
after edible mushrooms.
I picked these last autumn.

STEP 1

Sketch the shape of the mushrooms with pencil. Chanterelles come in all shapes and sizes, but are easily recognisable by the uneven caps and long gills underneath so be creative with it. Alternatively, trace the outline on page 230.

STEP 2

Ink the details of some little bits of dirt, which will sit on the bottom of the mushroom stalks and on the ground.

STEP 3

Ink the outlines of the mushrooms and and surrounding blades of grass. Add lines to the mushrooms: these will act as guides for yourself showing the direction of the gills, which run up and outwards from the stem.

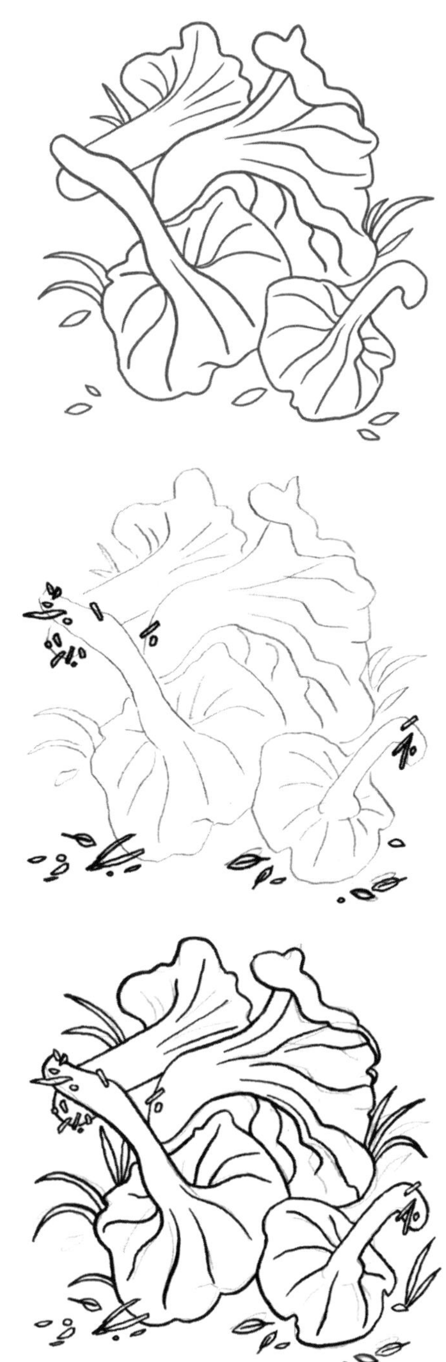

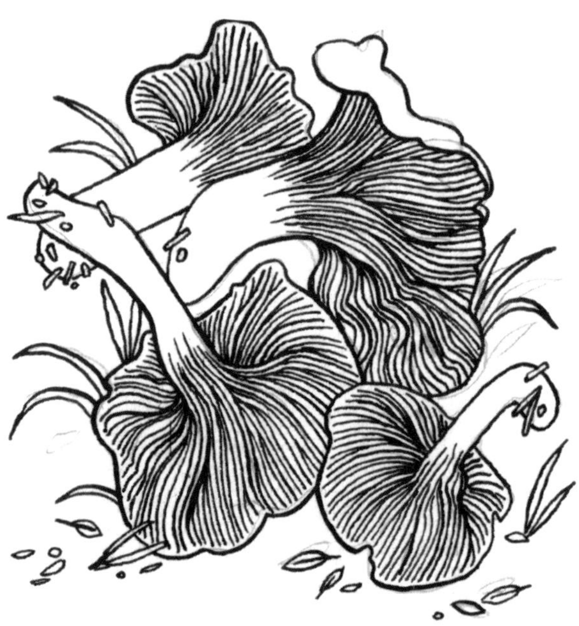

STEP 4

Draw in the thin lines underneath the chanterelle caps for the gills. I've stopped mine a little bit before they touch the edge of the cap.

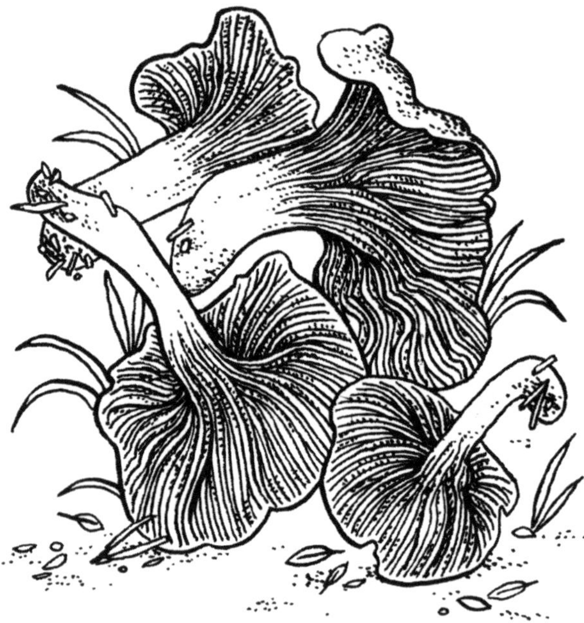

STEP 5

Add some dots for shading, paying special attention to the bottom of the stalks and underneath the caps. Add a little more detail to the ground. Once the ink is completely dry, erase your pencil lines.

Project 11

Horse chestnut

There is something magical about the pure size of horse chestnut trees, and the little spiky parcels underneath them. As kids we used to add little sticks for legs and turn them into hedgehogs.

STEP 1

Sketch the shape of the round, spiky horse chestnut and its pointed leaves lightly with a pencil, or trace the outline on page 230.

STEP 2

Ink the outline, following your sketch, and add extra pointed bits towards the tips of the leaves. Do not ink the midline down the centre of the leaves.

STEP 3

Using the midline of each leaf as a guide, draw out a double grid of veins pointing up and away from the centre.

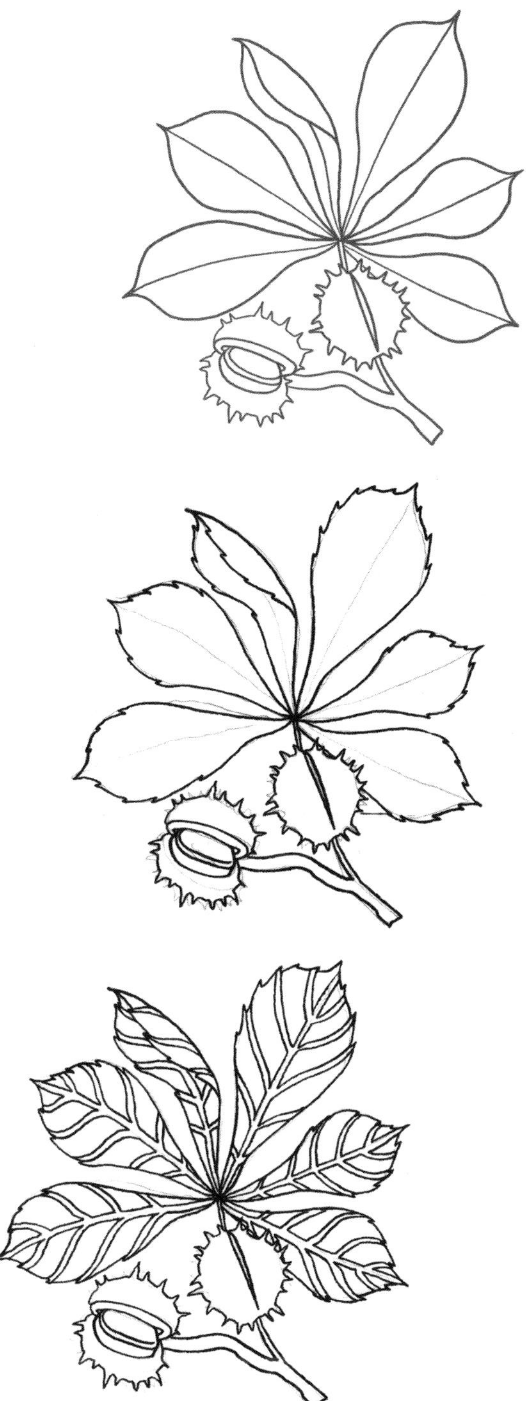

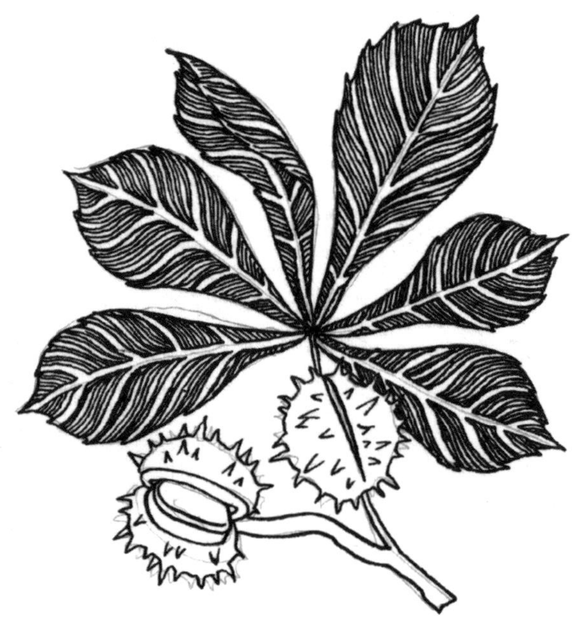

STEP 4

Fill in the grid with parallel, slightly curved lines, going in the same direction each time. Add a couple of spikes to each of the chestnut halves, pointing away from the centre.

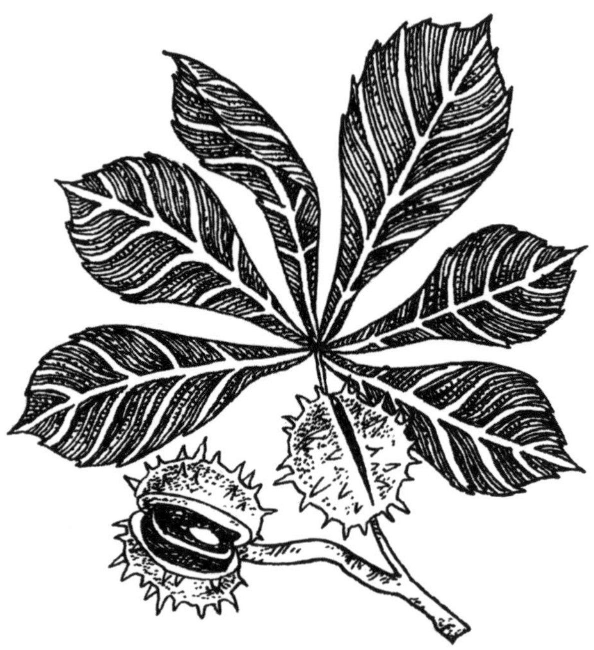

STEP 5

Use dots to shade the branch, chestnut and the areas of the leaves closest to the centre. Colour in the chestnut, but leave a round or oval highlight. Once the ink is completely dry, rub out your pencil lines.

Project 12

Morel

A morel is another lovely mushroom. It's so fun to draw the characteristic ridges and pits on their caps, which make them look a bit like honeycomb.

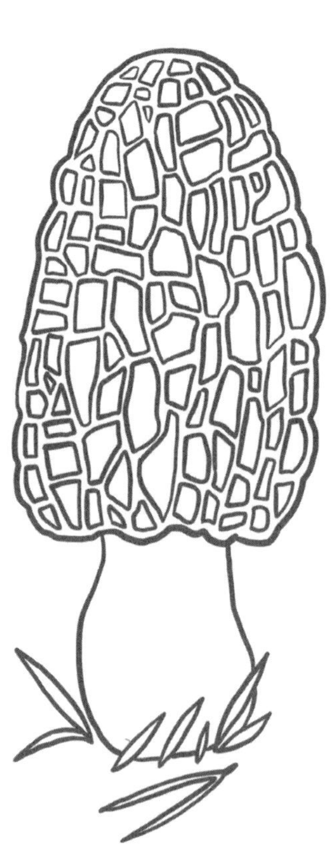

STEP 1

Sketch the bumpy outline of the morel, filling the mushroom with random geometric shapes, or trace the outline on page 230.

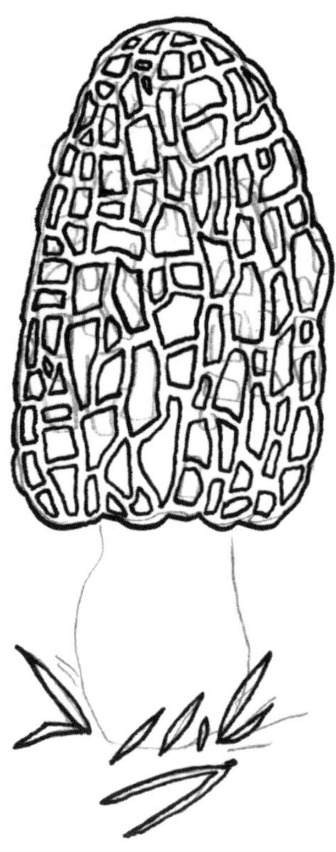

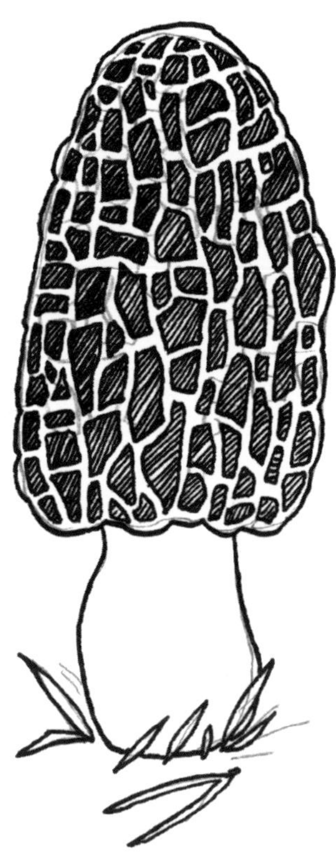

STEP 2

Ink some grass next to and overlapping the stem. Follow your sketch to ink the cap of the mushroom, including all the geometric shapes inside the cap outline.

STEP 3

Draw the stalk behind the grass. Fill in the shapes on the cap with diagonal lines.

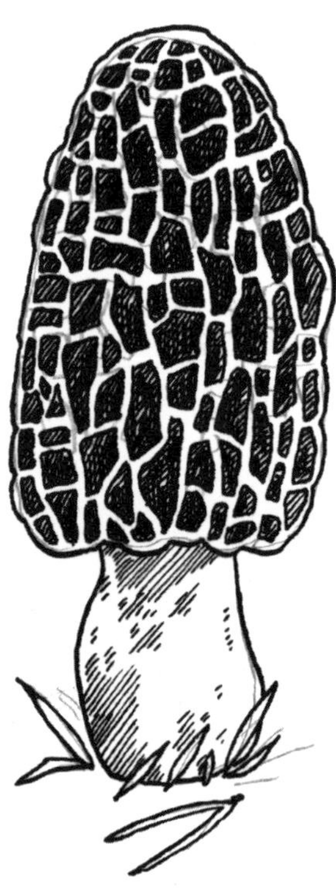

STEP 4

Add vertical lines or a scratchy texture to build shadow and texture in the morel shapes. Next, add diagonal lines on the stalk to shade underneath the cap and along the bottom.

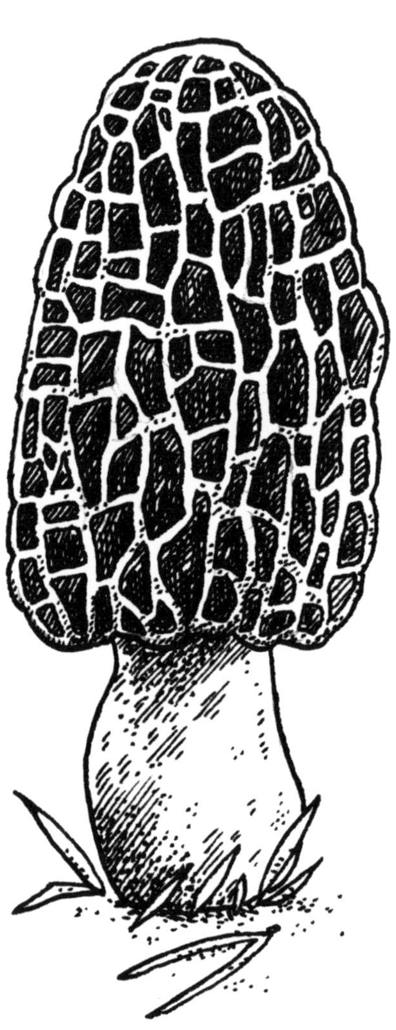

STEP 5

Add dots for shading and texture to bring the drawing together. I've added a few on the cap, but most are on the stem and ground. Once the ink is completely dry, rub out your pencil lines.

Project 13

Rowan

A rowan is usually one of the first pops of bright red I spot every autumn before the trees have changed their colouring, and it reminds me how much I love this time of year. You could use red ink to draw this, if you like.

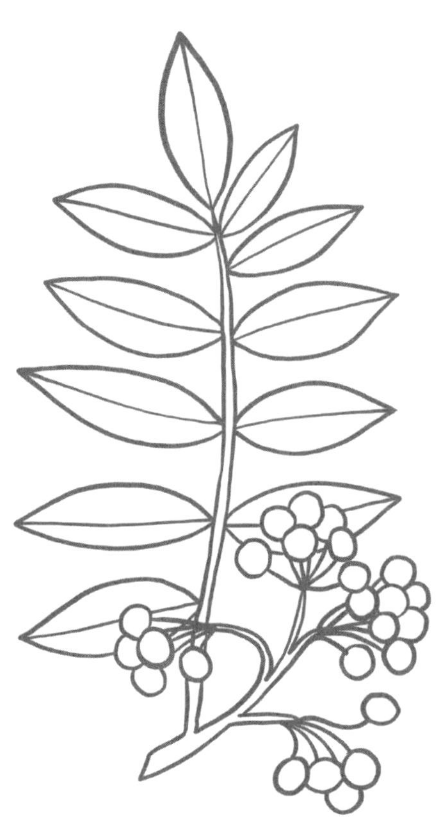

STEP 1

Sketch the shape of the berries and leaves. Rowan berries grow in clusters, and the leaves have tiny spikes, but I've kept my sketch simple for now. I will add those details at the next stage. Alternatively, trace the outline on page 231.

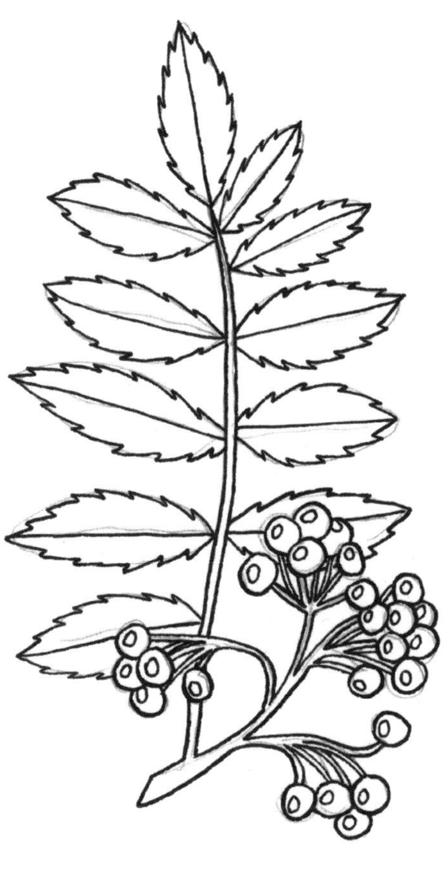

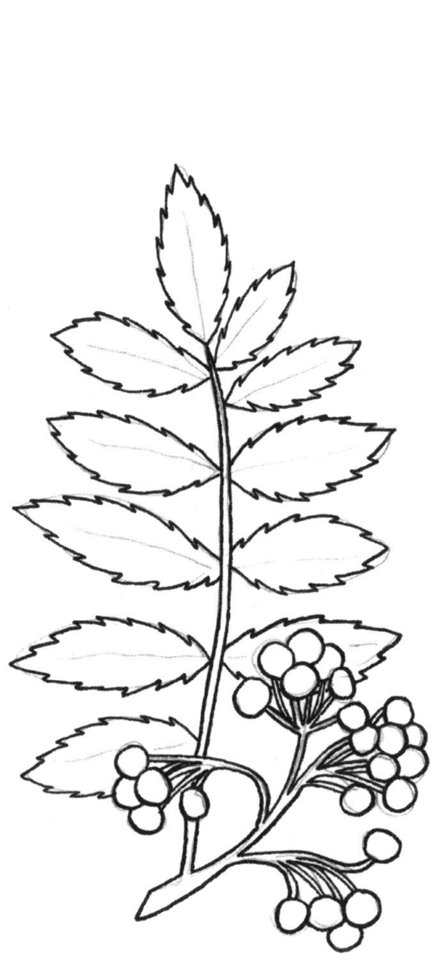

STEP 2

Ink the outline using your sketch as a guide. I've drawn double lines for the stems attached to the berries, but you could also draw single lines for them. When outlining each leaf, add small spike-like shapes around the edges and tips.

STEP 3

Add a midline to each leaf and a small circle to each berry to mark the highlight.

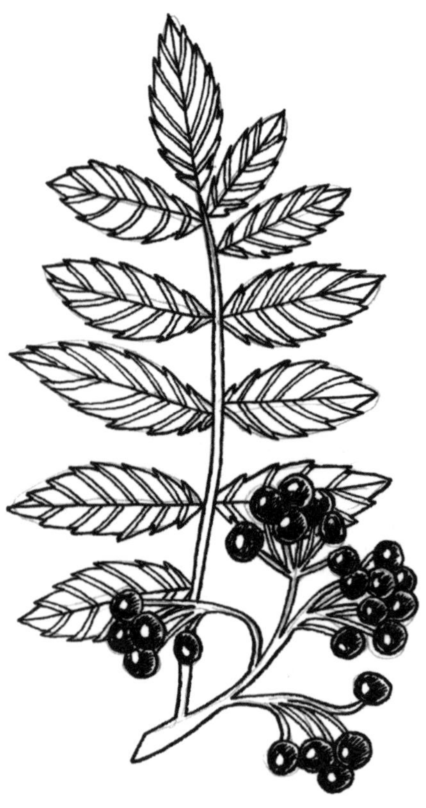

STEP 4

On every leaf, draw two thin parallel lines from each spike to the centre. Colour in the berries around the highlight, and leave a thin white space along the right edge.

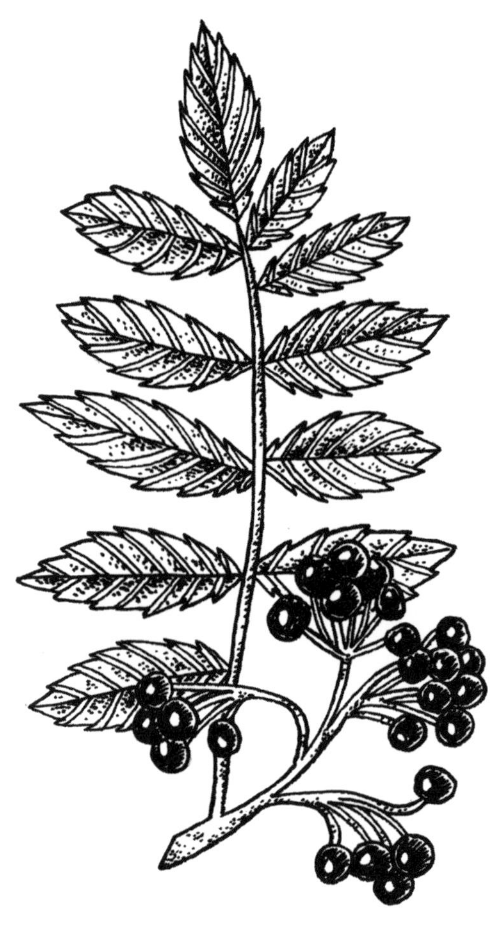

STEP 5

Shade the stem and leaves with dots. I've placed more dots on the left side of the leaf than on the right. Once the ink is completely dry, erase your pencil lines.

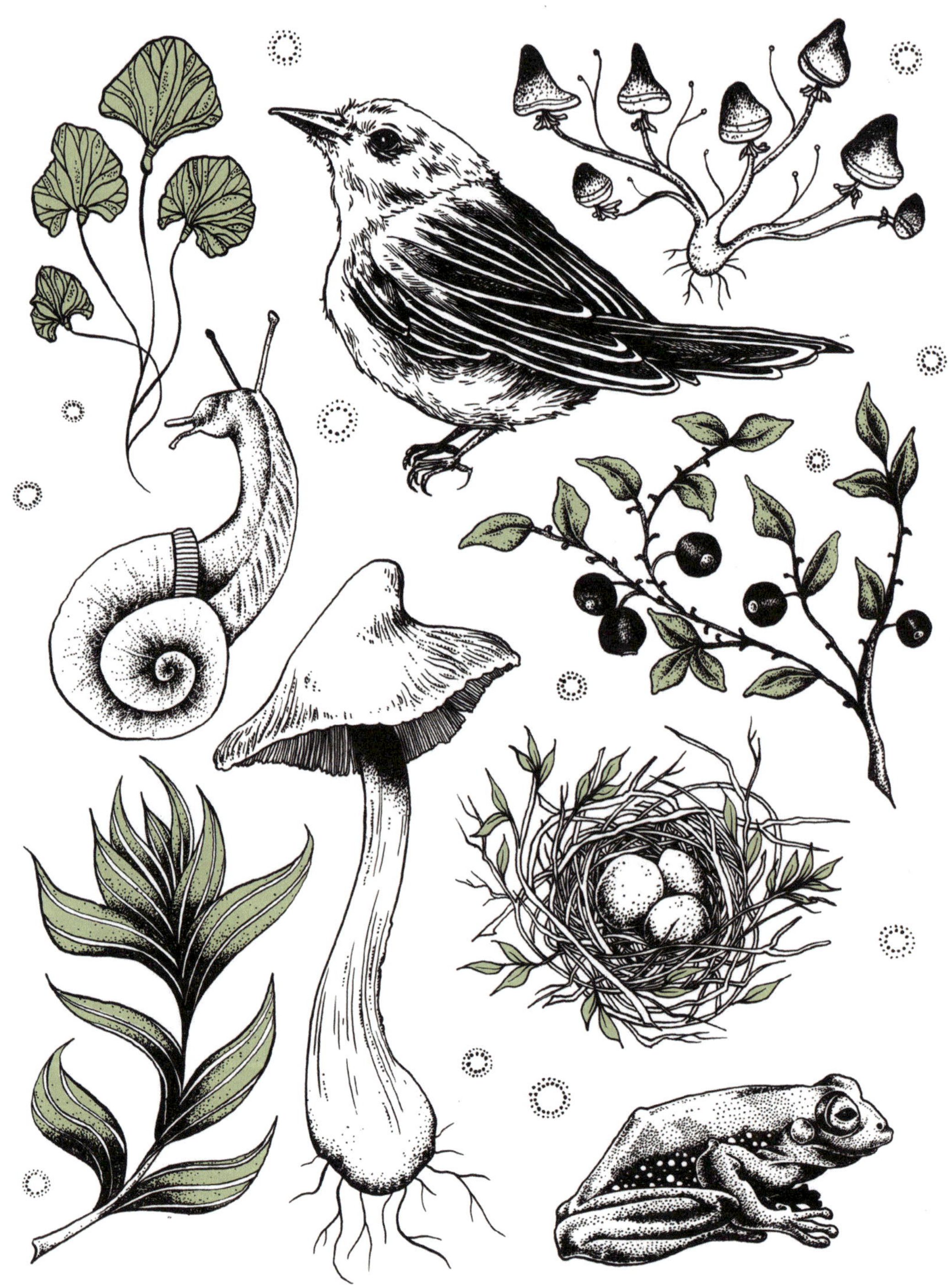

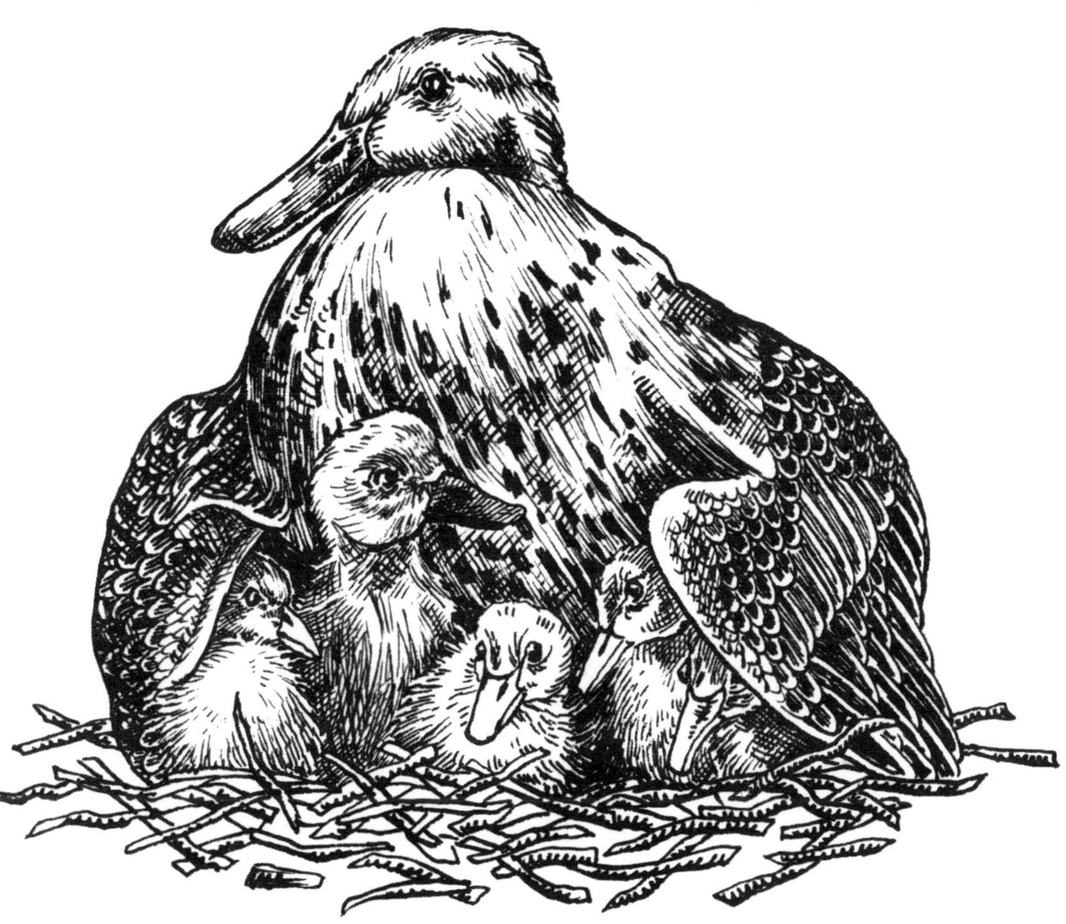

Project 14

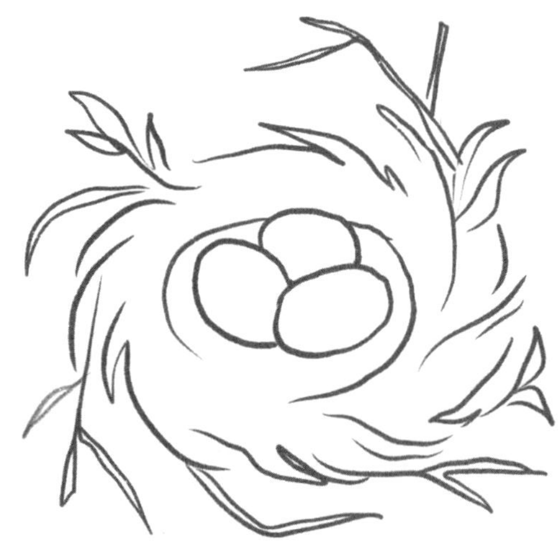

Bird's nest

Bird's nests come in many varieties and sizes, and can be made from the strangest materials. I've gone for a classic one of branches and leaves, but adding some moss, feathers or grass would also be a nice touch.

STEP 1

Lightly sketch out the shape of a bird's nest with a few eggs in the middle. This is only a guide, so the basic shape is enough for now. Alternatively, trace the outline on page 231.

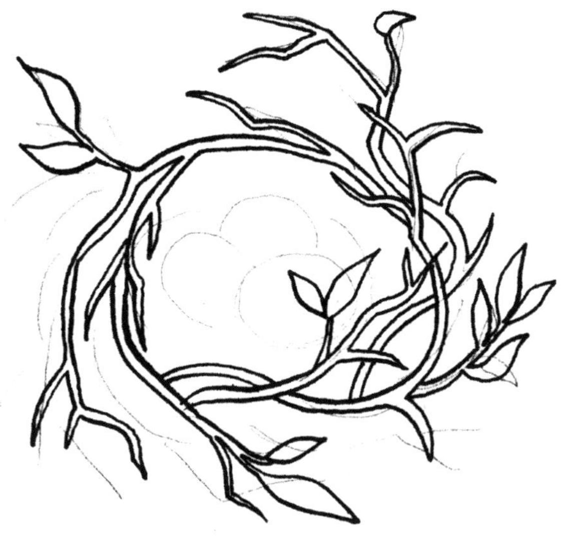

STEP 2

With a subject as busy as this, we have to work from the top to the bottom (or foreground to background). Ink a few branches and leaves in a wreath shape, a few of them with leaves on.

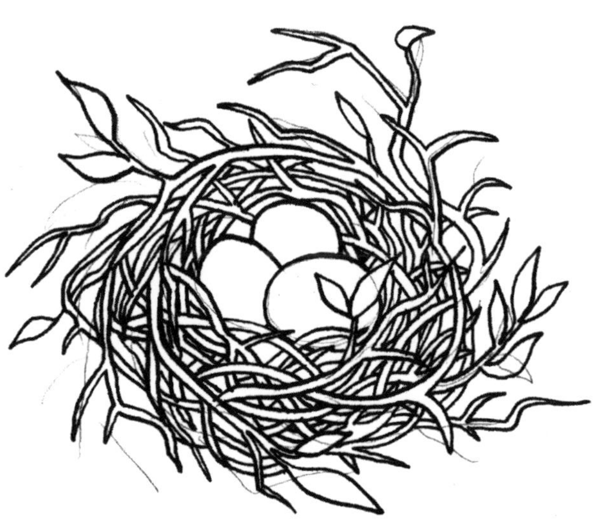

STEP 3

Add depth by adding more branches and leaves and filling out the shape. Keep all the new branches behind the ones you've already drawn. The more random these branches are, the better. Ink the eggs in the middle of the nest.

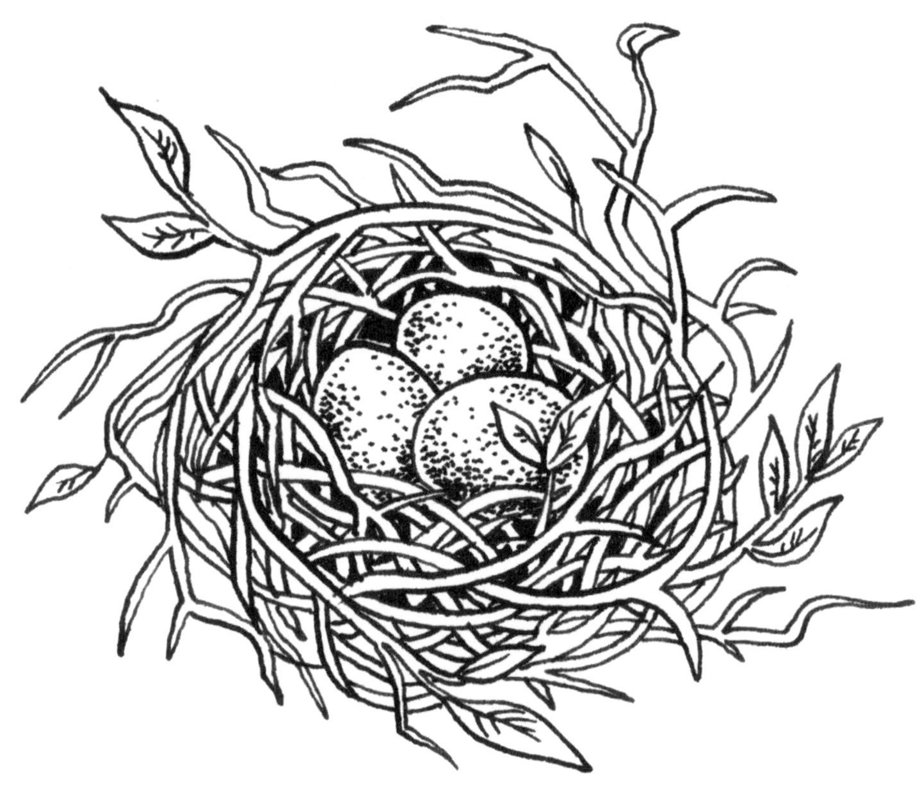

STEP 4

Add texture and the final touches by filling in the smallest gaps closest to the eggs with ink, then adding vein details to the leaves. Dot speckles on the eggs. I used a nib pen for these drawings, but another great tool for speckles would be an old toothbrush, to give a less controlled look. Once the ink is completely dry, rub out your pencil lines.

Project 15
Feather

A feather is a classic favourite find while out hiking in the woods or beachcombing. You can experiment with texure and tone by varying the strokes you use.

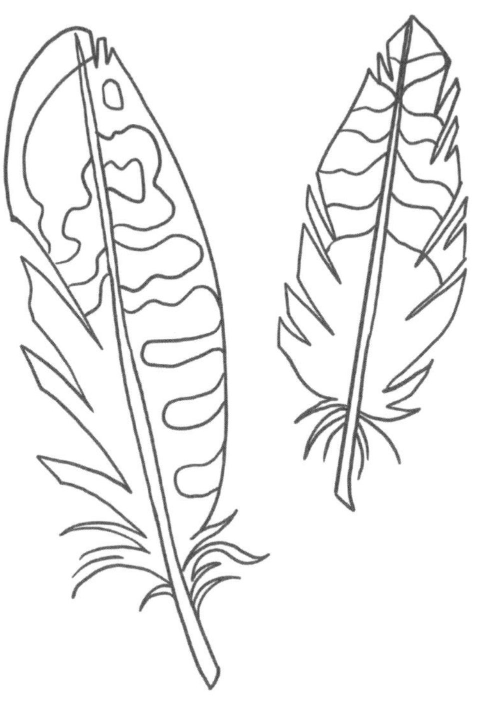

STEP 1

Sketch the shape of the feathers and roughly outline the pattern using wavy lines, or trace the outline on page 231.

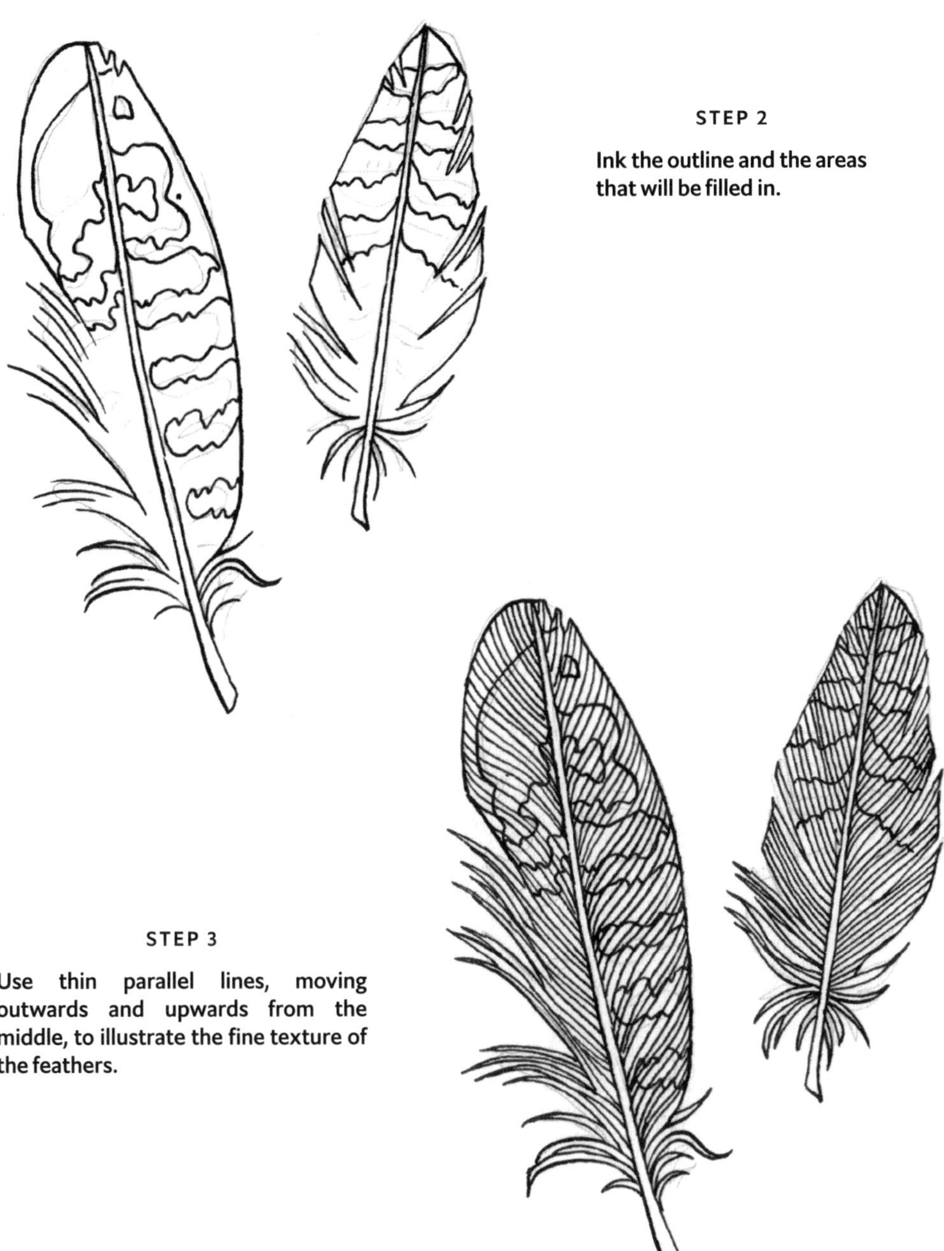

STEP 2

Ink the outline and the areas that will be filled in.

STEP 3

Use thin parallel lines, moving outwards and upwards from the middle, to illustrate the fine texture of the feathers.

STEP 4

Fill in the shapes you marked out in step 2 to add pattern. Be as thorough (or not) as you'd like. Personally, I quite like the scratchy texture that comes from adding quick, random strokes – I find a bit of light shining through really brings it to life!

STEP 5

Add depth and shading with dots along the centre line, following the guide you have made with your existing lines. Once the ink is completely dry, rub out your pencil lines.

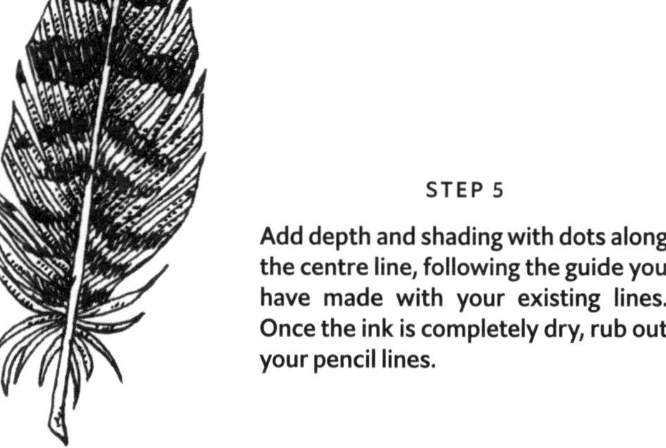

Project 16

Mushroom basket

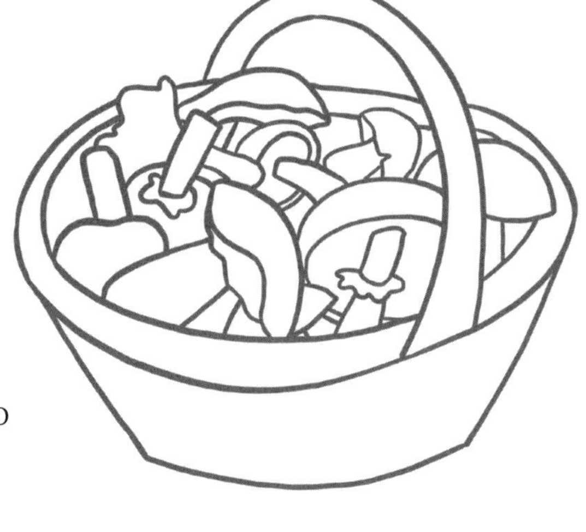

It was only two years ago that I was introduced to mushroom-picking, an activity I've since fallen absolutely in love with. It doesn't matter if I find mushrooms or not – I just love wandering in the woods looking for them.

STEP 1

Sketch the basic shape of the round basket and its handle as well as some rough mushrooms or trace the outline on page 231.

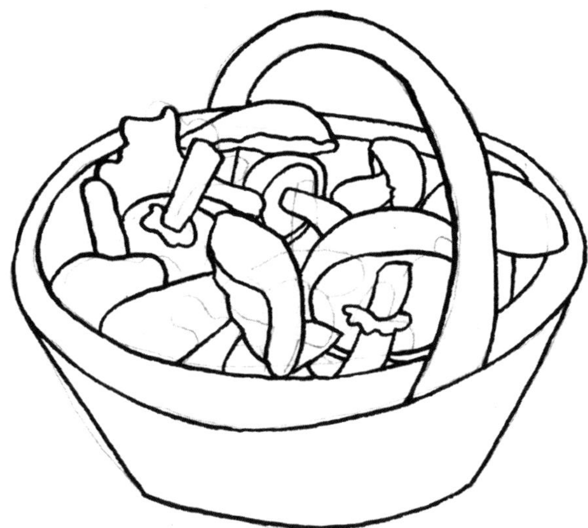

STEP 2

Ink the outline, following your sketch. I've filled my basket with mushrooms of various shapes and sizes, showing some from the side, top and some from underneath.

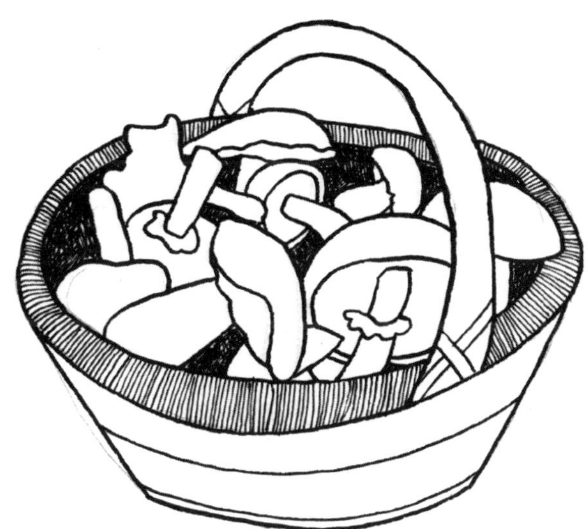

STEP 3

Add a cross detail where the handle meets the basket, then add detail to the rim using small parallel lines. Fill in the inside of the basket and between the mushrooms, using either solid black or a scratchy texture.

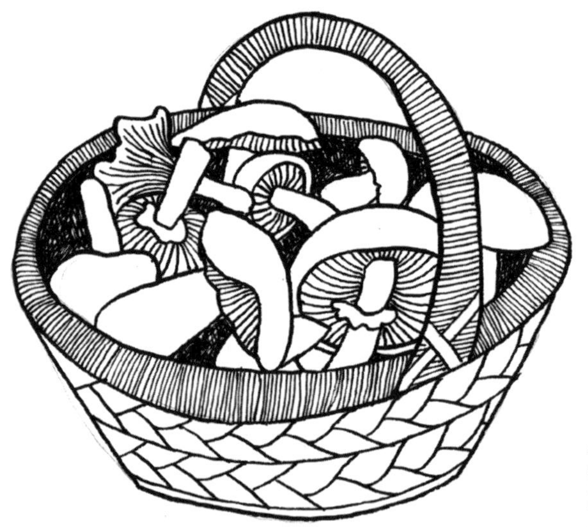

STEP 4

Add lines to the handle of the basket, to match the rim. Add slightly curved lines underneath the mushroom caps for the gills. Then add two lines of a braided pattern to the basket's body, starting on the left, with a short diagonal line. Keep building diagonal lines from the middle of your previous line, alternating direction each time, until you reach the end. Repeat the process for the second braid below.

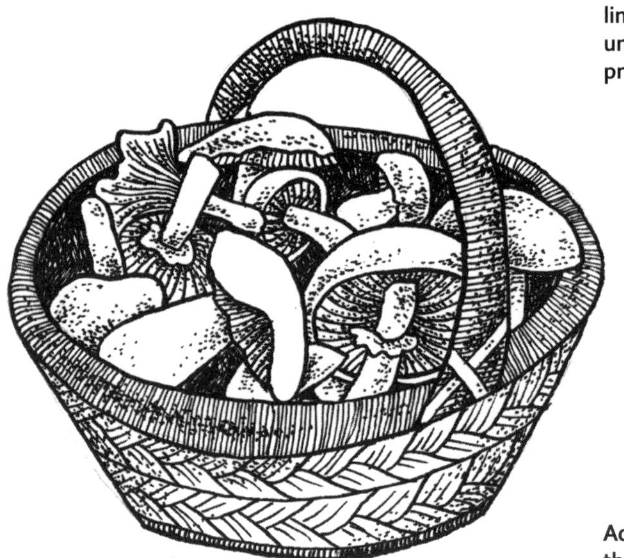

STEP 5

Add short lines to give detail to the braids, then use pointillism to shade the basket and mushrooms, mostly towards the outer edge and underneath the mushroom caps. Once the ink is completely dry, erase your pencil lines.

Project 17

Pine cone

The pine cone is such a familiar object to most of us, yet when I sat down to draw it from memory the first time, I was completely lost and started to doubt if I really knew what it looked like. Here, I've broken it into simple shapes, and I hope this helps you too.

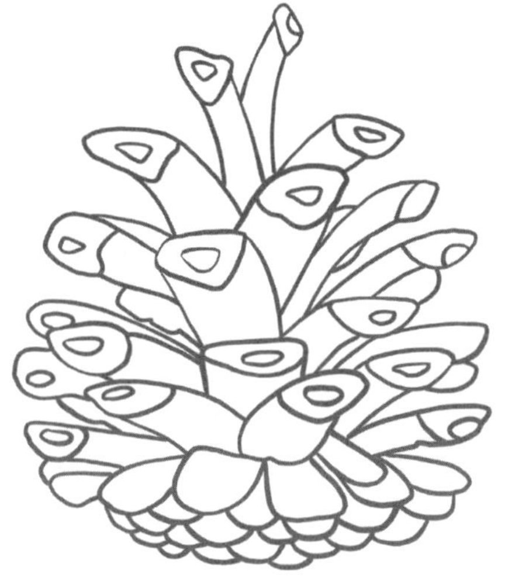

STEP 1

Sketch the shape of the pine cone. I sketched an egg shape before starting to add individual seed scales. Start from a third of the way up the egg. Random and crooked seed scales look good – just make sure they point up and outwards. Alternatively, trace the outline on page 232.

STEP 2

Trace your outline in ink and add little rounded triangles to the middle of the biggest seed scales. Use half circles to ink the ones at the bottom, which are bunched together.

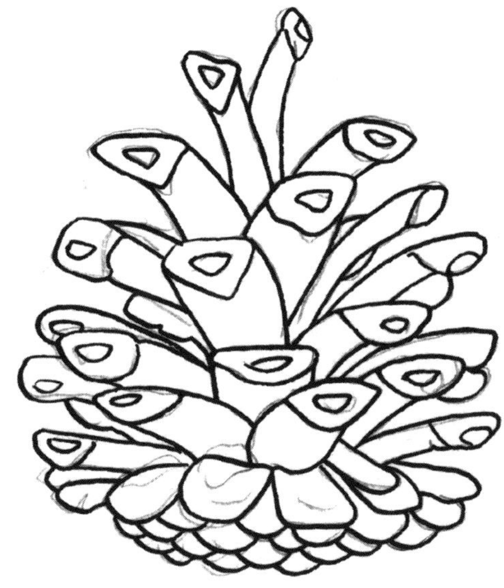

STEP 3

Draw thin lines on the individual seed scales, pointing outwards, leaving out the half circles at the bottom for now.

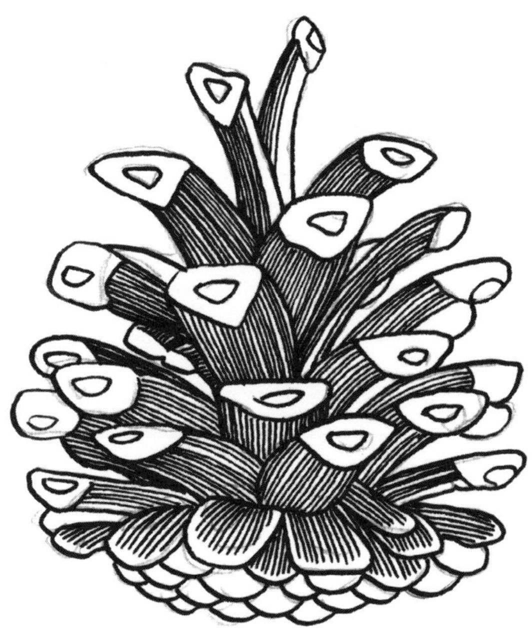

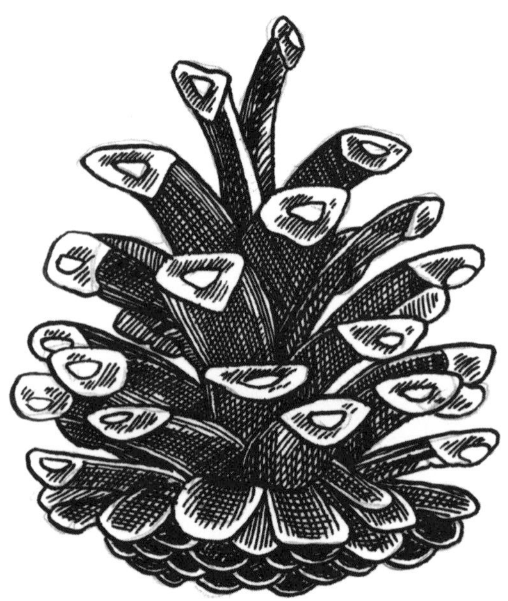

STEP 4

Draw half circles with the bottom scales and fill them in. Use a second layer of lines (in a different direction to the first) to make the shaded areas on the higher, individual scales even darker.

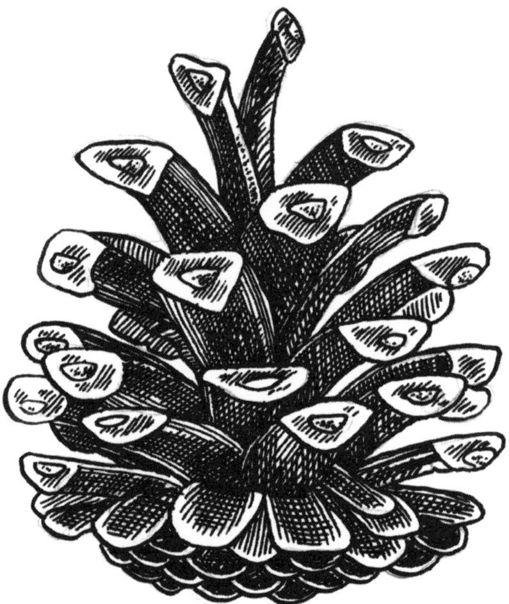

STEP 5

Use dots and short lines to add depth and textural details to the pine cone. Once the ink is completely dry, rub out your pencil lines.

Project 18

Quartz

I love anything in nature
that gives the impression
it may have been owned
by a witch, so naturally
I had to include some
kind of crystal.

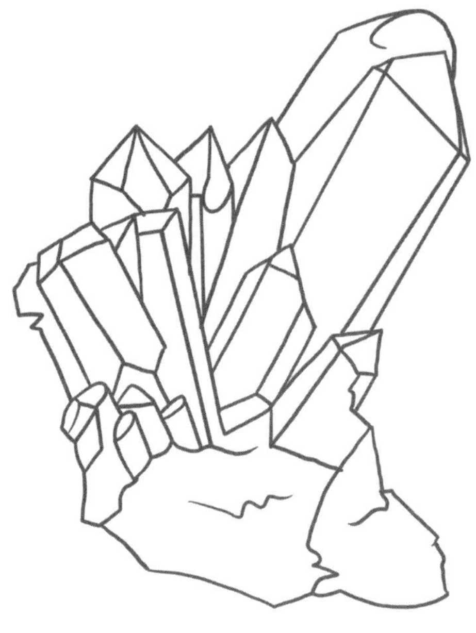

STEP 1

**Sketch the shape of the
crystal, or trace the outline
on page 232.**

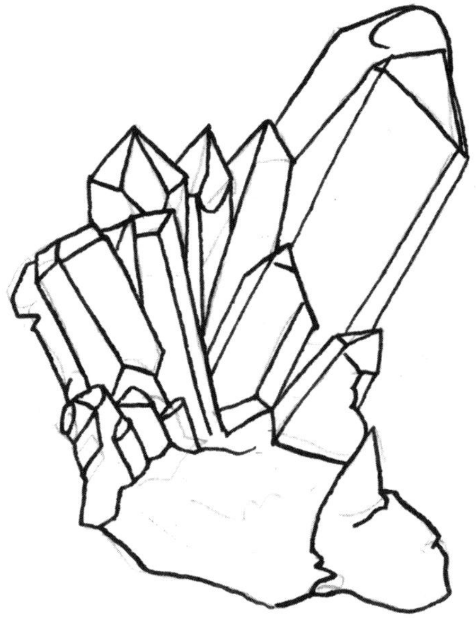

STEP 2

Ink the outline following your sketch, using mostly straight lines.

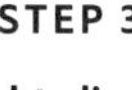

STEP 3

Use straight lines to add the first (lightest) layer of shading.

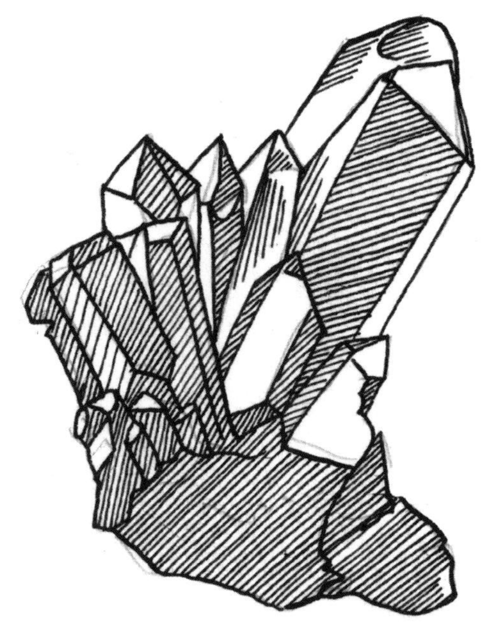

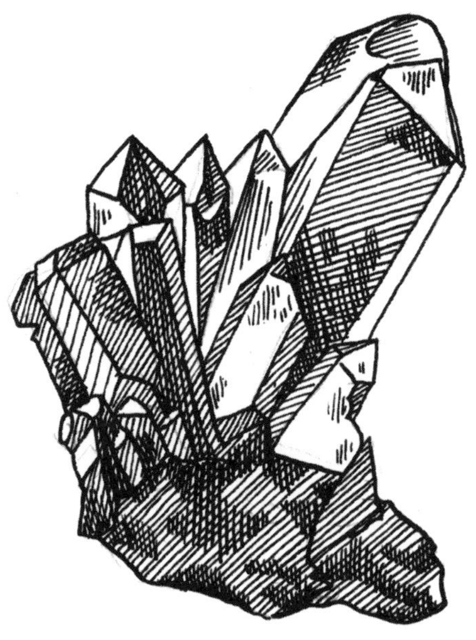

STEP 4

Use straight lines in a different direction to add the second, slightly darker layer of shading.

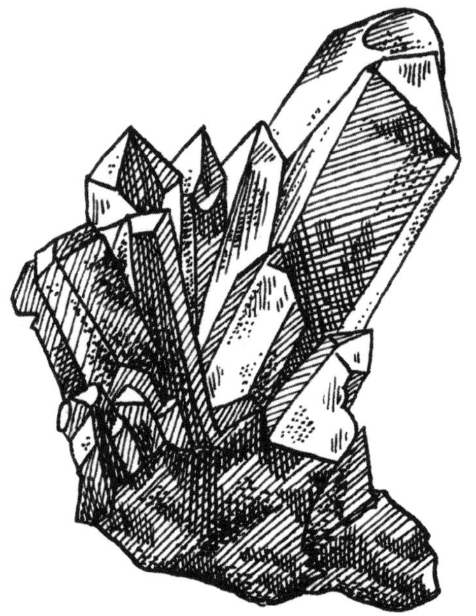

STEP 5

Use dots to add another texture and layer of shading. Erase your pencil lines once the ink is completely dry.

Project 19

Sycamore

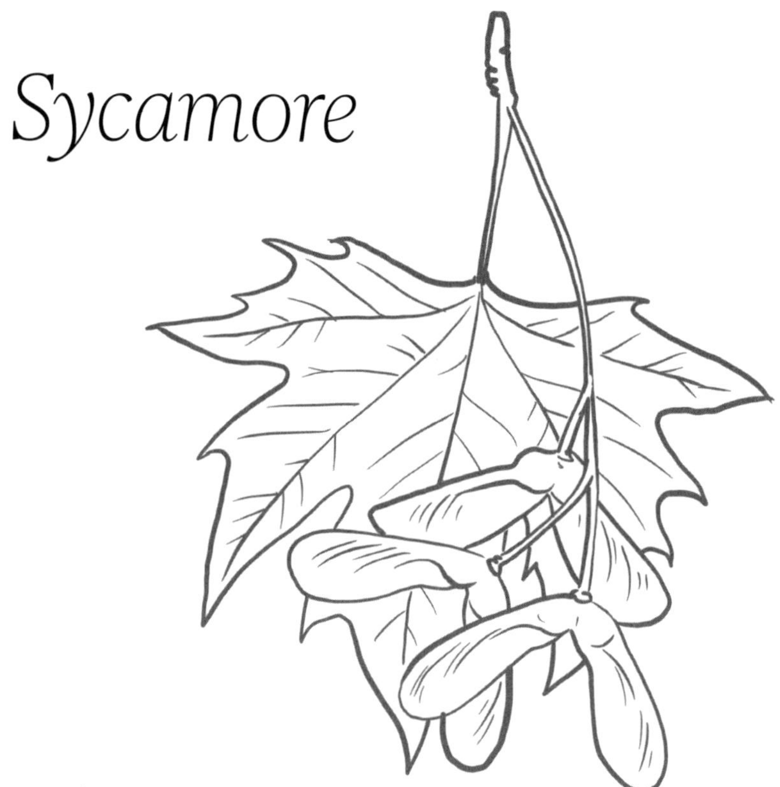

Sycamore seeds are great fun to draw, and fascinating as they resemble little helicopters as they fall in slow motion from the sky.

STEP 1

Sketch the spiky shape of the sycamore leaf and the rounded shape of the seed pods, or trace the outline on page 232.

STEP 2

Use your sketch as a guide to outline the leaf and its pointy edges, stem and the three seed pods.

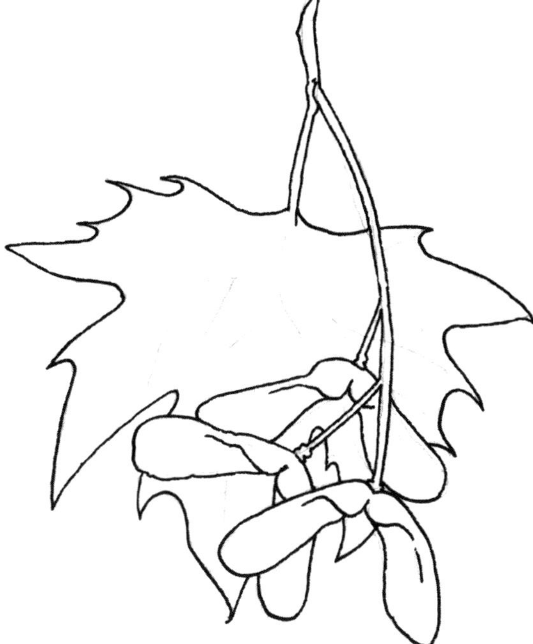

STEP 3

The veins in the leaf will stay white, so draw around your sketch lines from the stem to create a grid with double lines. Give the seed pods some texture and shape by drawing a combination of long and short curved lines on their wings.

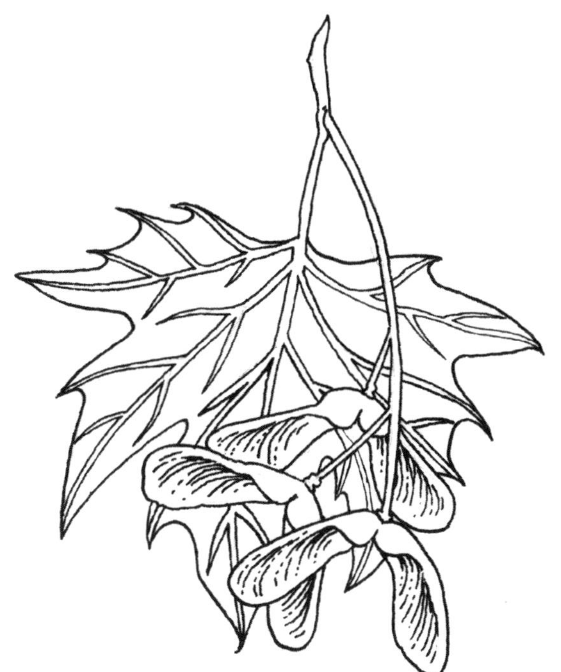

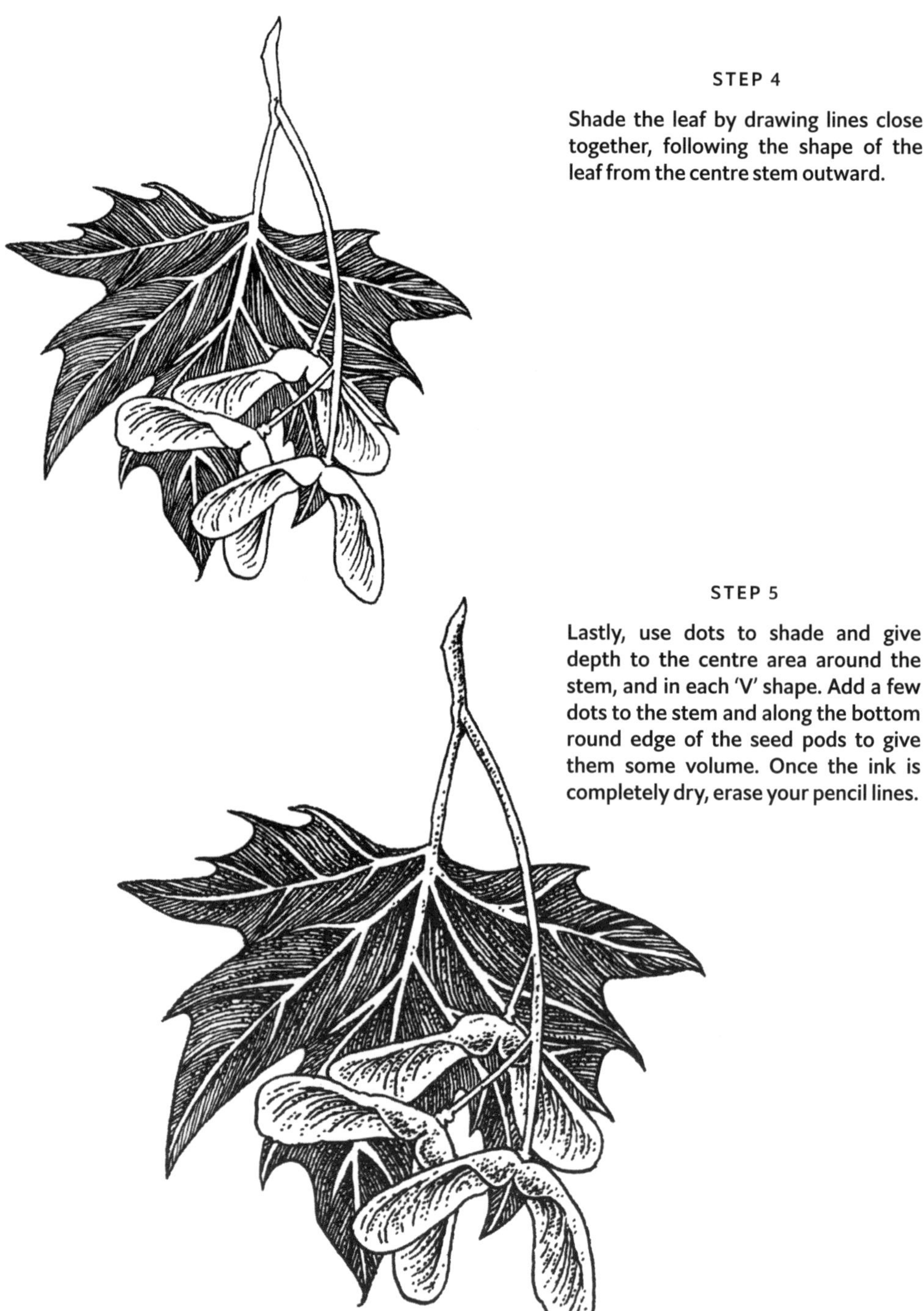

STEP 4

Shade the leaf by drawing lines close together, following the shape of the leaf from the centre stem outward.

STEP 5

Lastly, use dots to shade and give depth to the centre area around the stem, and in each 'V' shape. Add a few dots to the stem and along the bottom round edge of the seed pods to give them some volume. Once the ink is completely dry, erase your pencil lines.

Project 20

Tree stump

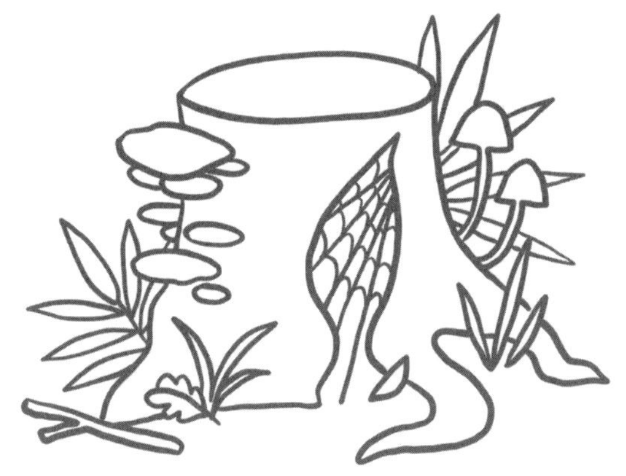

Tree stumps, especially really overgrown ones, are one of my favourite things to encounter and draw on forest walks. Whether they've been cut down or taken down by weather or beavers, they are a breeding ground for mushrooms, moss and lichen. I like to count the growth rings and imagine who lives inside.

STEP 1

Sketch the shape of the tree stump and the foliage that surrounds it. I've opted for mushrooms, grass, leaves and a stick, and I want a cobweb in the crack of the stump. Add whatever plants you'd like, or trace the outline on page 233.

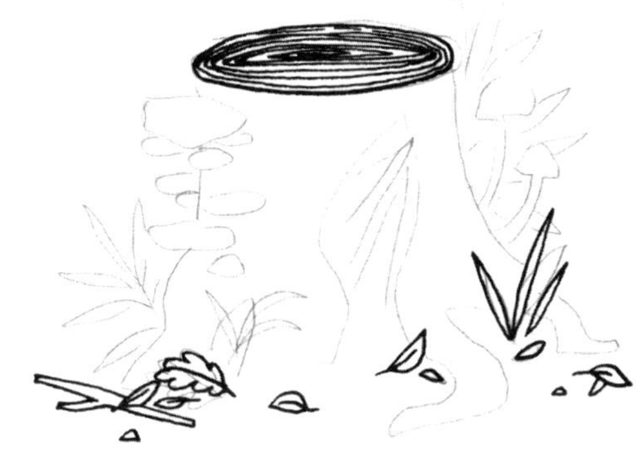

STEP 2

Ink the oval on top of the tree stump and the growth rings inside. The spiral does not have to be perfect; as long as we hint at it, the eye will still read it as the top of a cut tree. Next, draw the grass and leaves that lie on the ground in front of the stump.

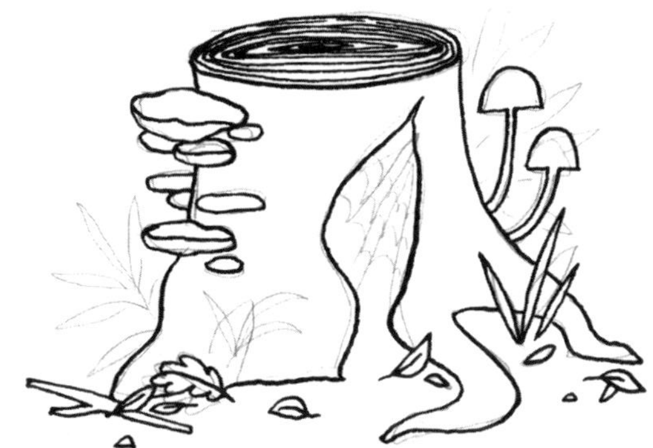

STEP 3

Ink the shape of the stump and the mushrooms that are growing on it.

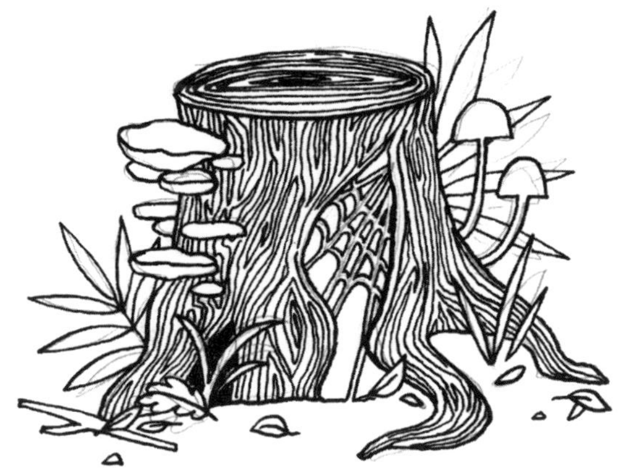

STEP 4

Fill in the tree stump with continuous lines in spirals and long strokes to make the bark pattern. Add the bits of larger foliage growing behind it. Follow your cobweb sketch, drawing around it with double lines to map out the white area of your web.

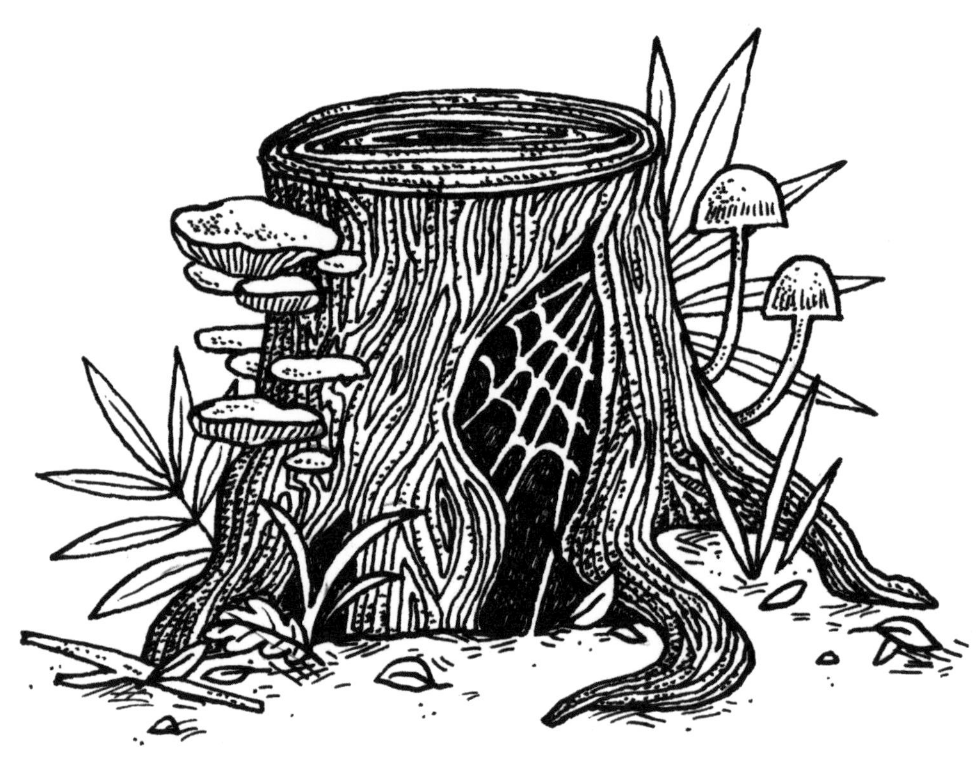

STEP 5

Fill in the gaps between the lines of your cobweb. Add detail to the mushrooms and leaves, as well as some texture and shadow on the ground. Finally, use a few dots to shade and give shape to the stump. Add lines along the bottom of the roots and the base of the stump for shadow. Once the ink is completely dry, erase your pencil lines.

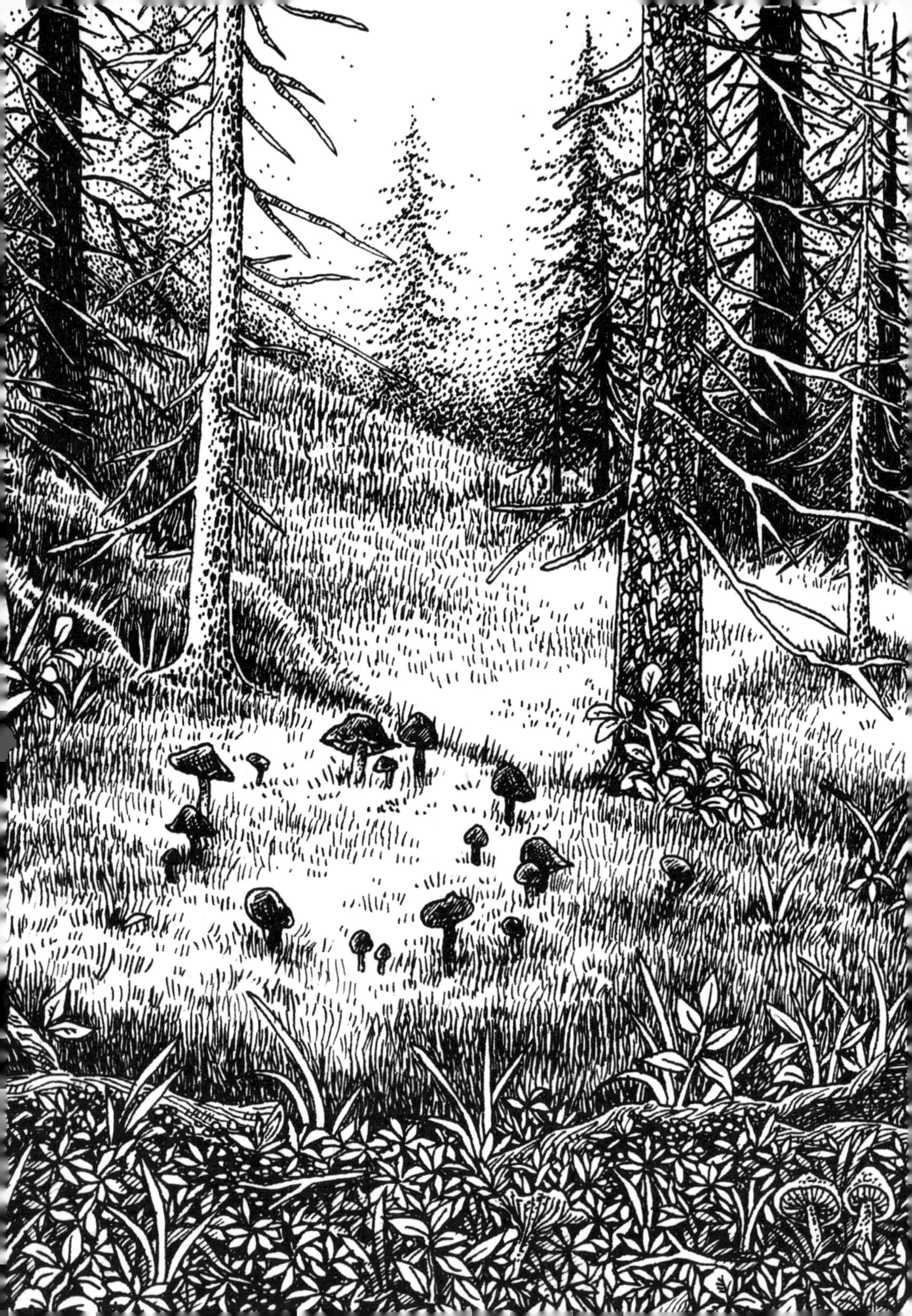

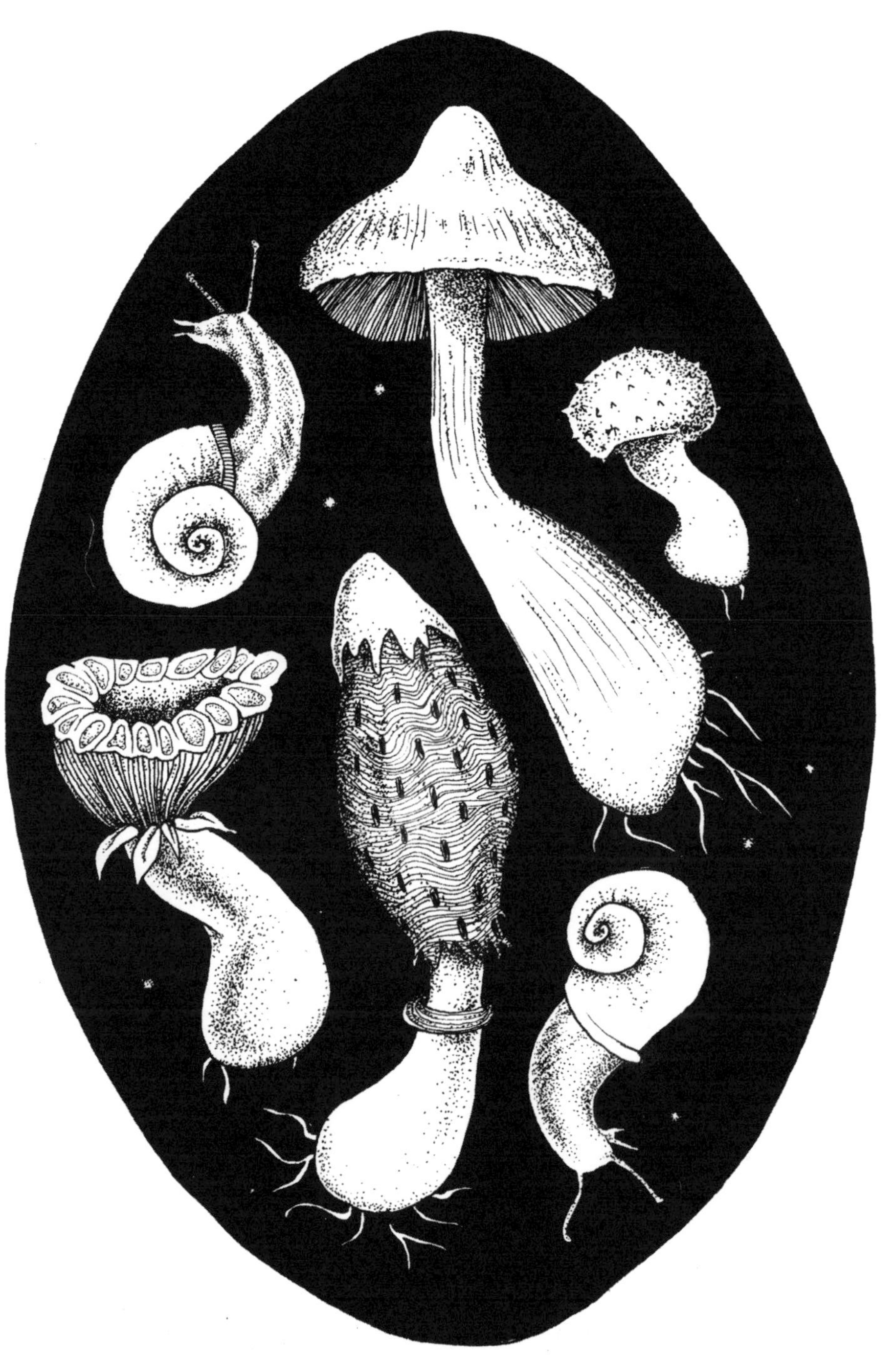

Project 21

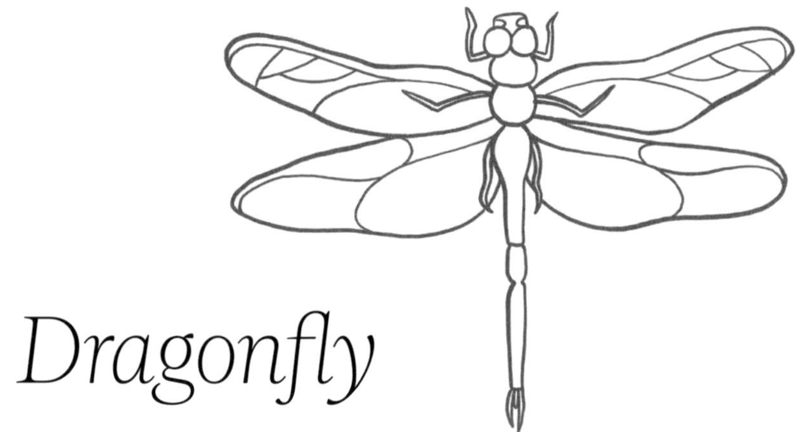

Dragonfly

I love the intricate patterns of dragonflies, and there is so much room for variation and experimentation here. If you have more time, try making a few, perhaps even a group?

STEP 1

Sketch the shape of the dragonfly's body and wings, or trace the outline on page 232.

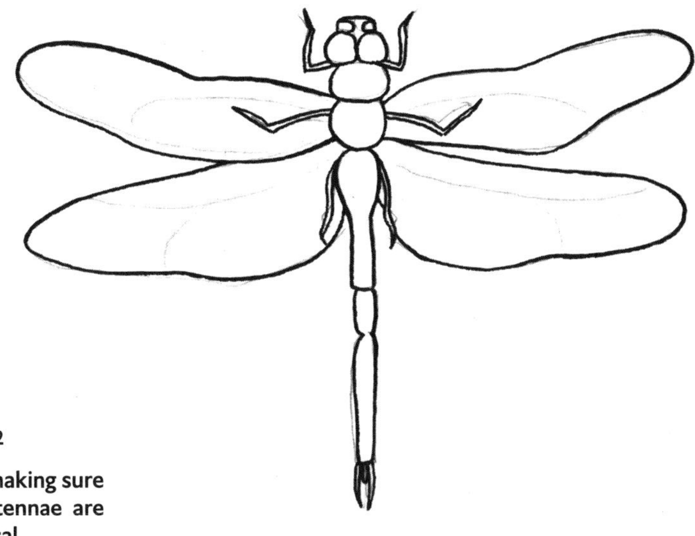

STEP 2

Ink the outline, making sure the legs and antennae are pretty symmetrical.

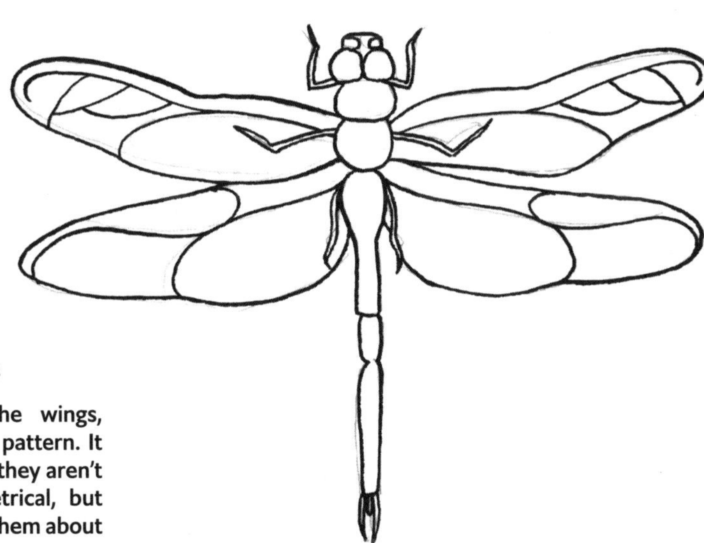

STEP 3

Add lines to the wings, mapping out the pattern. It doesn't matter if they aren't perfectly symmetrical, but I aim for making them about the same.

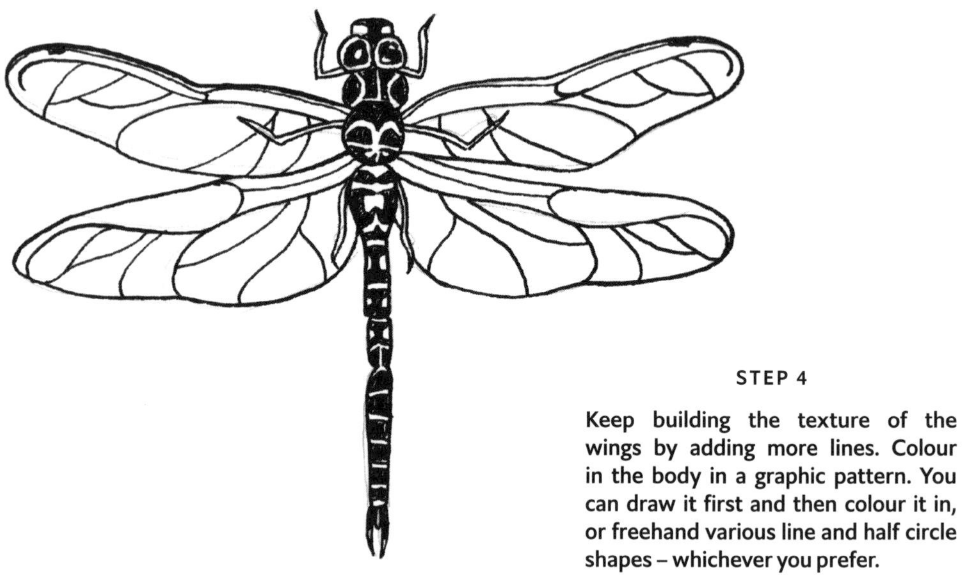

STEP 4

Keep building the texture of the wings by adding more lines. Colour in the body in a graphic pattern. You can draw it first and then colour it in, or freehand various line and half circle shapes – whichever you prefer.

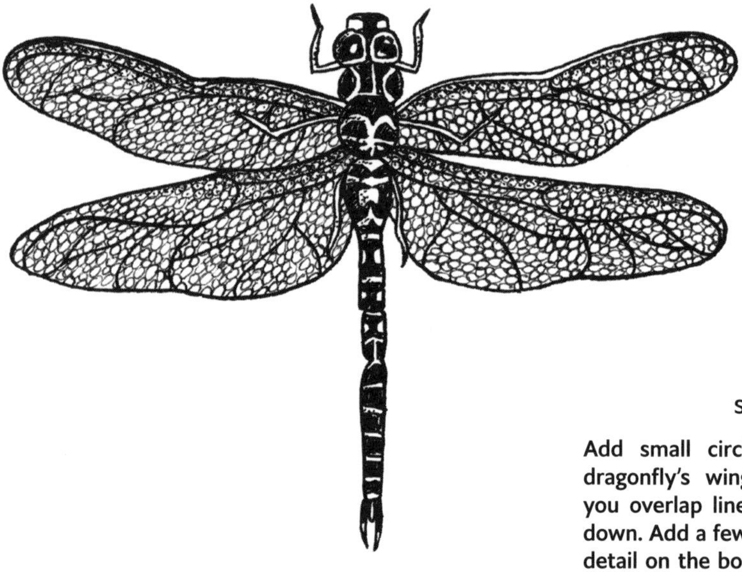

STEP 5

Add small circles covering all the dragonfly's wings – don't worry if you overlap lines you've already put down. Add a few dots for shading and detail on the body, and along the top edge of all four wings. Once the ink is completely dry, erase your pencil lines.

Project 22

Frog

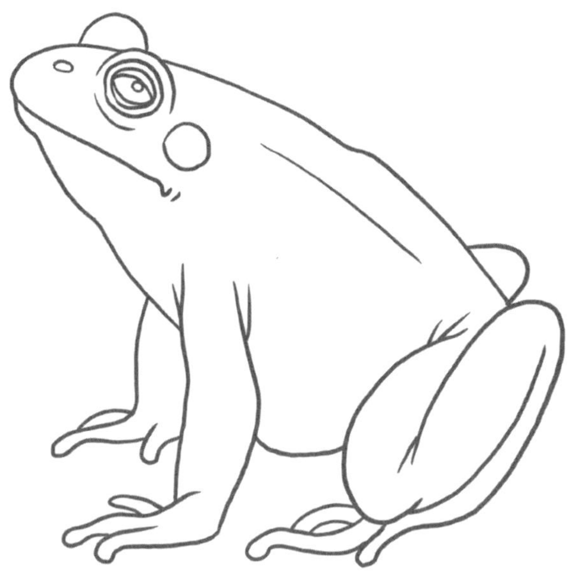

Frogs have been frequent
in my work for the longest
time. I think it is the big
expressive eyes, grumpy face
and human-like proportions
that make them incredibly
characterful and fun to draw.

STEP 1

Sketch the shape of the frog, giving it big eyes that sit on top of the head, folded back legs and long fingers. Alternatively, trace the outline on page 233.

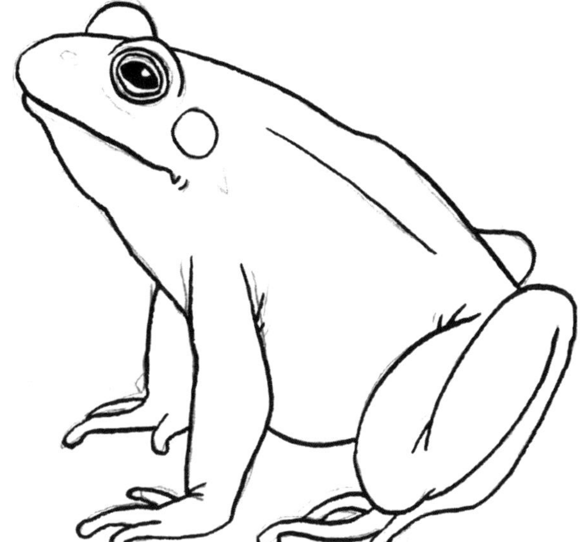

STEP 2

Ink the outline and add small marks to emphasise the skin folds on the arms and legs. Fill the eyeball in black, leaving a small, round highlight. Don't forget about the circle next to the frog's eye – this is its eardrum!

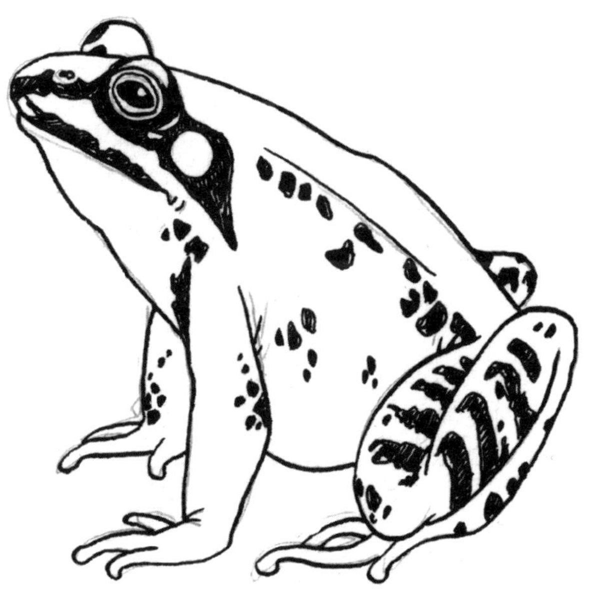

STEP 3

Add markings to the frog's body and colour them in. You needn't be too precious about making them a solid black; I quite like the scratchy texture of the nib and for the paper to shine through.

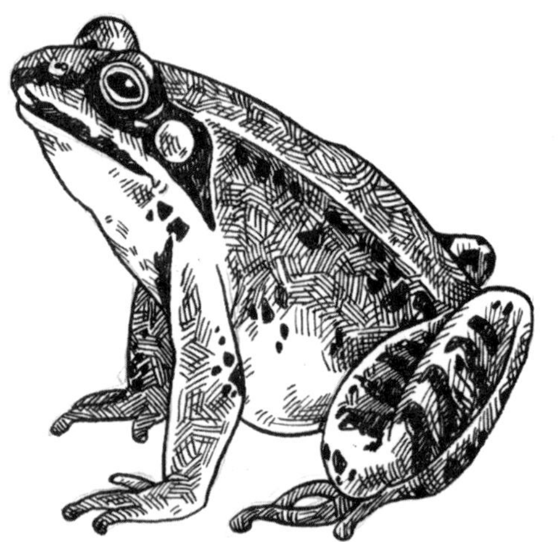

STEP 4

Use crosshatching to build a layer of shadow. Leave a white line across the frog's back and leave light areas at the throat and belly.

STEP 5

Add some dots around the throat, stomach and knee. Use a little bit more crosshatching to bring out the deep shadows along the lower back, hip, behind the elbow and the far leg. Once the ink is completely dry, rub out your pencil lines.

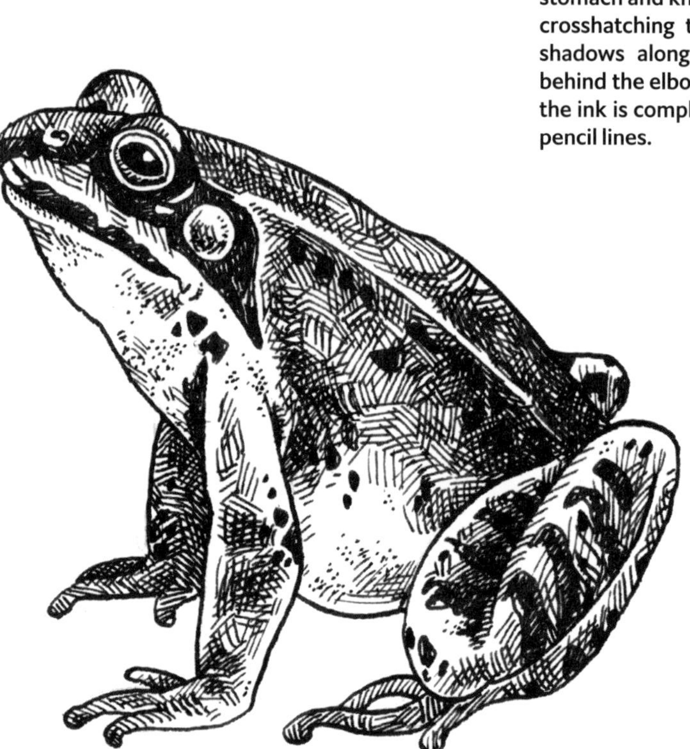

Project 23

Rabbit

A countryside favourite that I simply had to include in this book.

STEP 1

Sketch the shape of your rabbit, making sure to include its long, pointed ears and short tail, or trace the outline on page 233.

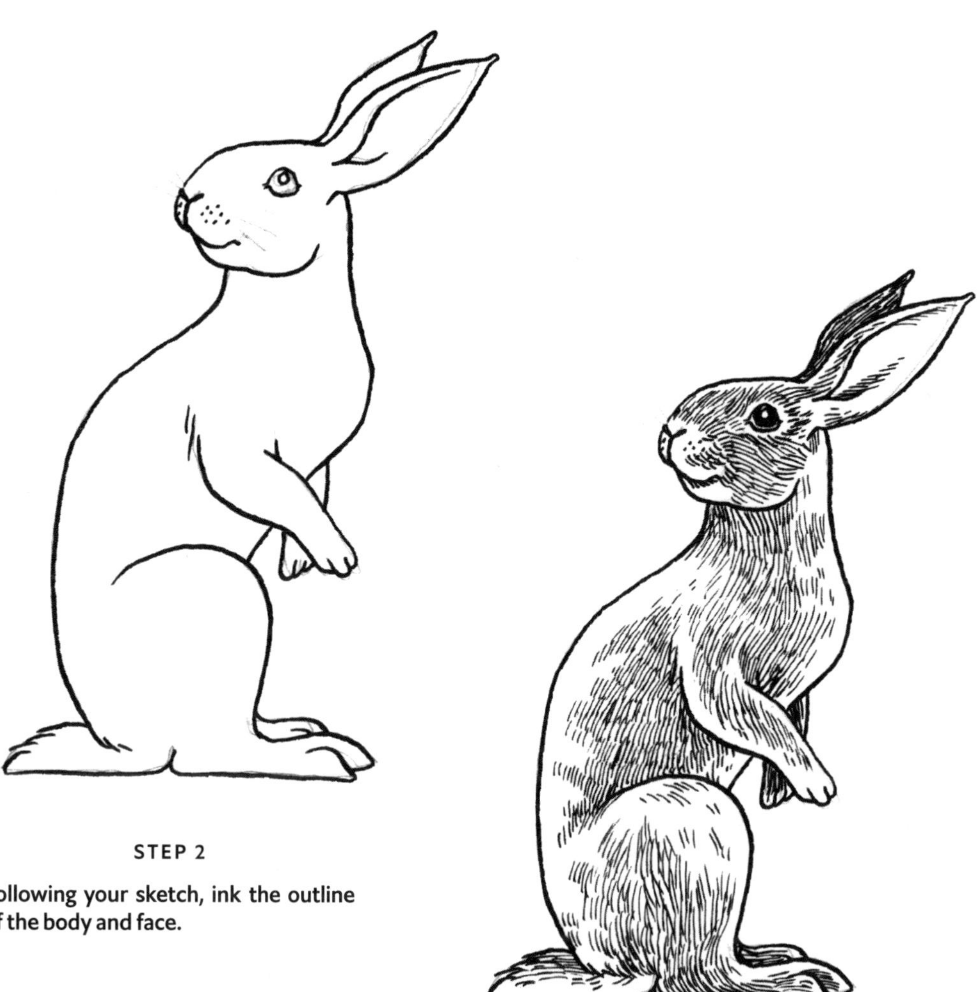

STEP 2

Following your sketch, ink the outline
of the body and face.

STEP 3

Use small lines in the direction of the fur to shade
the rabbit. Leave out the outer edges of its body,
which will make it look as if the light source is
coming from behind. Fill in the eyes, leaving a
small highlight.

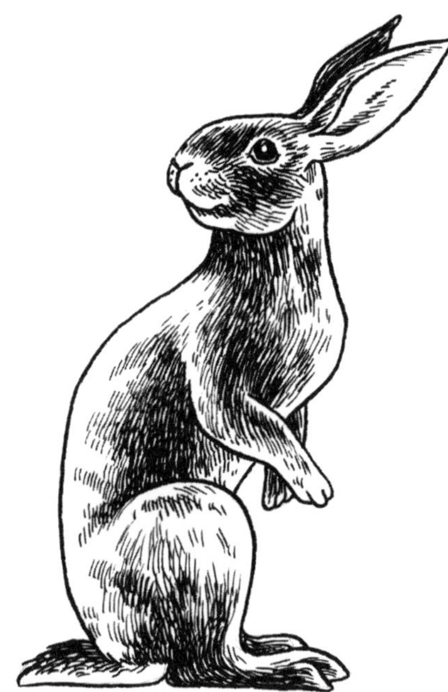

STEP 4

Keep adding more tiny lines to build shadow in the fur. The darkest areas will fall on the ear furthest away, underneath the chin, on the arm, above the hip, and along the bottom of the feet.

STEP 5

Add whiskers and use dots to add detail and pull the drawing together. Once the ink is completely dry, erase your pencil lines.

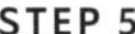

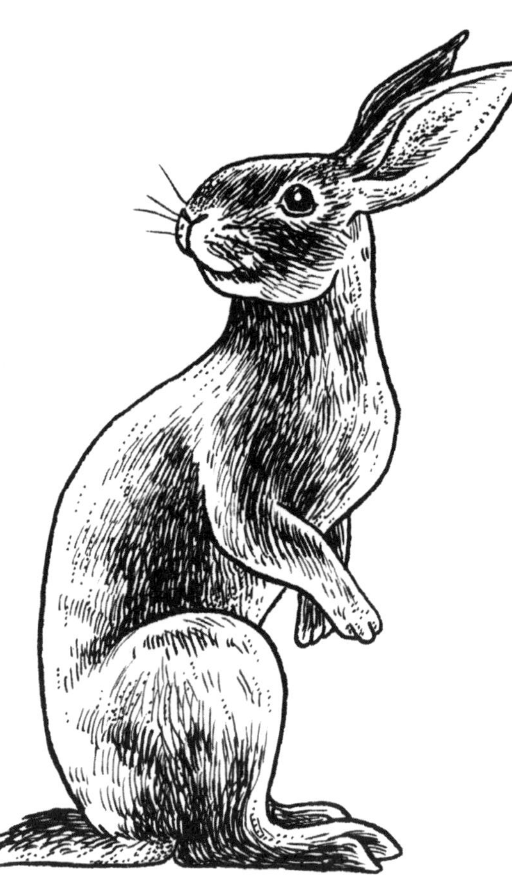

Project 24

Fox

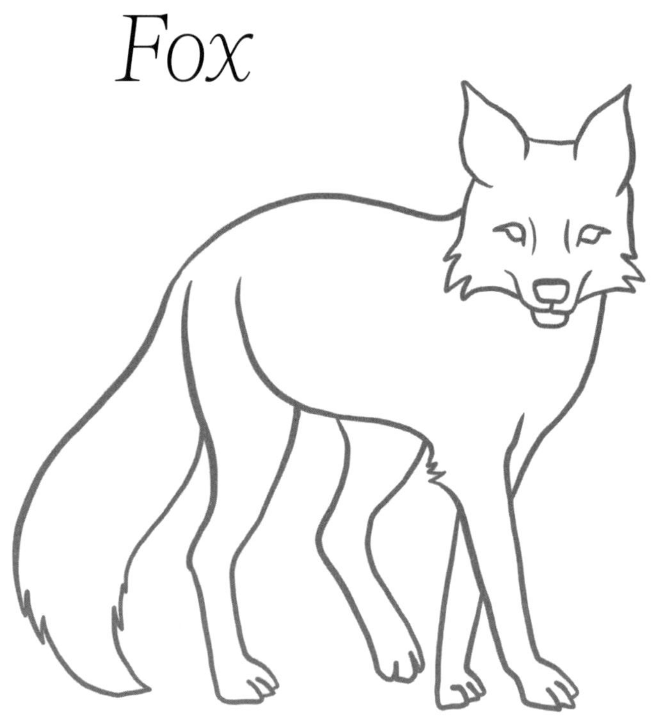

Foxes are a staple in any woodland, fairytale or folktale adventure – always cunning and smart. Fur is also excellent for playing around with texture, to give the fox character.

STEP 1

Sketch out the fox's body, legs, pointed ears and big bushy tail, or trace the outline on page 233.

STEP 2

Ink the outline using your sketch as a guide.

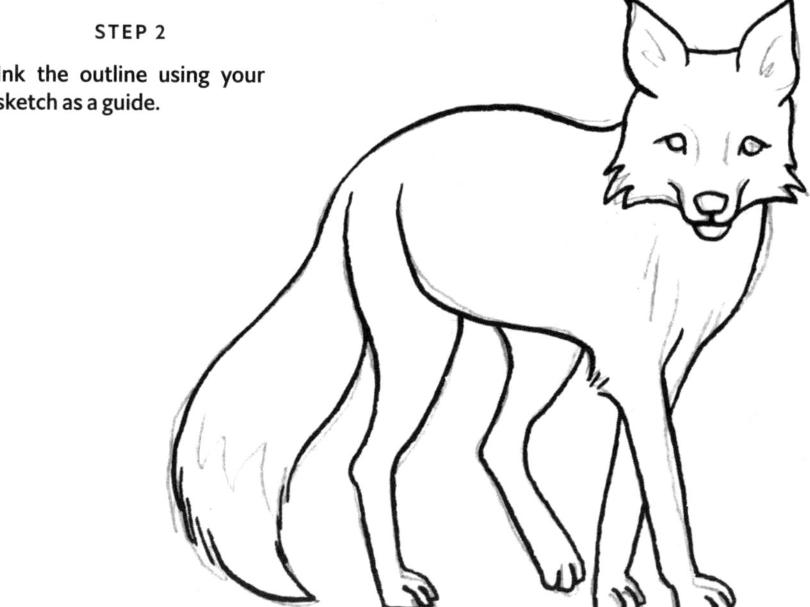

STEP 3

Use short strokes in the direction of the fur's growth, avoiding the areas where the fox has white markings (tip of the tail, ears, chest and face). I have also left out the feet as they are black and you will fill them in later.

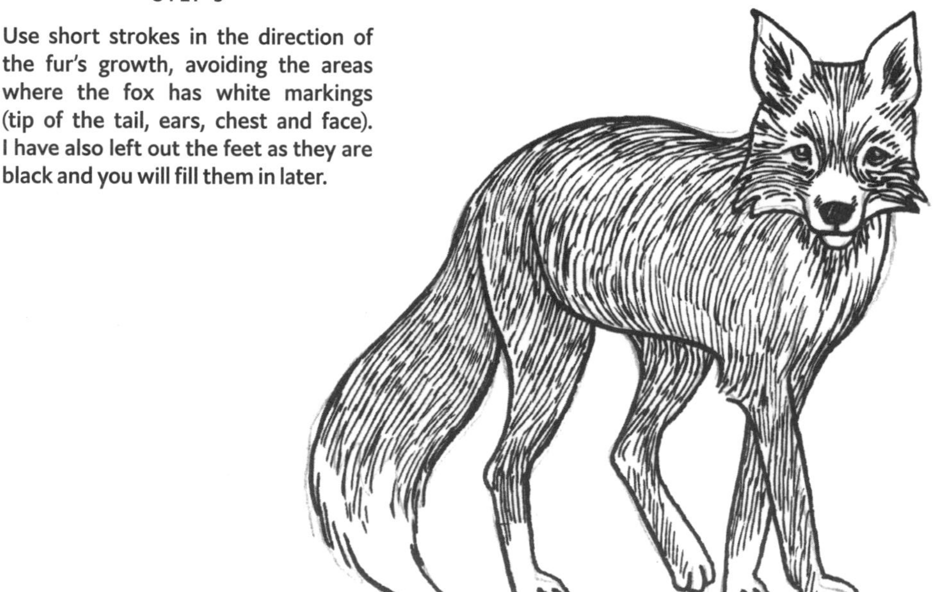

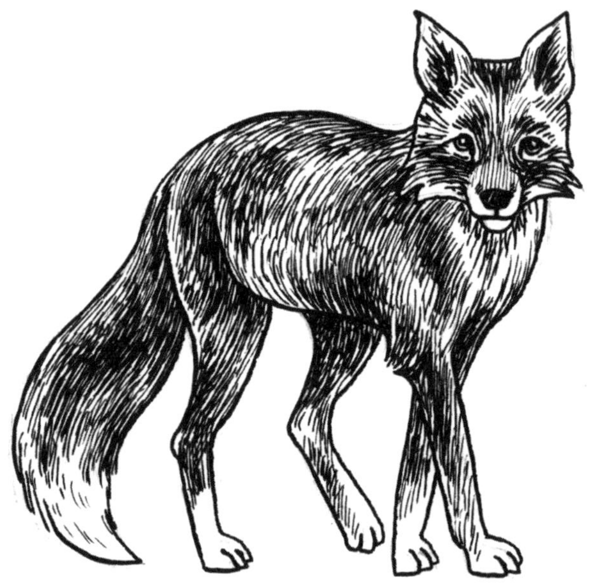

STEP 4

Using the same short strokes, build the texure of the fur and create darker areas for shadow.

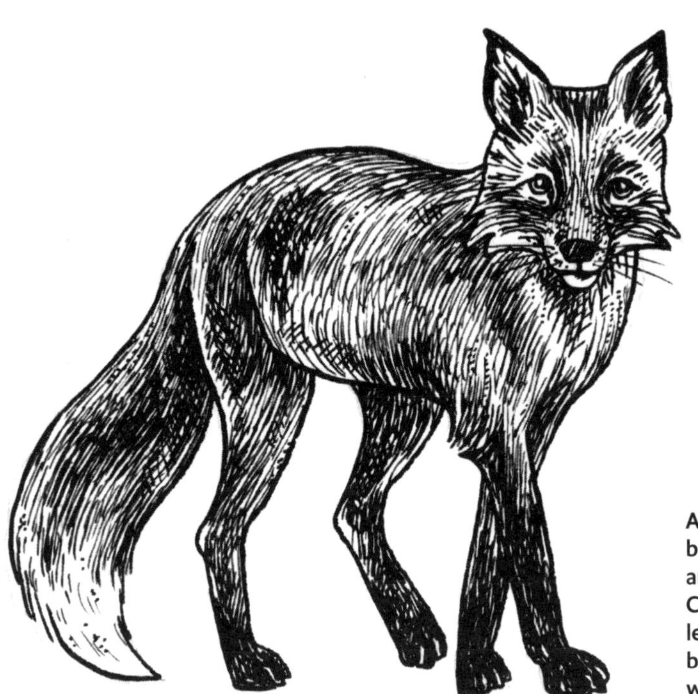

STEP 5

Add a few dots and lines to bring some visual interest and variation to the fur. Colour the feet black, leaving small white areas between the paws, and add whiskers. Once the ink is completely dry, erase your pencil lines.

Project 25

Tawny owl

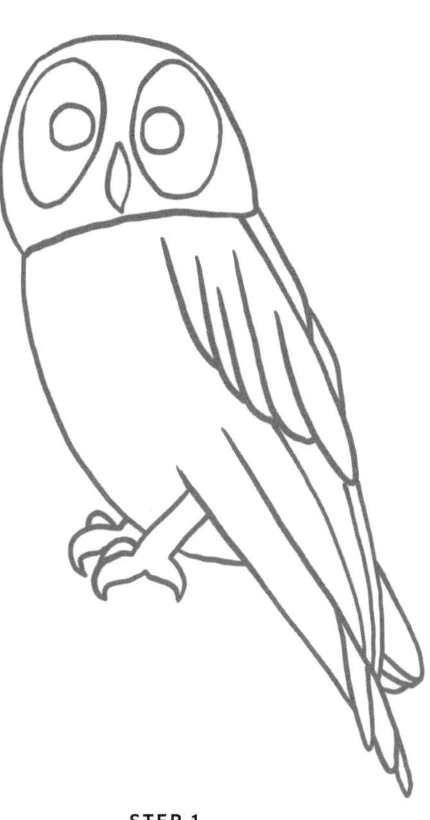

This nocturnal bird of prey is common throughout Europe. Because of its haunting call and night-time hunting it has traditionally, and unfairly, been thought of as a bad omen, so we're going to draw one here to show its beauty.

STEP 1

Sketch your owl with its big eyes, feathery tail and talons, or trace the outline on page 234.

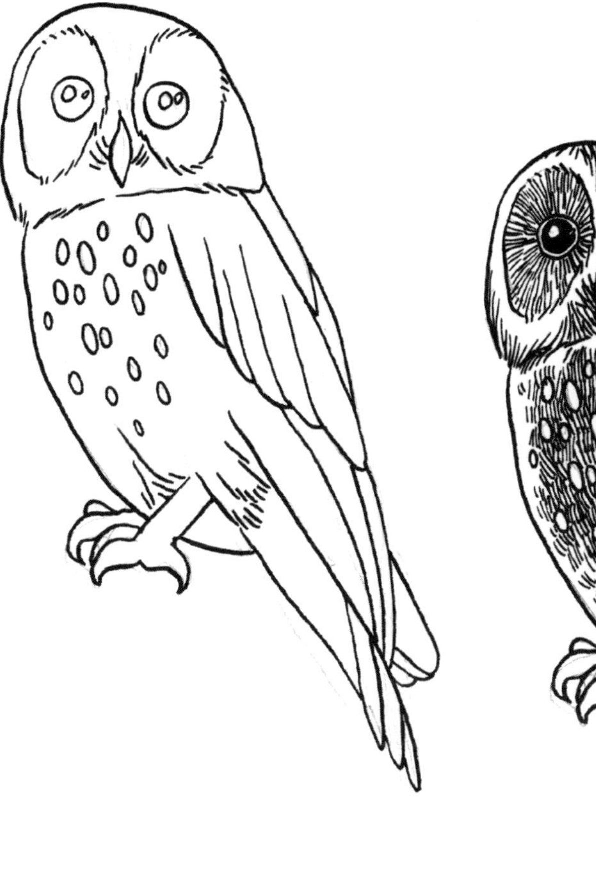

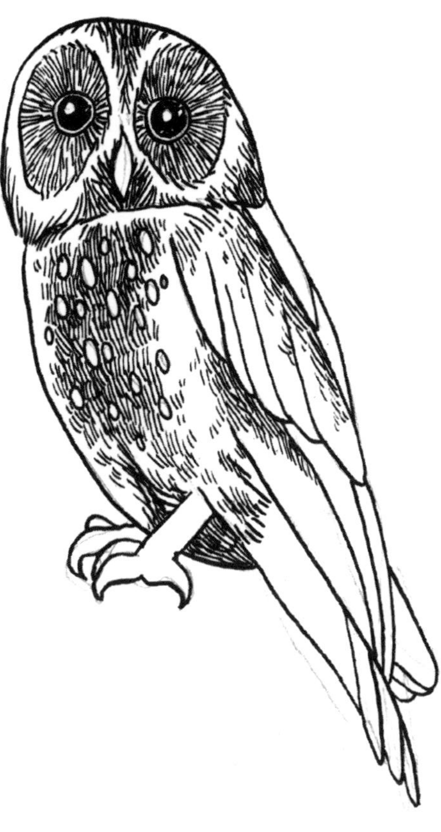

STEP 2

Use your sketch as a guide to ink the outlines of the owl, as well as the shape of the feathers and the circular pattern on its chest.

STEP 3

Colour in the owl's eyes, leaving two small highlights. Use lines to shade in the chest (around the circular pattern), the edges of the wing and the head. For the area around the eyes, make sure your strokes run from the eye outward, in the same direction as the feather pattern.

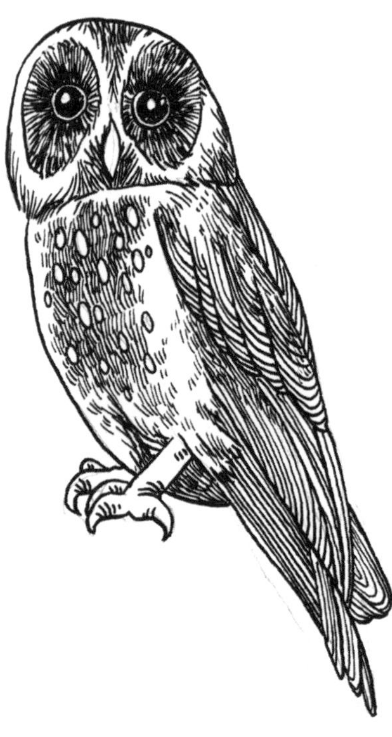

STEP 4

With strokes in the same direction, add more shade around the eyes. Add lines to the wings and feet.

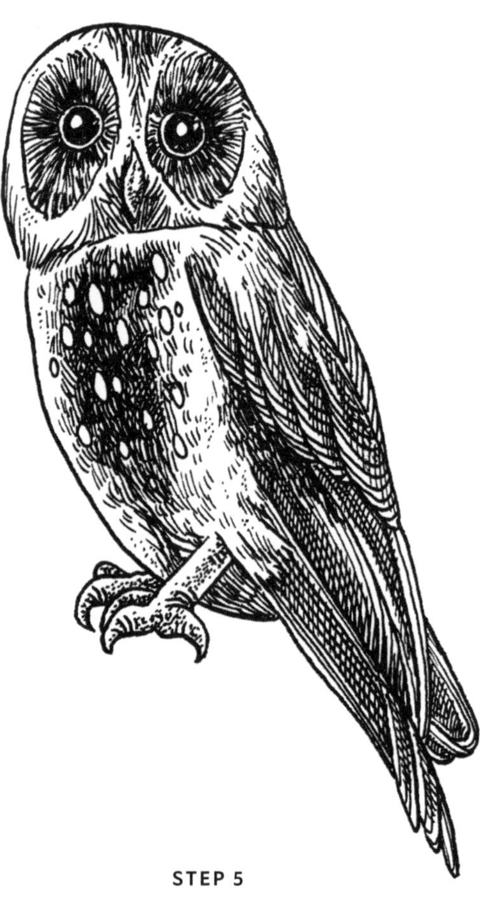

STEP 5

Darken the area in the middle of the chest with crosshatching, and add straight lines (in a different direction to the first) to shade the wing and tail feathers. Add a few dots for detail, including on the claws and beak. Once the ink is completely dry, erase your pencil lines.

Project 26

Stag beetle

There are about 12,000 species of stag beetle in the world – why not try experimenting with a few different types? The males are easily recognisable by their large, antler-like jaws, which they use for showing off and fighting other beetles.

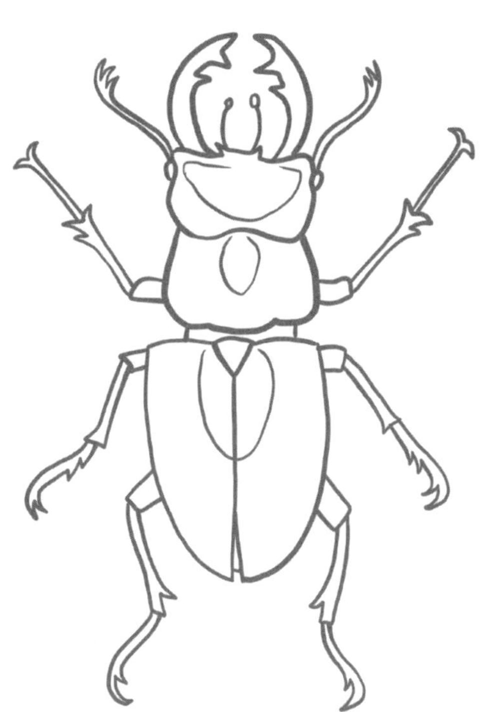

STEP 1

Sketch the shape of the beetle's body, legs and jaws or trace the outline on page 234.

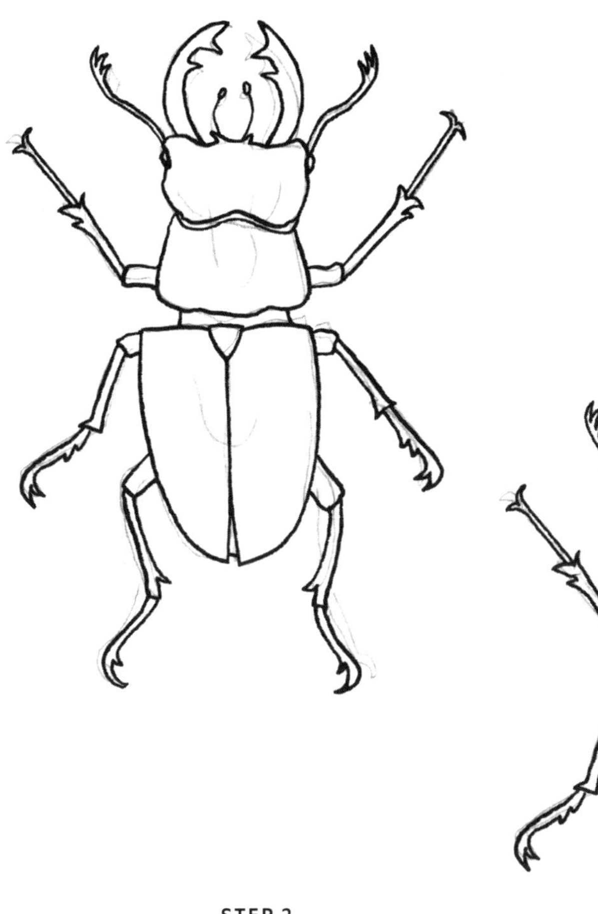

STEP 2

Follow your sketch and ink the beetle's outline. It doesn't need to be perfectly symmetrical, but make sure that pairs of limbs are about the same length.

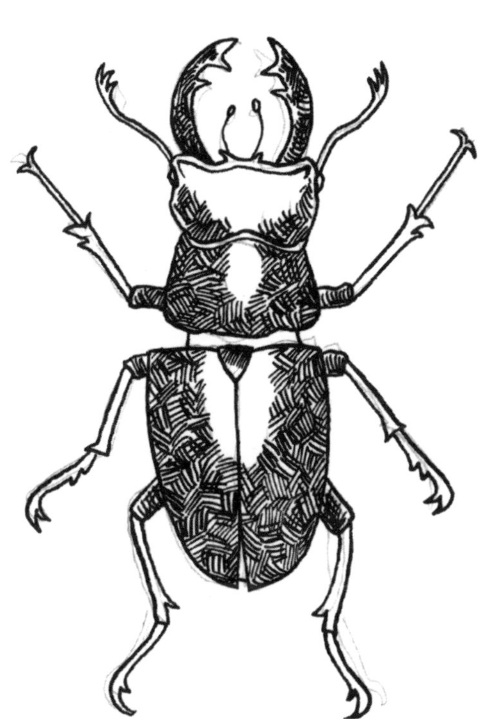

STEP 3

Use crosshatching to shade the outer edges of the beetle's body and jaws.

STEP 4

Build more shadow and tone with another layer of crosshatching. The beetle is darkest on the outer edges of its body. Colour in the legs, but leave a small highlight on the side of any leg that faces up or outwards.

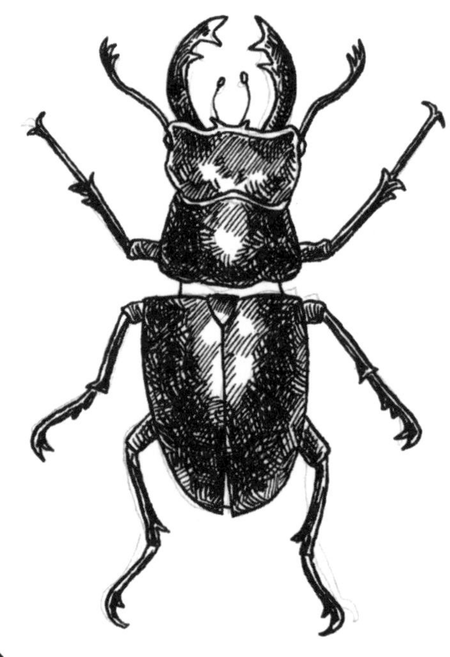

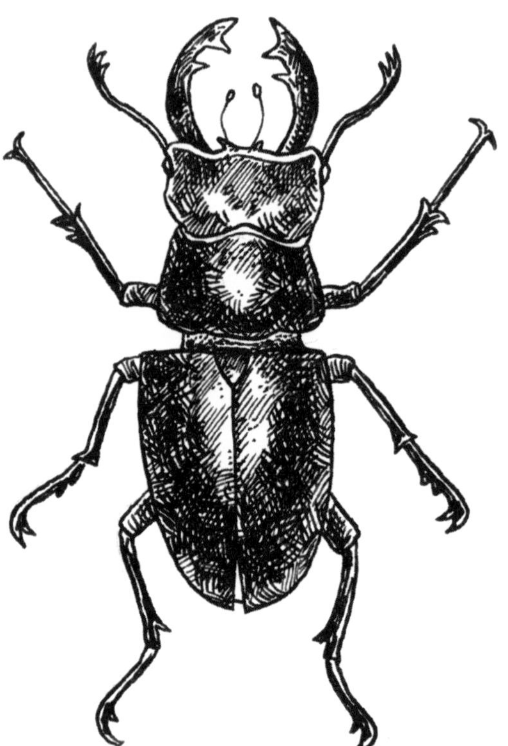

STEP 5

Use dots to add final details and shading. Once the ink is completely dry, rub out your pencil lines.

Project 27

Bat

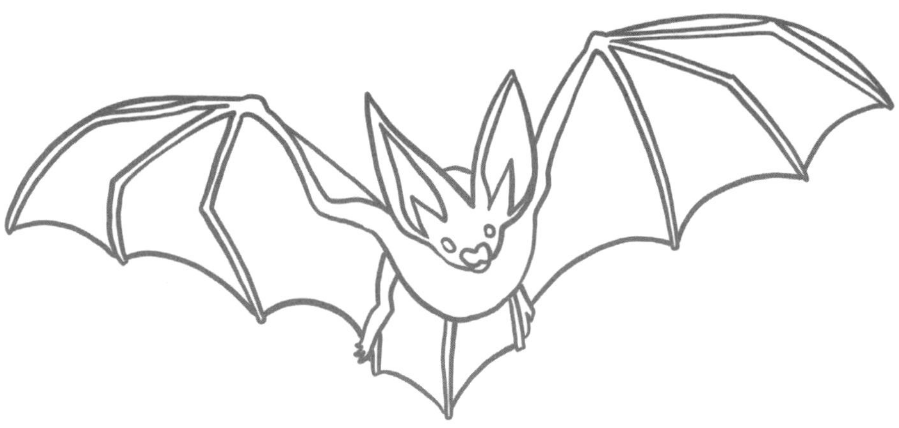

This bat, the common pipistrelle, is so small it can fit in a matchbox. It's both the smallest and the most common bat in the UK. You can draw yours any size you like!

STEP 1

Sketch the shape of the bat with extended wings, or trace the outline on page 234.

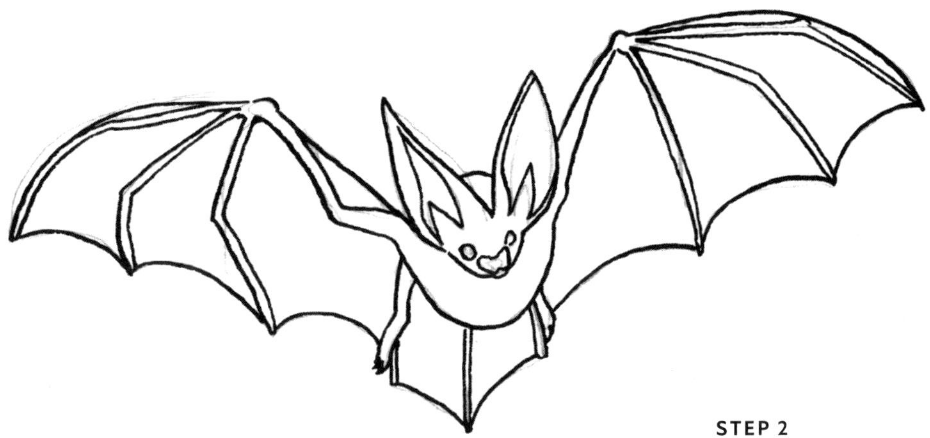

STEP 2

Using your sketch as a guide, ink the outline.

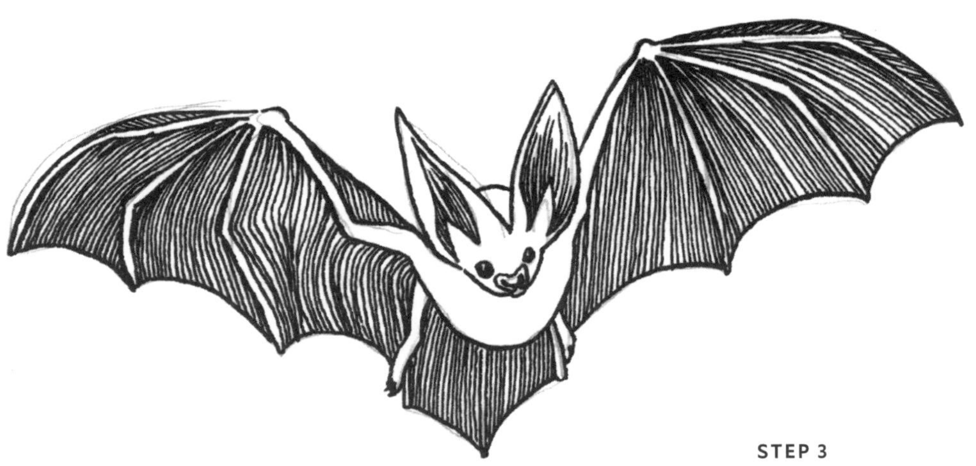

STEP 3

Add thin parallel lines to the wings and ears, following the outline of the shape you are filling in. The lines should be vertical, but not straight. Fill in the eyes and nose, leaving small circular highlights on the eyes and top of the nose.

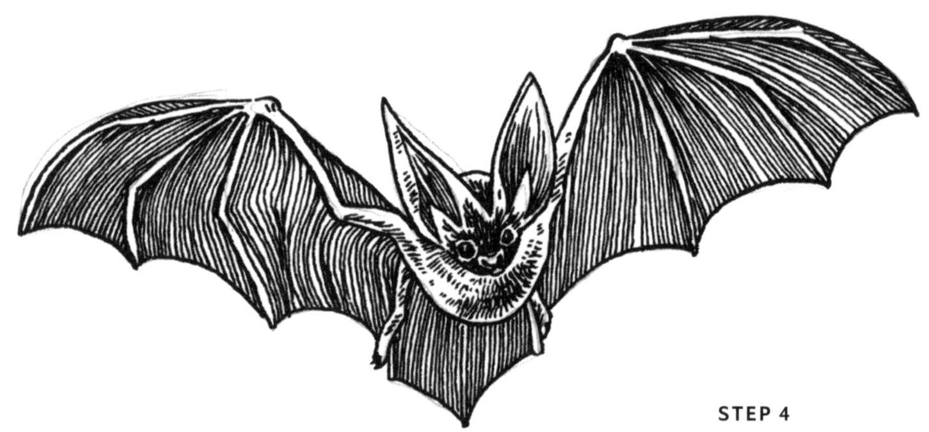

STEP 4

Add small lines to shade the bat's body to give the impression of fur. Shade the ears.

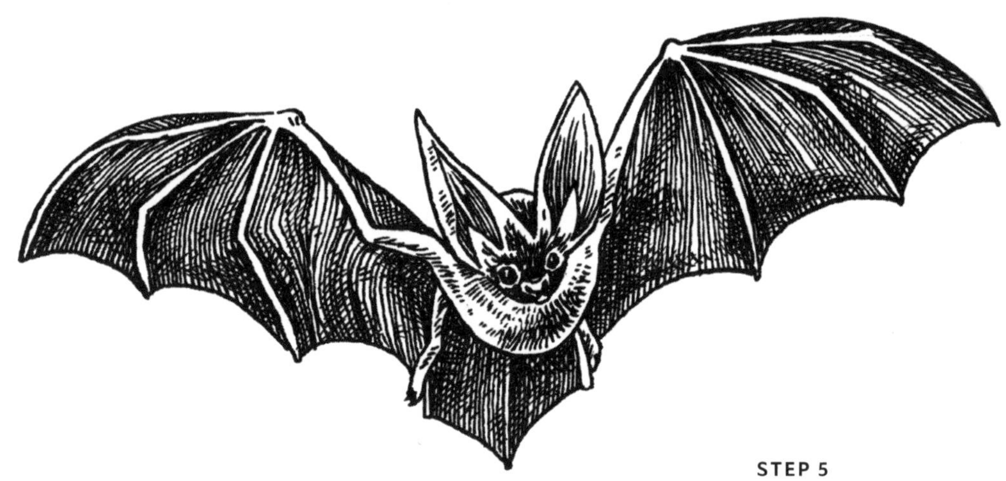

STEP 5

Crosshatch the wings to shade and give depth. I don't place lines in any particular direction, but slowly build shaded areas at the top and bottom of the wings. Once the ink is completely dry, rub out your pencil lines.

Project 28

Chaffinch

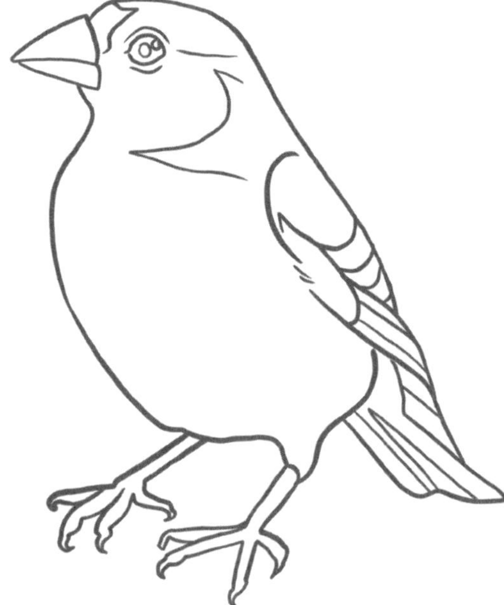

Chaffinches are common garden (and bird feeder) visitors, so I had to include one. In the 19th Century, chaffinches were highly valued for their song, and caged for use in competitions.

STEP 1

Sketch the shape of the chaffinch with its pointed beak and round belly, or trace the outline on page 234.

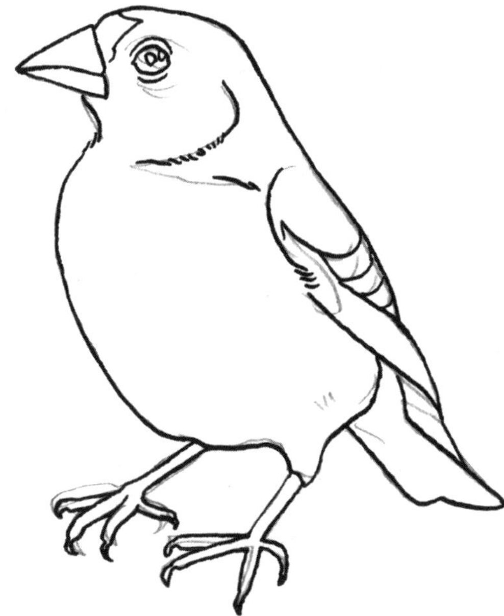

STEP 2

Ink the outline, making sure to give the bird big eyes and small pointed claws.

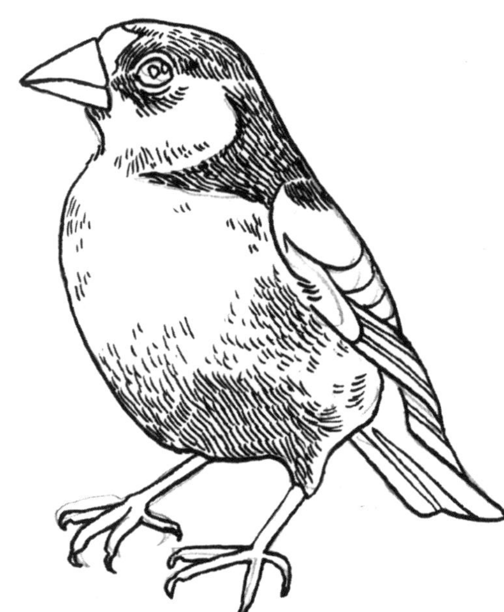

STEP 3

Draw lines on the wing to map out the pattern. Next, use small lines (a little like fur texture) to hint at the feathery texture of the bird – darker around the head and belly, and lighter underneath the eye and on the breast.

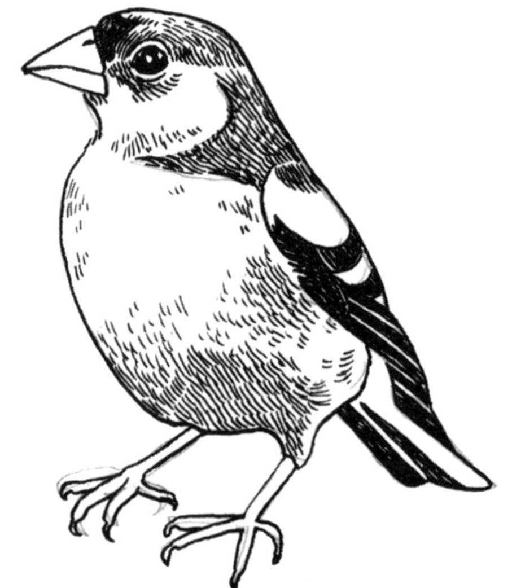

STEP 4

Colour in the dark parts of the wings and eye, as well as the dark marking on the forehead.

STEP 5

Use small lines to darken the areas on the belly, throat and head. Draw thin parallel lines on the end of the tail. Finally, use dots to shade the feet and add a little more detail to the body. Once the ink is dry, erase your pencil lines.

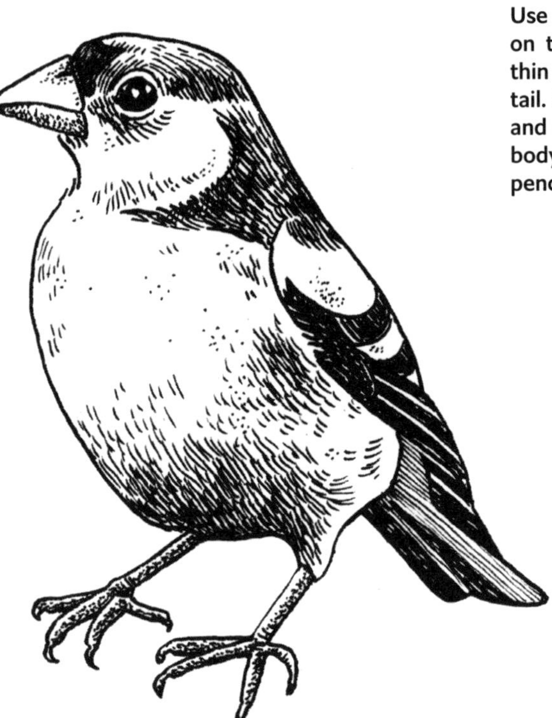

Project 29

Hedgehog

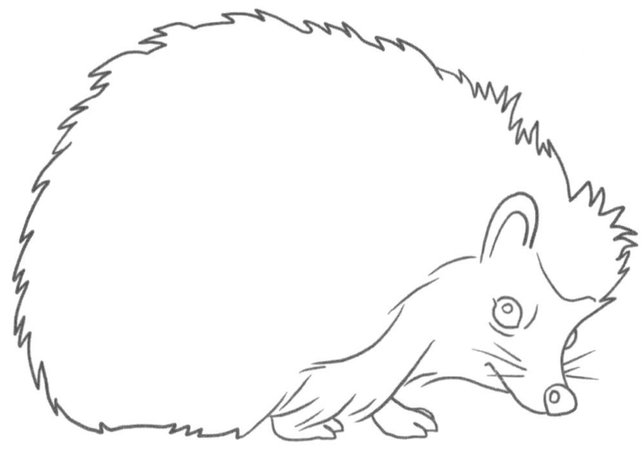

I'll take any excuse to draw what is (probably) the UK's most popular spiky mammal. They are a lot of fun to draw because of their simple body shape, paired with tiny legs and an adorable face.

STEP 1

Sketch the outline of the hedgehog. A pointy snout and big eyes are a recipe for a cute face! Alternatively, trace the outline on page 235.

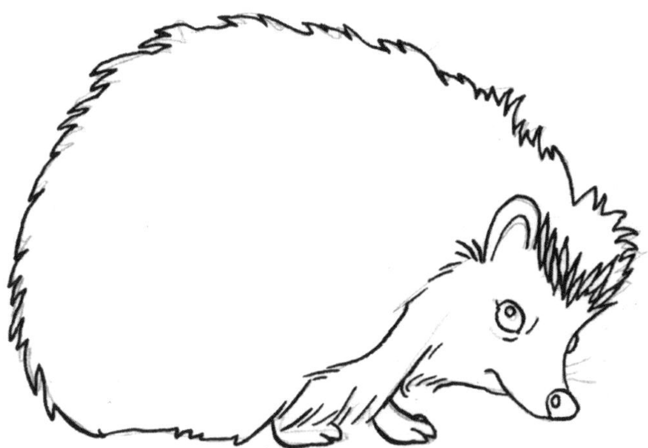

STEP 2

Ink the outline, marking out small spikes along the back of the hedgehog.

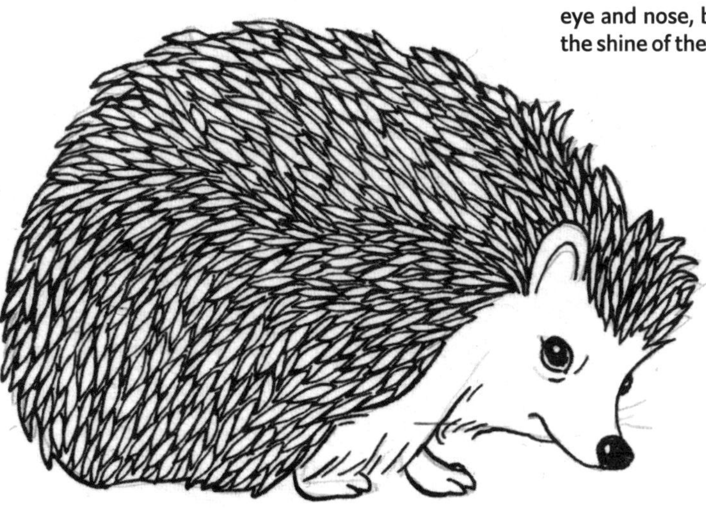

STEP 3

Build the hedgehog's spikes by drawing small pointy ellipse shapes across its back, a bit like rice grains (see detail, left). Begin around the face, and keep building spikes behind each other until the back is covered. Fill in the eye and nose, but leave a highlight for the shine of the eye and the nostril.

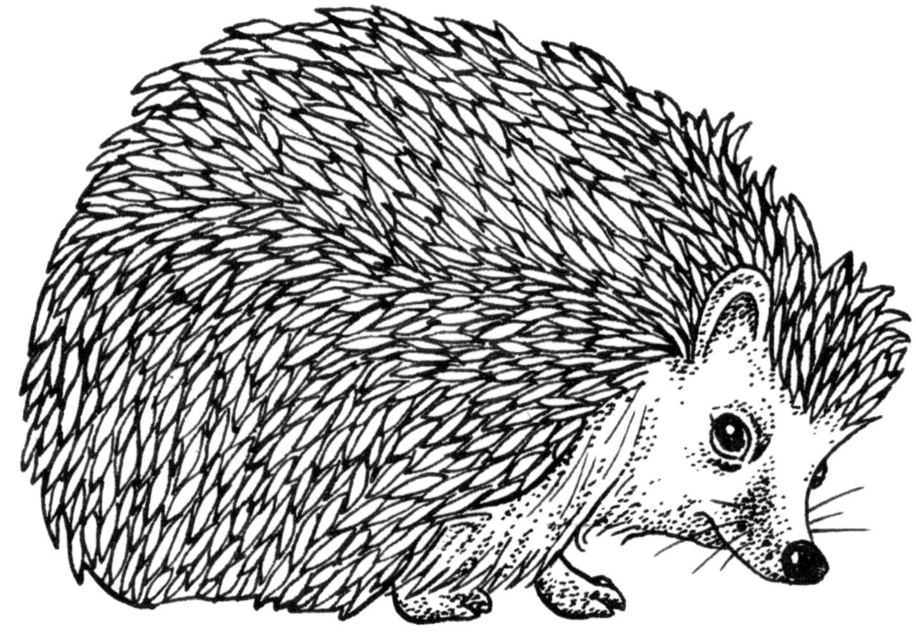

STEP 4

Use pointillism to shade the face and front feet. Less is usually more, but add a little shadow under and above the eye. Lastly, add some whiskers. Once the ink is completely dry, rub out your pencil lines.

Project 30

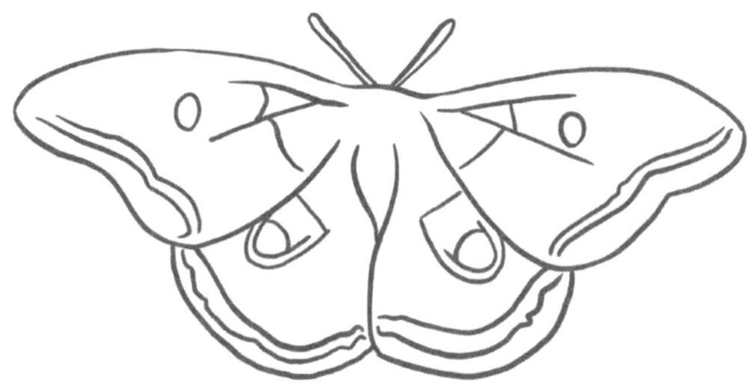

Moth

Although they are usually outshone by butterflies, moths are just as beautiful in their own right. They're a bit stouter in build, fluffier and less colourful, which makes them a great candidate for ink drawing.

STEP 1

Sketch the outline of the moth, giving it four large wings and two antennae, or trace the outline on page 234.

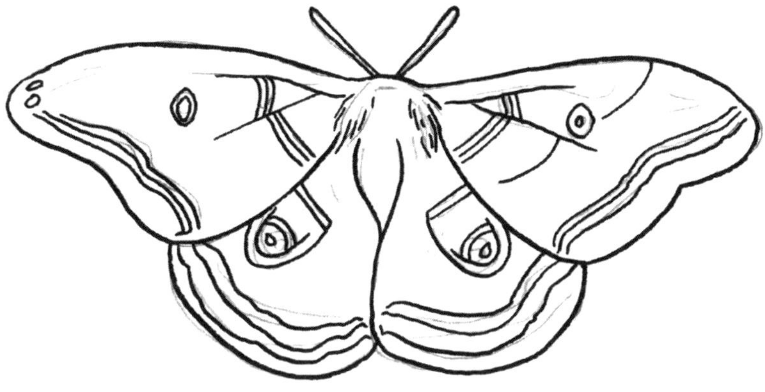

STEP 2

Ink the outline of your sketch, adding three uneven lines to the bottom of each wing, and short lines around the fluffy part of the body.

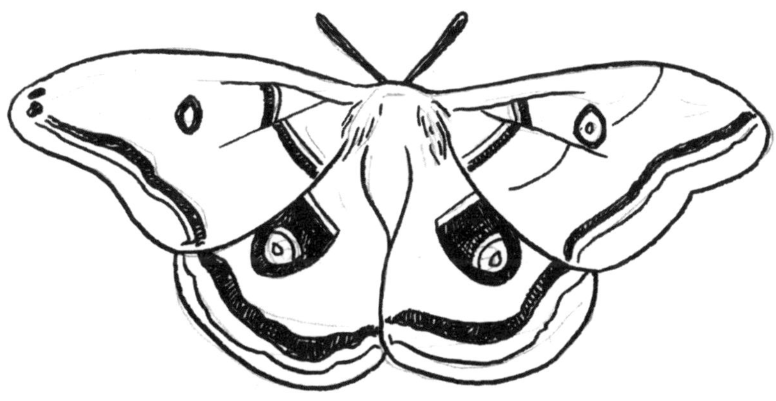

STEP 3

Fill in the antennae and the pattern you have created on the wings using scratchy texture or crosshatching. You will have a thick, filled in line, with a single line next to it.

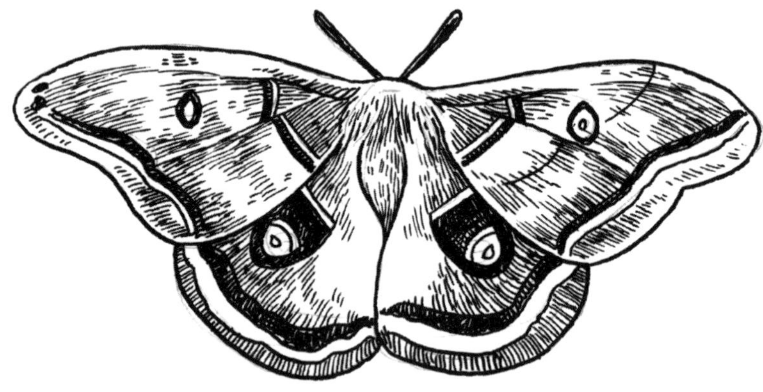

STEP 4

Use short lines, all pointing towards the head, to map out the dark areas of the moth's body. Leave the middle of the wings, and the middle line on the wings, white.

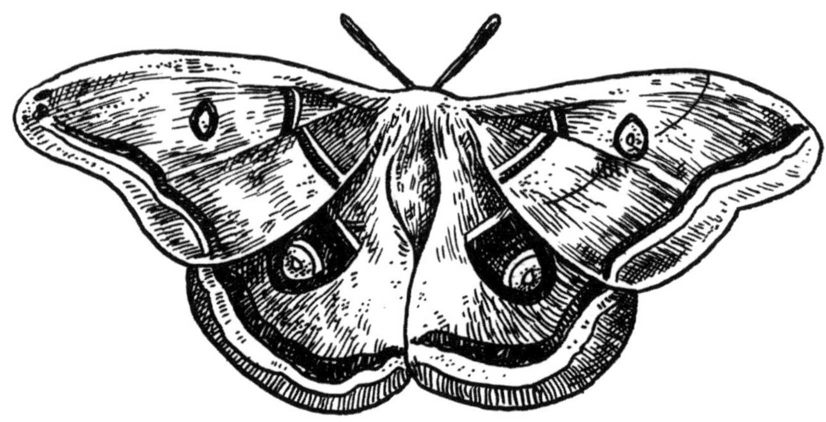

STEP 5

Use dots and small lines to build texture and depth. The colour is darkest under the area where the top set of wings overlap the bottom set, as well as on the bottom wings where they attach to the body. Once the ink is completely dry, erase your pencil lines.

Project 31

Sleeping squirrel

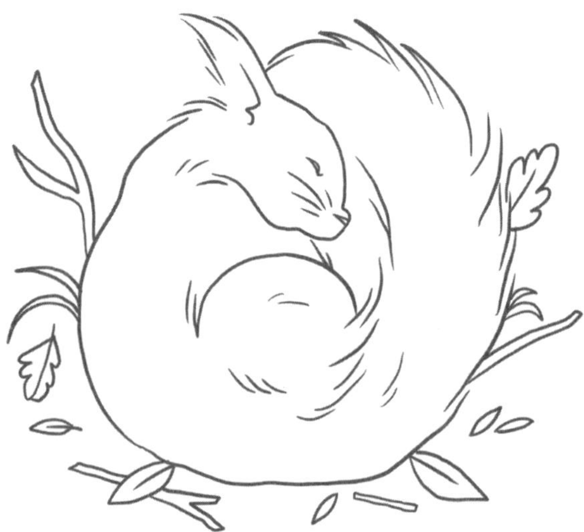

A sleeping squirrel is essentially a big ball of fur with facial features. I love the repetitiveness of drawing fur and, with a little bit of foliage for context, the squirrel comes to life.

STEP 1

Sketch the shape of the squirrel inside a big circle. Add a small pointy nose, long ears, the shape of the hip and a big, bushy tail. Alternatively, trace the outline on page 235.

STEP 2

Ink the outline in the direction of the fur, using small strokes but leaving white space in between.

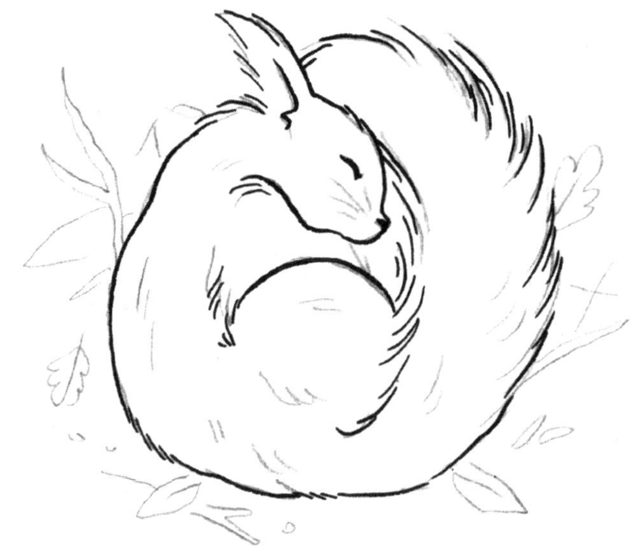

STEP 3

Again using light strokes, build fur texture, always in the same direction.

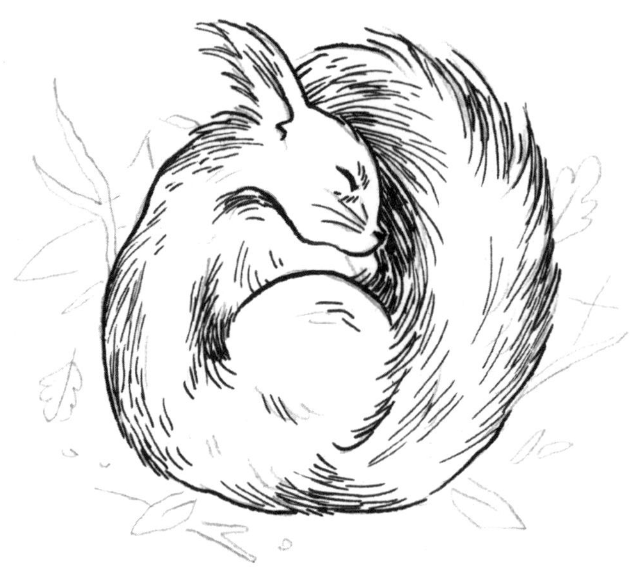

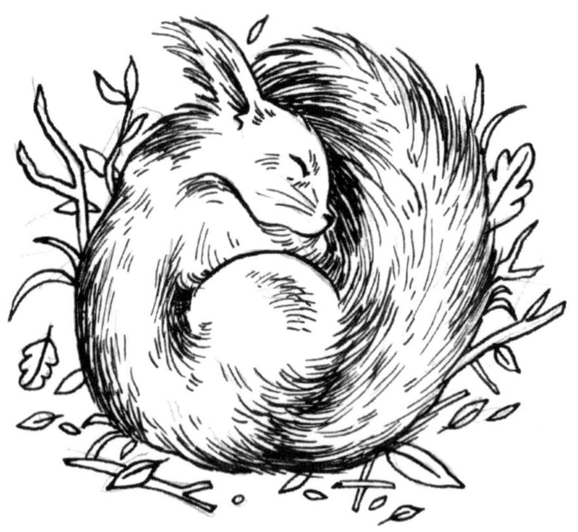

STEP 4

Add sticks, leaves and grass underneath the squirrel. Keep building shade and depth in the fur. The darkest areas will be the tail section underneath its head, and the spine and the base of the tail.

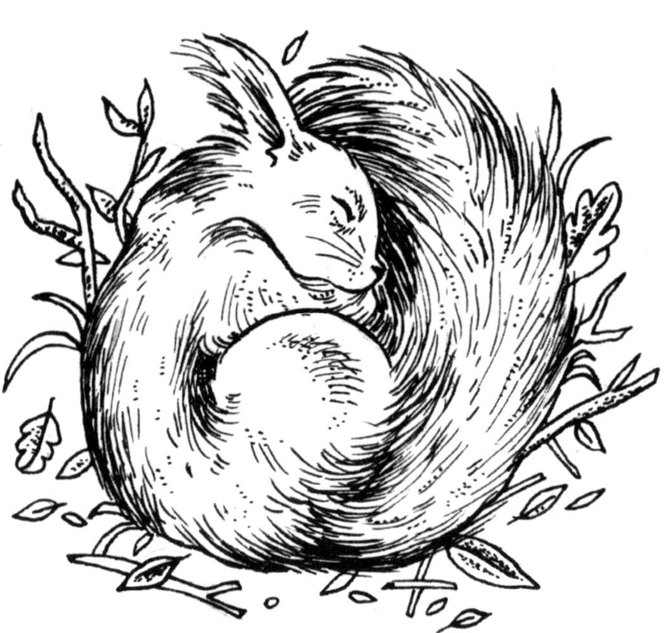

STEP 5

Add dots in small rows throughout the fur to add life and variation in texture. Using the same technique, shade some of the leaves and branches. Once the ink is completely dry, erase your pencil lines.

Project 32

Field mouse

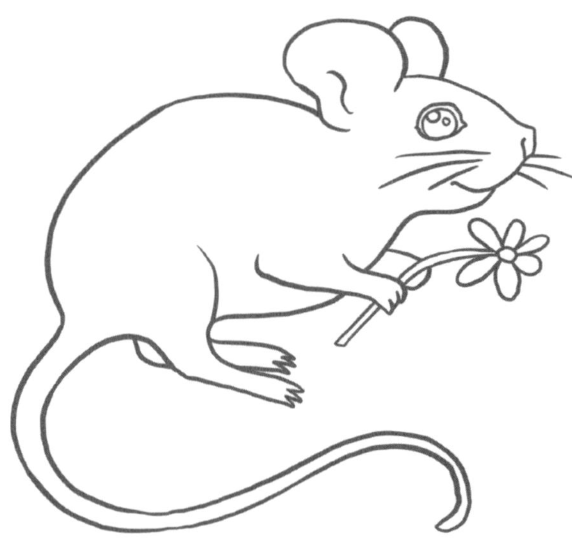

I grew up with Jill Barklem's *Brambly Hedge*, Beatrix Potter's *The Tailor of Gloucester* and Kenneth Grahame's *The Wind in the Willows*. Mice and other tiny forest creatures are always a joy to encounter, and I love imagining what little burrows they're hurrying away to as I draw them.

STEP 1

Sketch the outline of the mouse. I've given her big ears and big round eyes, as well as a little flower in her paw. Alternatively, trace the outline on page 235.

STEP 2

Follow your sketch in ink, outlining the body. Give the eye one big and one smaller highlight.

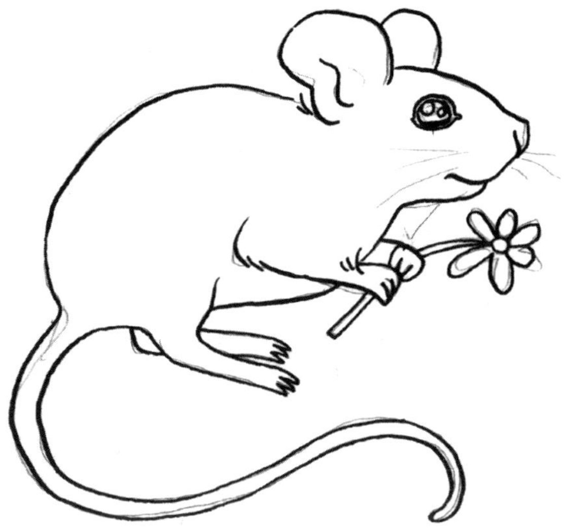

STEP 3

Use short strokes to indicate the direction of the fur on the mouse's body. Add little dots where the whiskers will go, and short lines to shade the ears.

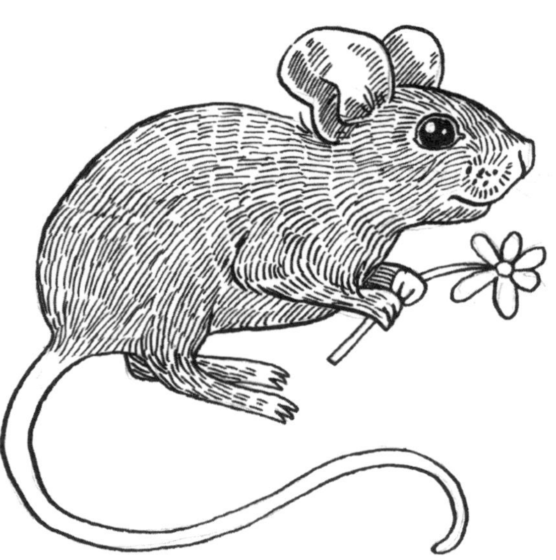

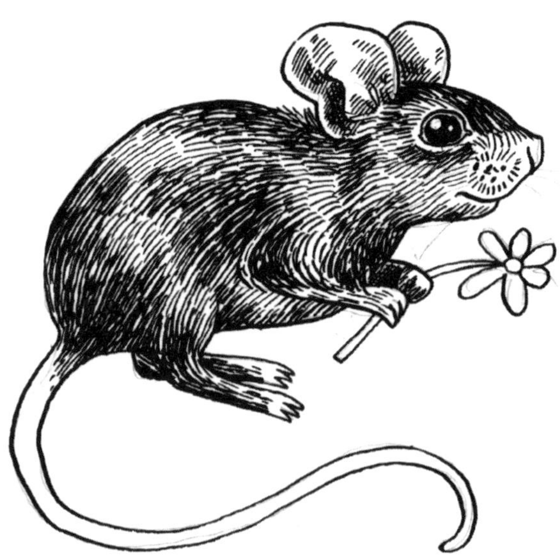

STEP 4

Using more of the same small strokes in the direction of the fur, keep building shadow and tone. It will be darkest on the forehead and spine, elbow and underneath the arm, as well as the seat, hip and back legs.

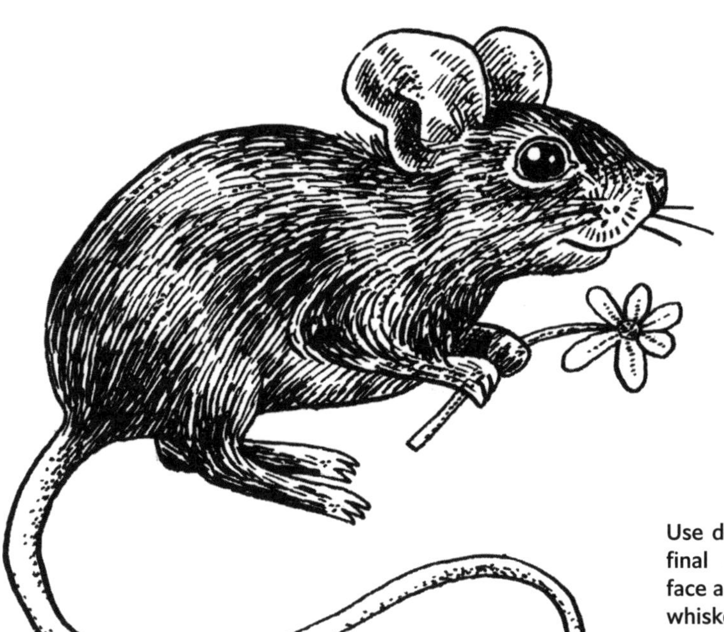

STEP 5

Use dots to add detail and final shading to the tail, face and flower. Finally, add whiskers. Once the ink is completely dry, rub out your pencil lines.

Project 33

Newt

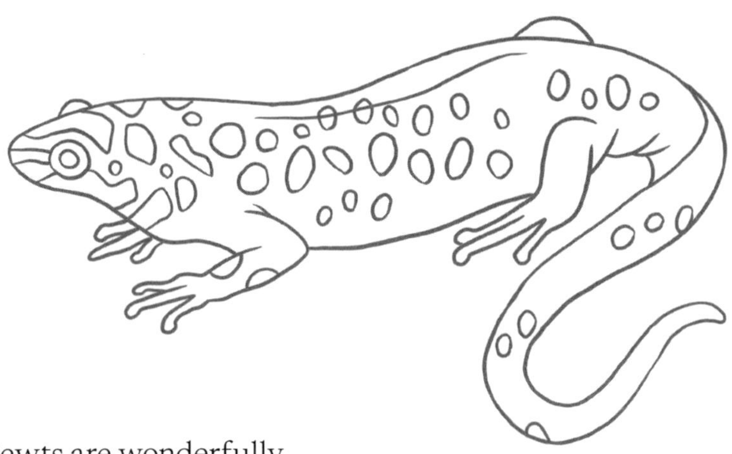

Newts are wonderfully weird, and a fun way to experiment with unusual shapes. They are widely spread across the UK, and a common inhabitant in garden ponds.

STEP 1

Sketch the outline of the newt and the pattern on its skin using asymmetrical, random and oval shapes, or trace the outline on page 235.

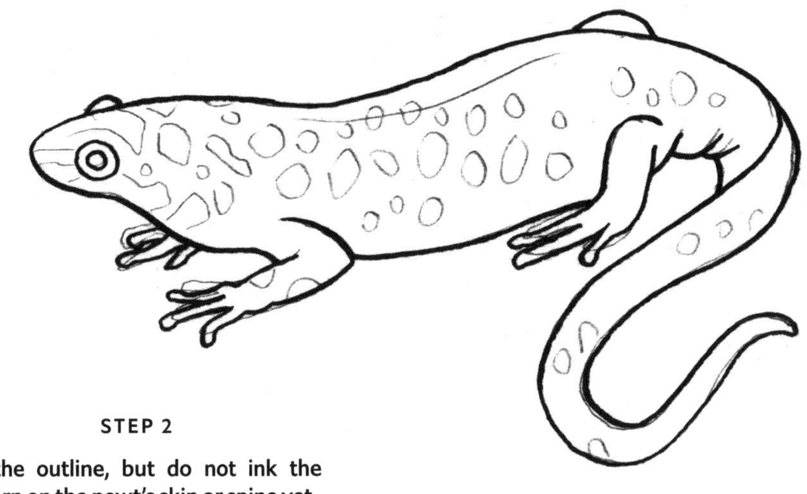

STEP 2

Ink the outline, but do not ink the pattern on the newt's skin or spine yet.

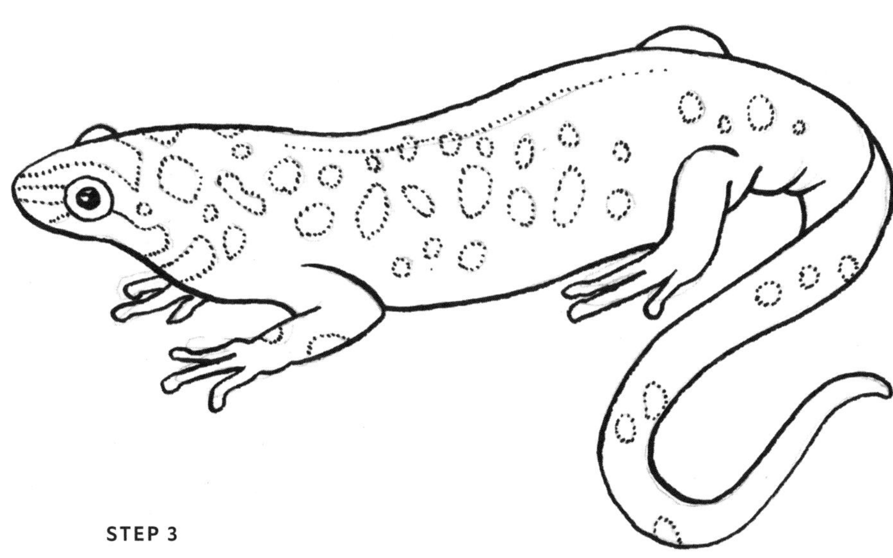

STEP 3

Use small dots to outline the pattern on the newt's back and the line along its spine. Fill in the eye, leaving a highlight.

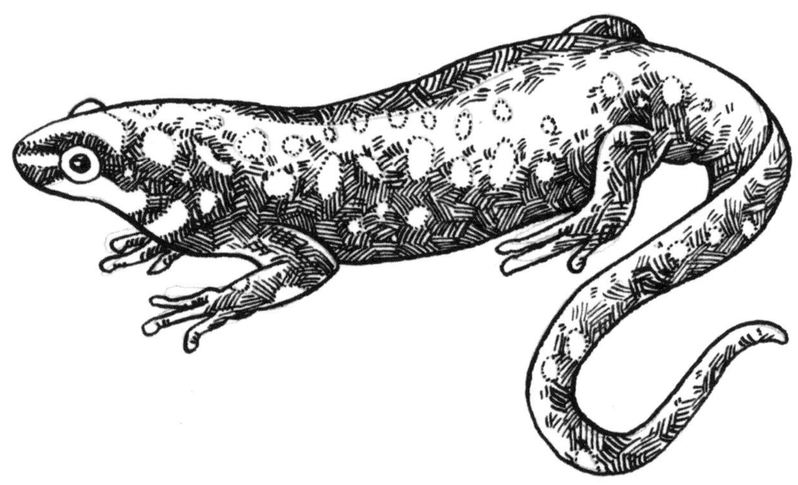

STEP 4

Use crosshatching to shade, leaving a white highlight along
the newt's back and the top of its tail.

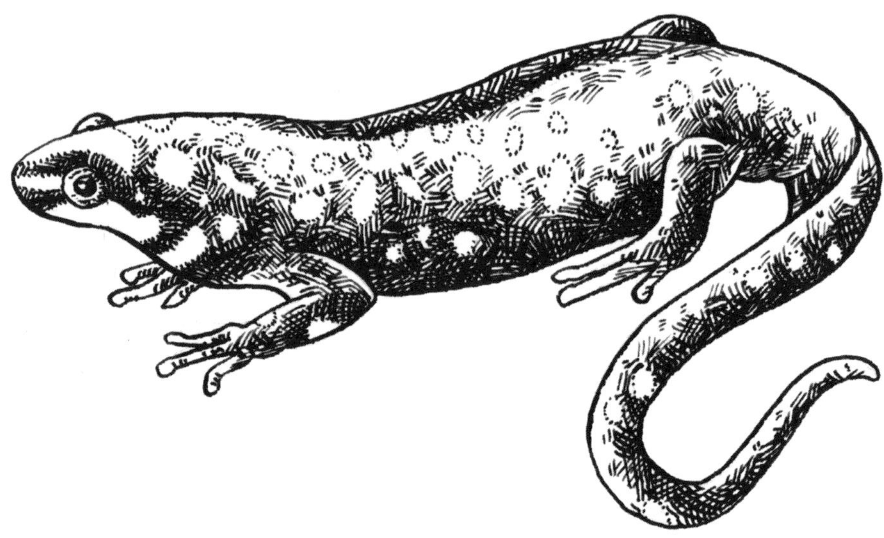

STEP 5

Add another, smaller layer of crosshatching top and bottom,
to darken the underside of the body and tail. Add a little
detail to the eye area using dots. Once the ink is completely
dry, rub out your pencil lines.

Project 34

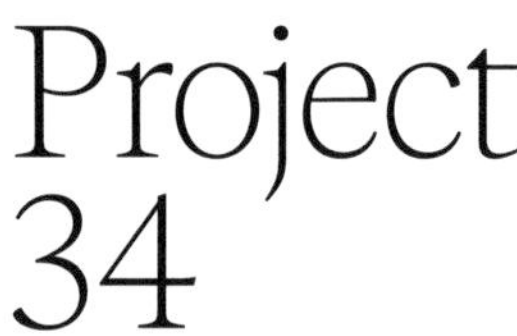

Lesser spotted woodpecker

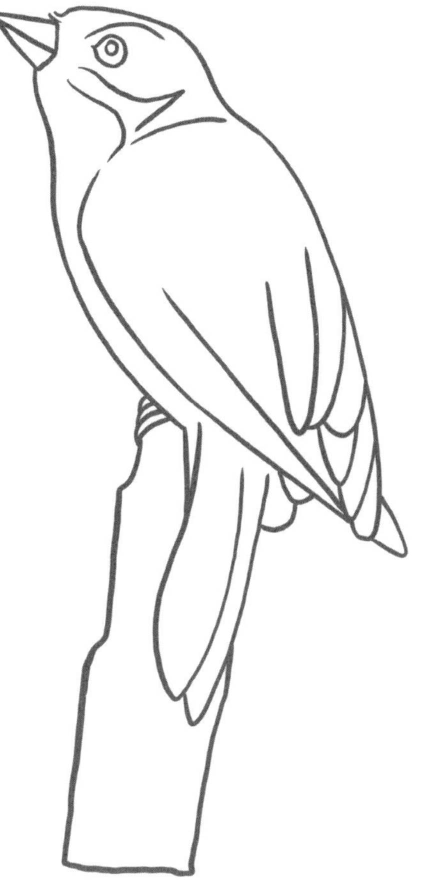

The smallest woodpecker found in the UK is a black and white bird with a crimson crown, which nests in holes in (usually dead) trees. There are so many textures here thanks to the branch, beak, feathers and tail.

STEP 1

Sketch out the shape of the woodpecker, along with a branch for context, or trace the outline on page 236.

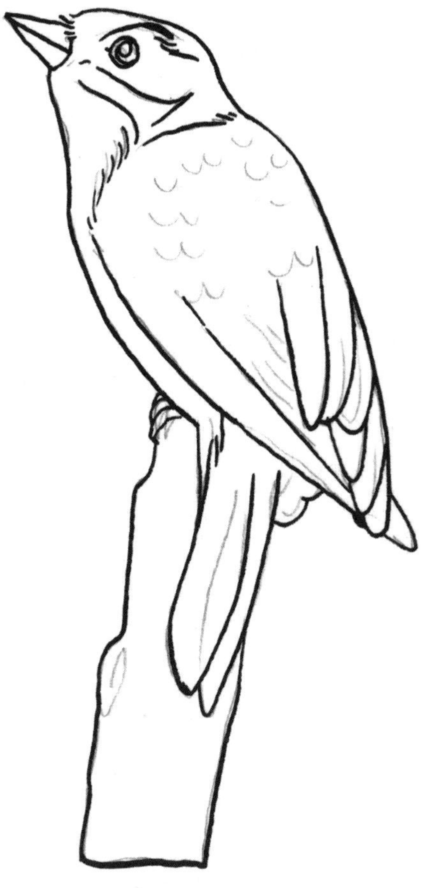

STEP 2

Outline your sketch with ink, adding a highlight to the eye, and using small whiskery strokes along the tail, throat, beak and above the eye to hint at feather texture.

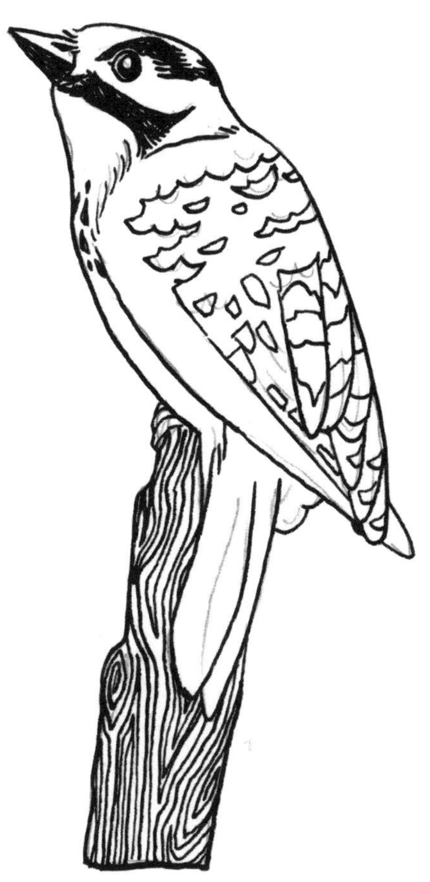

STEP 3

Fill in the markings on the face and lower beak. Draw the pattern on the woodpecker's back, using random and half circle shapes. Give the branch a tree-like texture by using thin lines in spirals and long, uneven lines. Carry all the line ends to the edge, so it looks continuous.

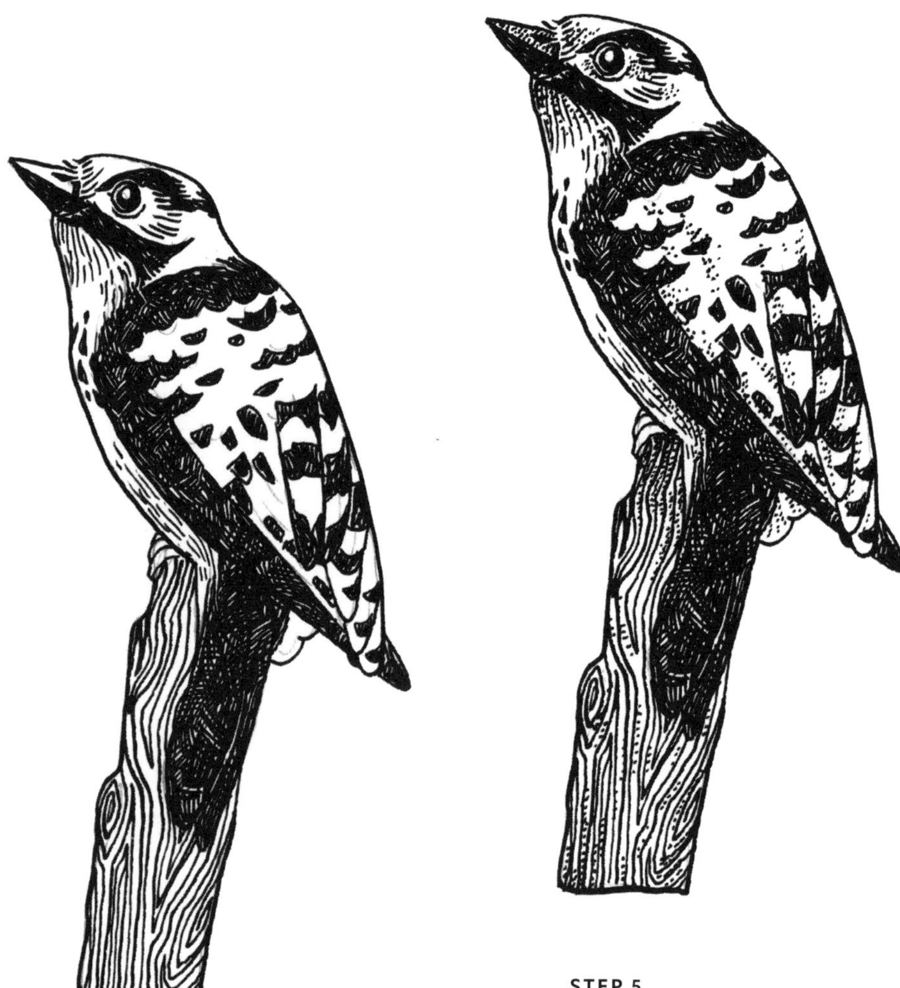

STEP 4

Crosshatch the breast, tail and the pattern you've mapped out on the wings. Add a line underneath the eye, as well as small lines in the direction of the feathers on the throat, top and side of the head, and on the feet.

STEP 5

Use pointillism for final shading and detail, especially on the branch underneath the body, around the eye and edge of the wing. Once the ink is completely dry, rub out your pencil lines.

Project 35

Fawn

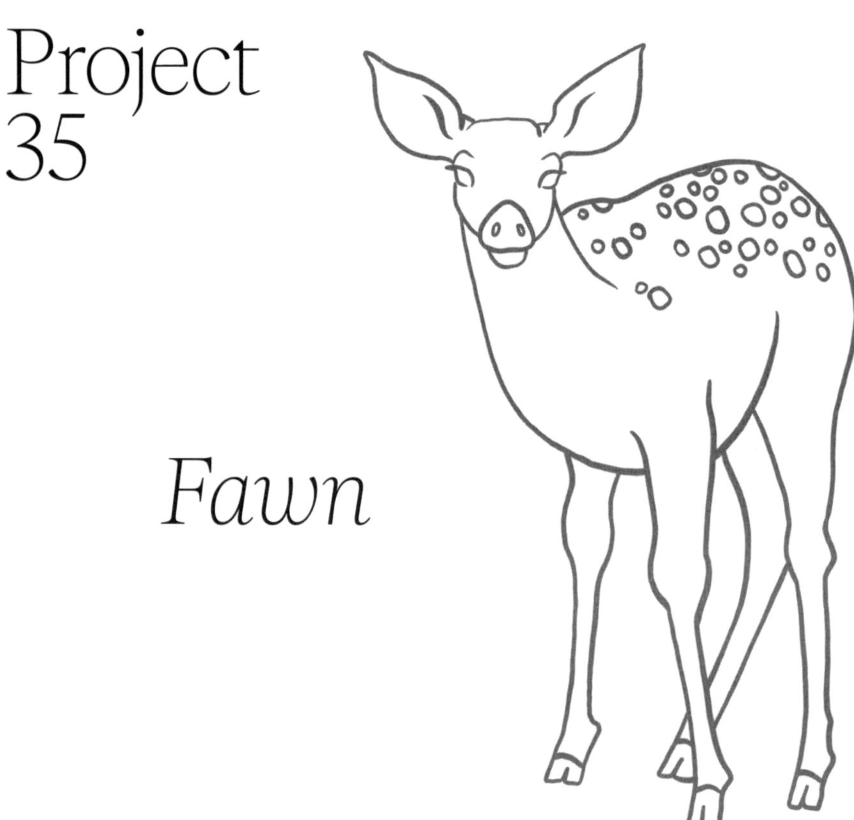

I love illustrating all animals, but nothing is sweeter than young ones with big eyes and legs that are disproportionately large for their bodies.

STEP 1

Sketch the fawn with long legs, big eyes and ears, and spots covering its back. Alternatively, trace the outline on page 237.

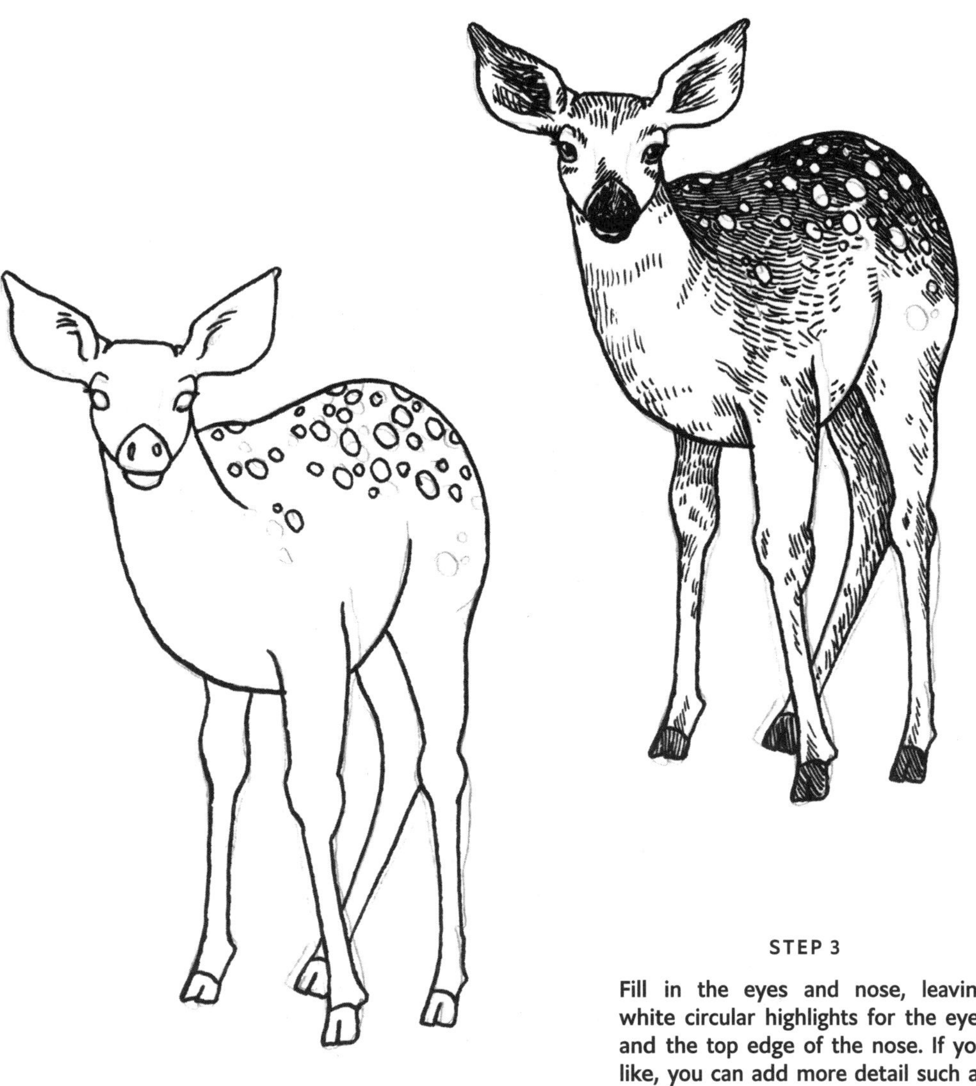

STEP 2

Ink the outline following your sketch.

STEP 3

Fill in the eyes and nose, leaving white circular highlights for the eyes and the top edge of the nose. If you like, you can add more detail such as nostrils, or keep it simple. Use short strokes to mimic the short fur in the direction it would grow, avoiding the white circles across its back. A fawn is darker on the back, and has white fur on its belly, so keep shading here to a minimum.

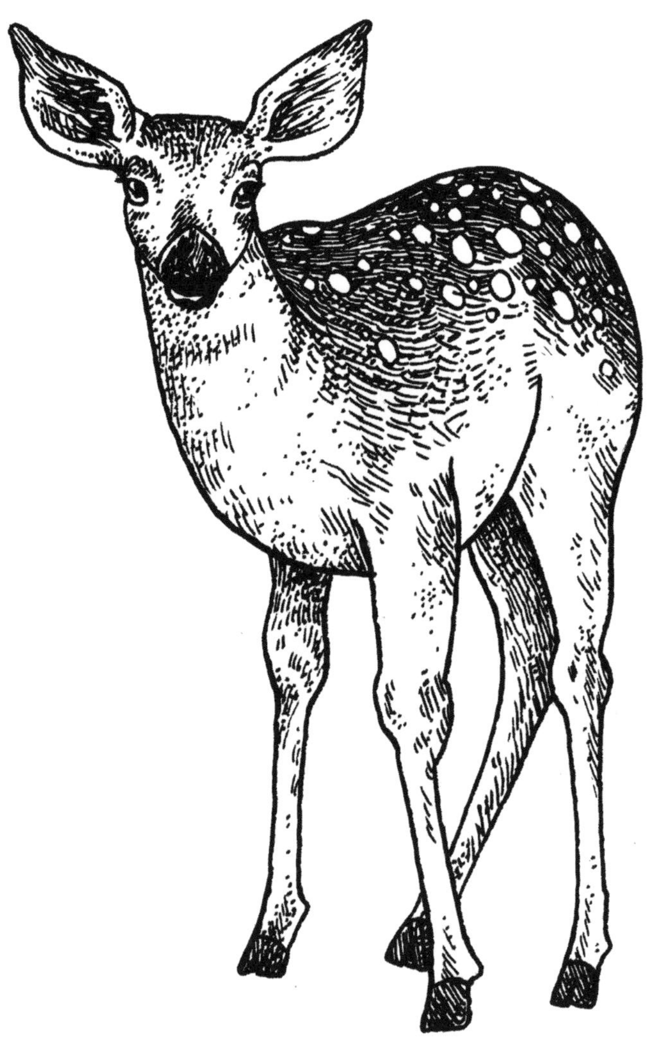

STEP 4

Use dots to add a little extra detail and shading where you
see fit. I've evened out the forehead and added a bit more
shading to the ears and around in the eyes. Once the ink is
completely dry, erase your pencil lines.

Project 36

Grey heron

Herons are a beloved and common sight in the UK, so I had to include one here. They hold an important place in British folklore, art and literature, and symbolise patience, resilience and adaptability.

STEP 1

Sketch the long body and legs of your heron and the round rock, or trace the outline on page 236.

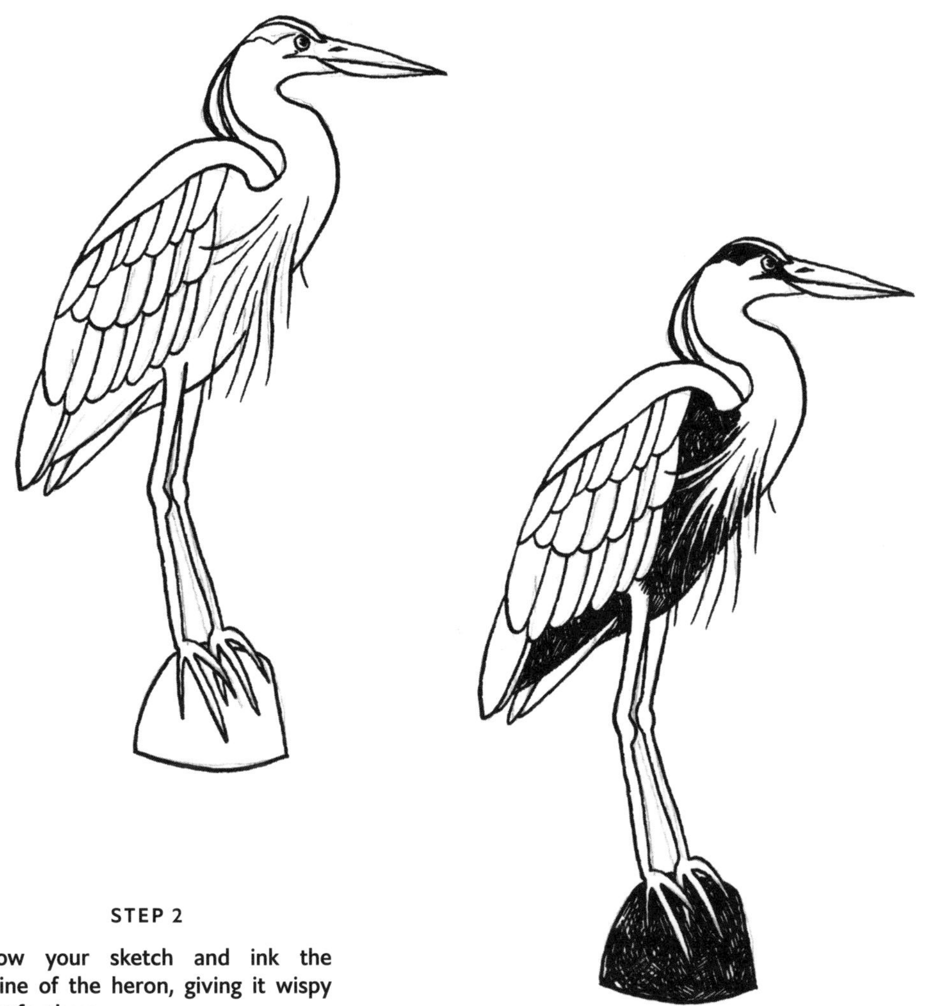

STEP 2

Follow your sketch and ink the outline of the heron, giving it wispy chest feathers.

STEP 3

Fill in the darkest areas with a scratchy texture (or solid black if you prefer). These will be the heron's head, chest, tail feathers and the rock it is standing on.

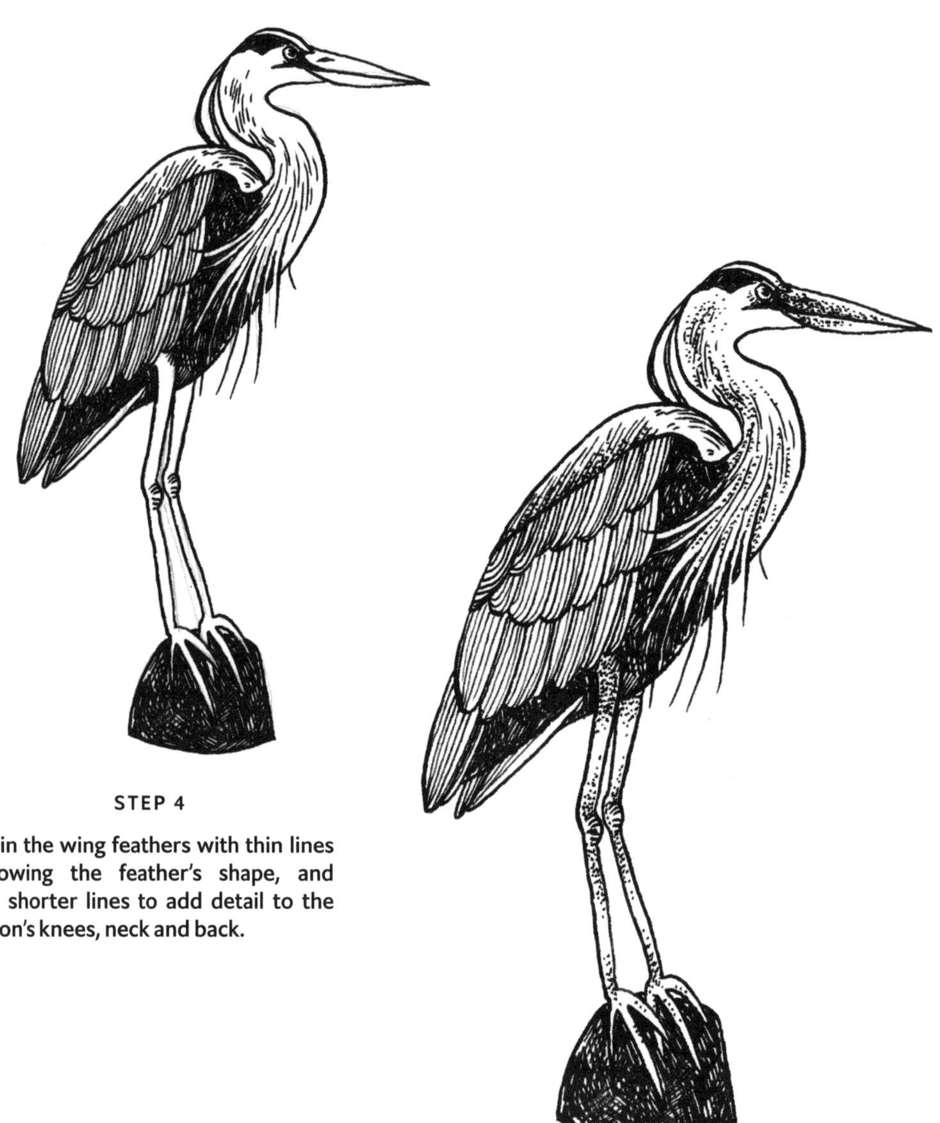

STEP 4

Fill in the wing feathers with thin lines following the feather's shape, and use shorter lines to add detail to the heron's knees, neck and back.

STEP 5

Use small dots to give the heron's beak, neck, back and legs detail. Once the ink is completely dry, rub out your pencil sketch.

Project 37

Snail

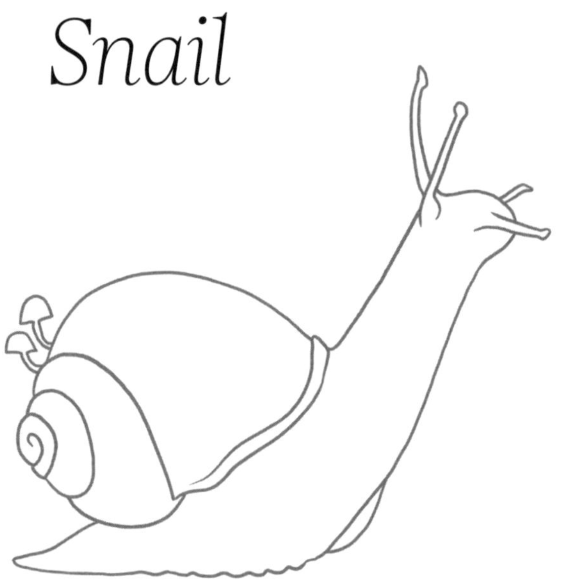

I'm not sure what it is about snails that make me return to them again and again in my drawings, but I love them and their shape, which is so familiar yet also alien.

STEP 1

Sketch the snail, or use the outline on page 236. I've added two little mushrooms to the snail's shell, which are incredibly unrealistic – but so cute. The beauty of snails is that you can draw one, and its shell, almost any shape you'd like and it will still look like a snail!

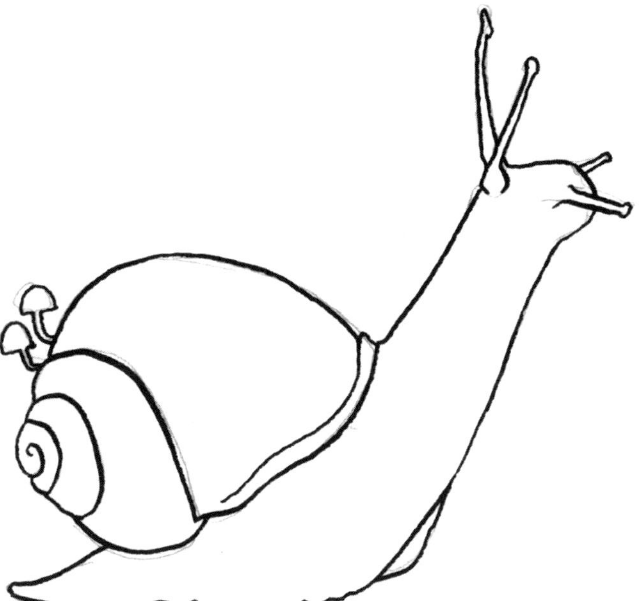

STEP 2

Ink the outline following your sketch.

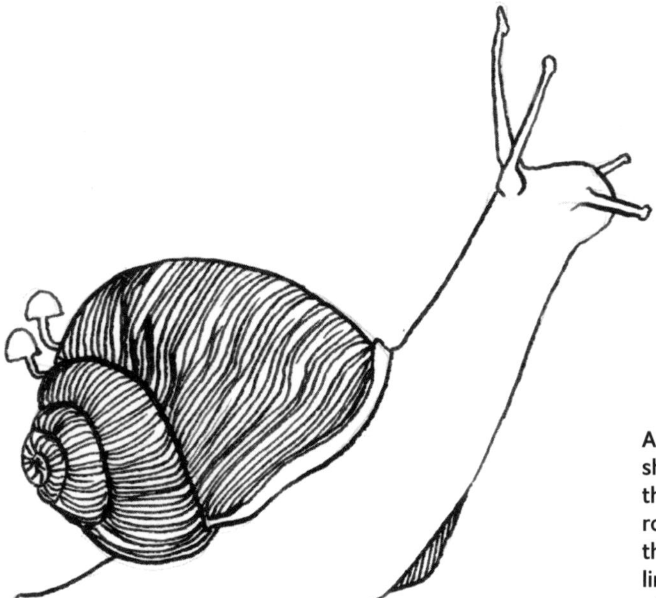

STEP 3

Add linework to the snail's shell for texture. Emphasise the shape of the shell by rounding the lines towards the edge of each spiral. Use lines to shade the front of the snail's foot, at the bottom right of the drawing.

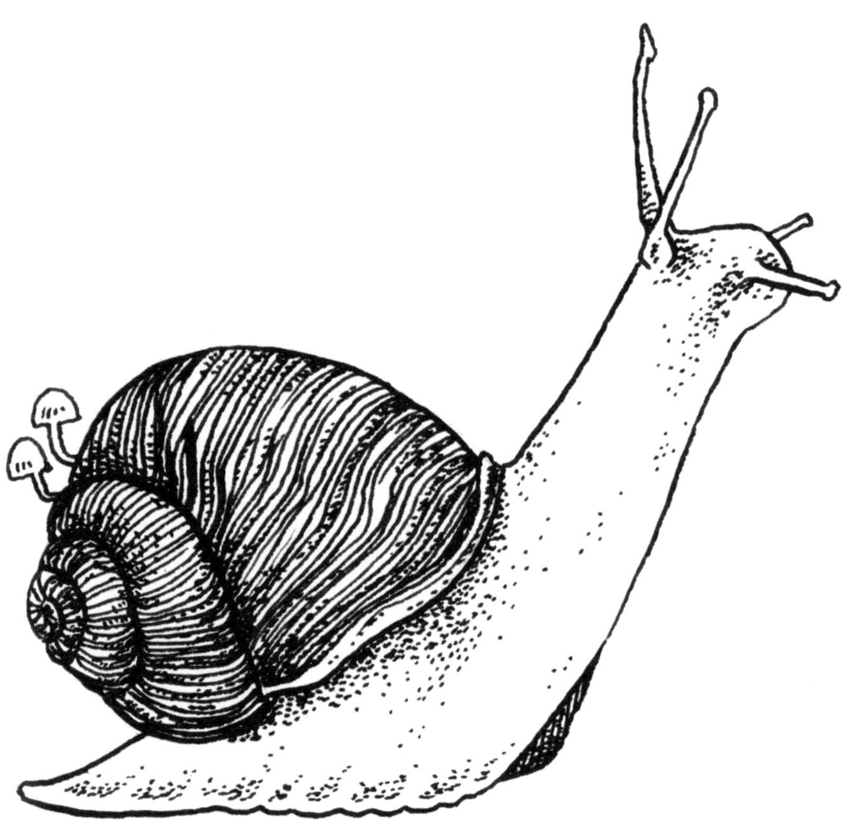

STEP 4

Use dots to add shading to the snail and shell. I've focused on the bottom of each spiral on the shell, as well as where the shadow would sit on the snail's back, underneath the shell, a little along the bottom of the foot and on its face. Add tiny stripes to the mushrooms. Once the ink is completely dry, rub out your pencil lines.

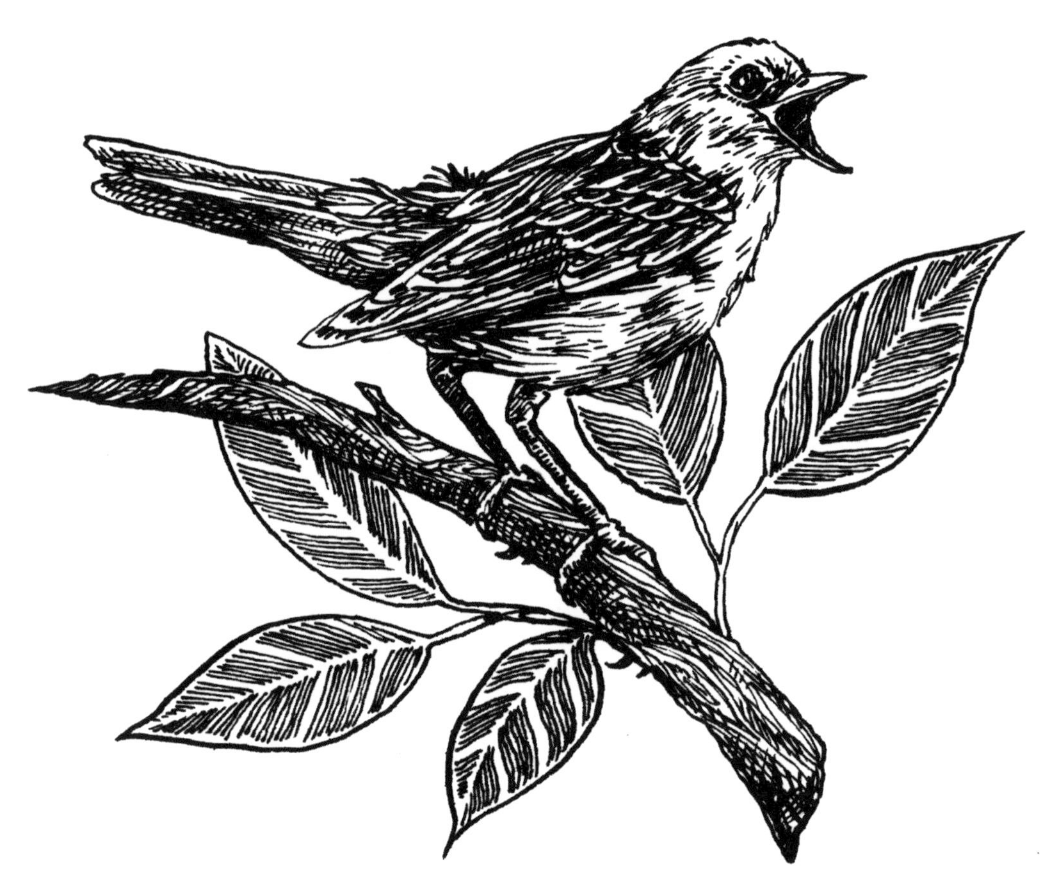

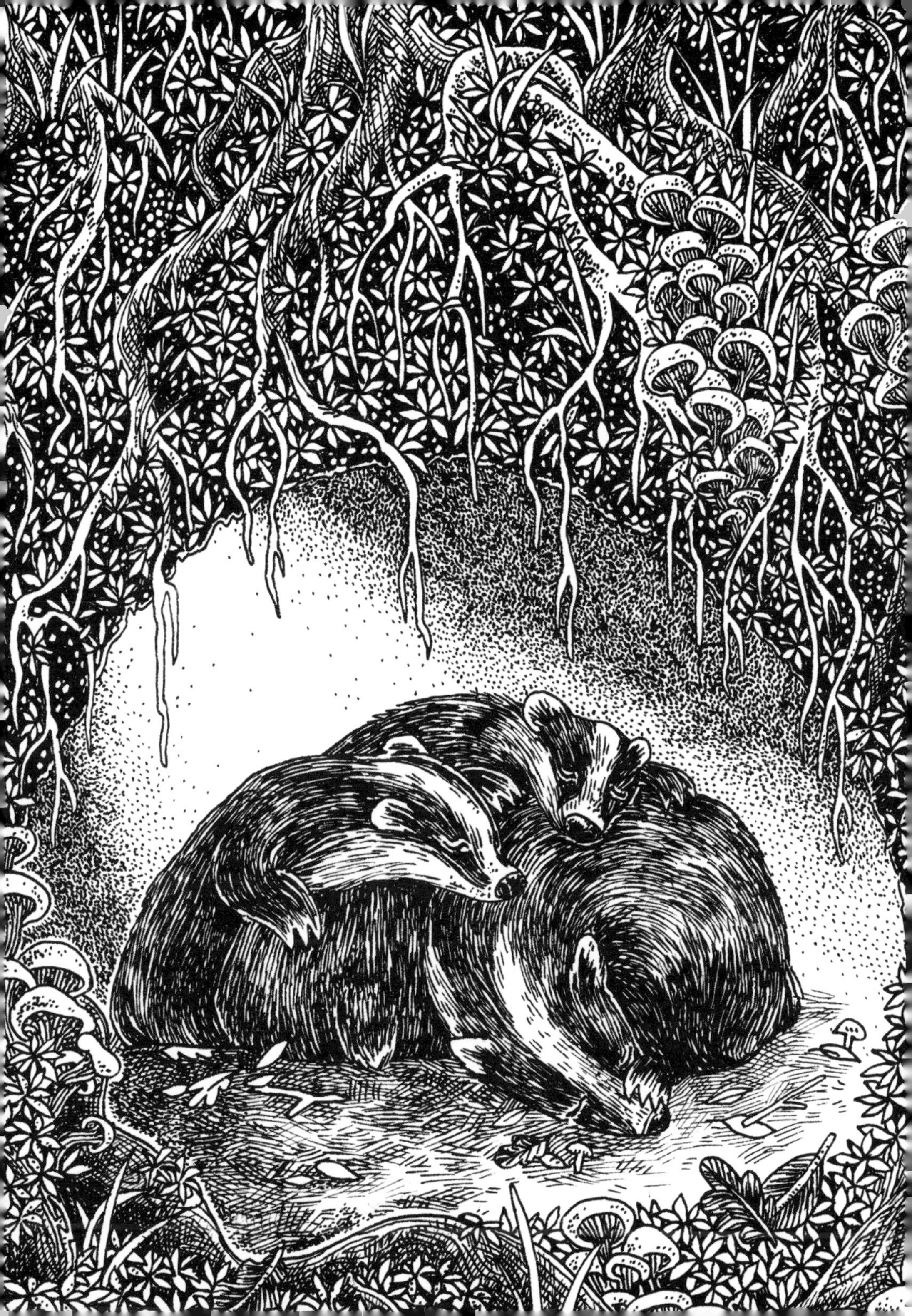

Project 38

Magnifying glass

A magnifying glass is
an essential tool for any
curious nature enthusiast.
I've given this a traditional
wooden handle, which is
great for experimenting
with pattern and line.

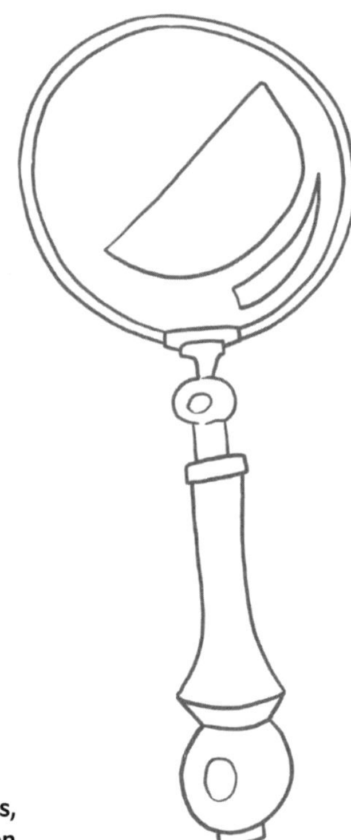

STEP 1

Sketch the magnifying glass,
or trace the outline on
page 236.

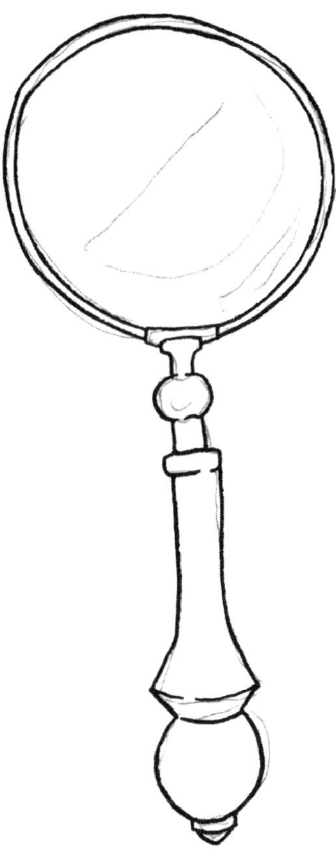

STEP 2

Ink the outline, but leave out the highlight on the glass.

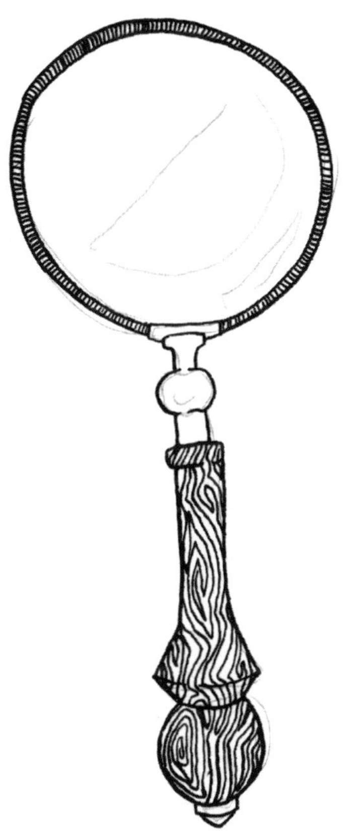

STEP 3

Use swirly lines on the handle to create a woody texture. Add small lines around the frame of the glass.

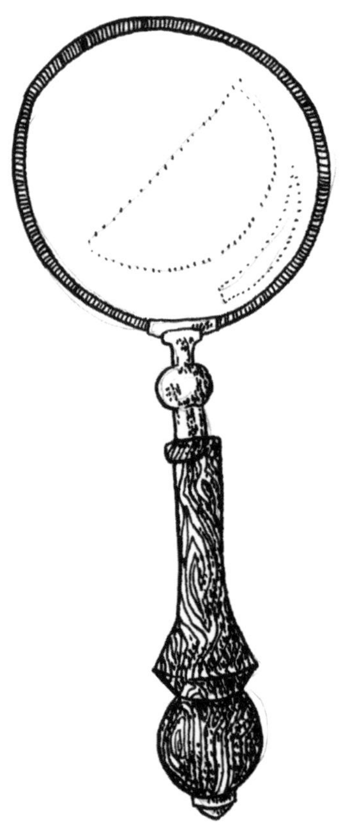

STEP 4

Shade the handle using dots, more towards the right edge where it is darkest, getting lighter towards the middle of the handle. Outline the highlight of the glass with a line of dots.

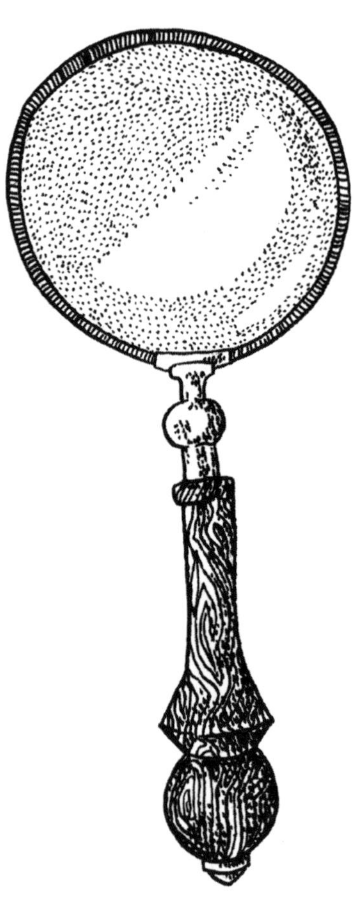

STEP 5

Fill the glass surface with small dots, leaving the highlight white. The closer together you place your dots, the darker the surface will become. Once the ink is completely dry, erase your pencil lines.

Project 39

Campfire

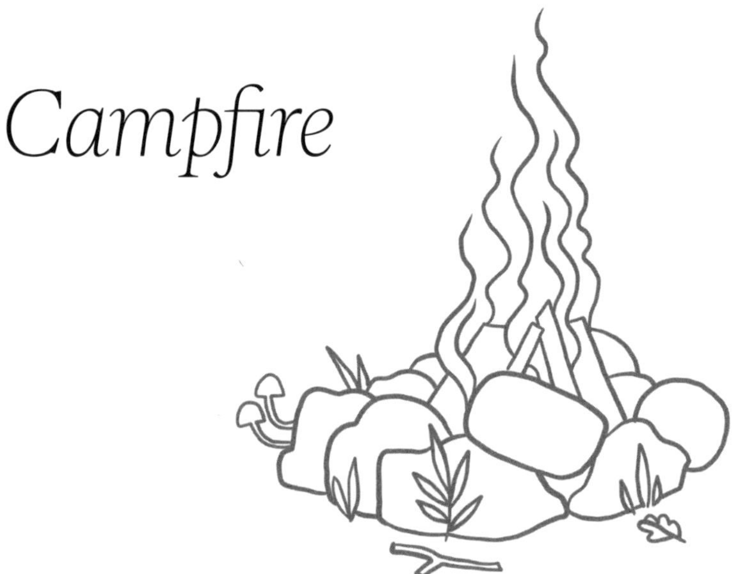

Drawing moving things can seem daunting, but if you give simple hints at light and shadow, your brain will fill in the rest of the information for you.

STEP 1

Sketch out the campfire scene by drawing some big rocks surrounded by grass, leaves and mushrooms. Draw a few logs and add the shape of the fire with wavy lines. Alternatively, trace the outline on page 237.

STEP 2

Draw grass, leaves and sticks on the ground in front of the campfire.

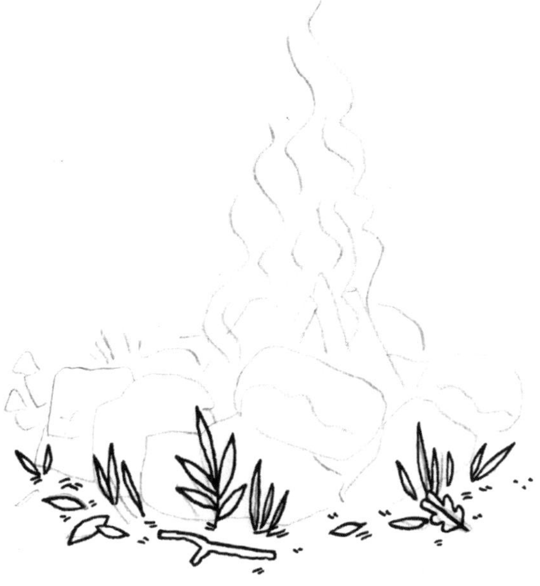

STEP 3

Behind the grass, draw the big, uneven rocks and bits of firewood, leaving little gaps for the flames to come up. Add more grass and a few mushrooms behind the rocks.

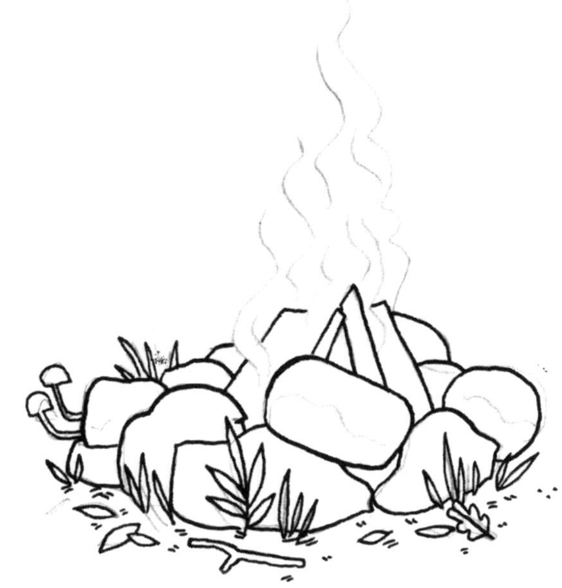

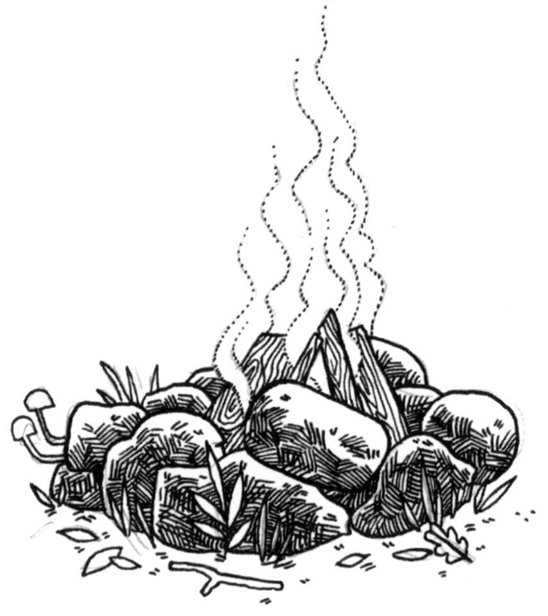

STEP 4

Use a line of dots to create the wavy fire lines. Add texture to the logs with a wavy striped pattern, and crosshatch the shaded parts of the rocks, leaving highlights on the top edges.

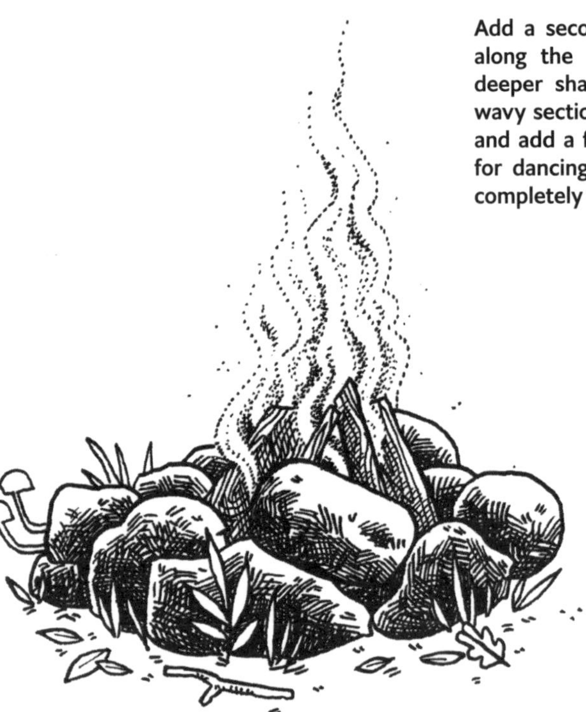

STEP 5

Add a second layer of crosshatching along the bottom of the rocks for deeper shading. Draw more dots in wavy sections to bring the fire to life, and add a few dots scattered around for dancing embers. Once the ink is completely dry, erase your pencil lines.

Project 40

Camping lantern

Although most people switched to battery-powered torches a long time ago, drawing these traditional lanterns makes me feel like I'm wandering around the woods in a fairytale.

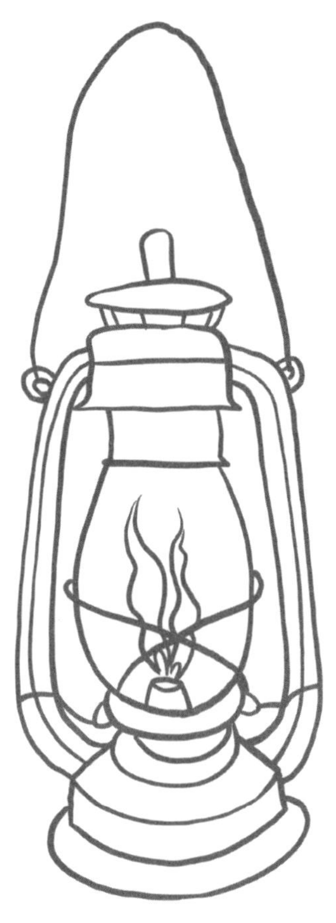

STEP 1

Sketch the camping lantern, or trace the outline on page 237.

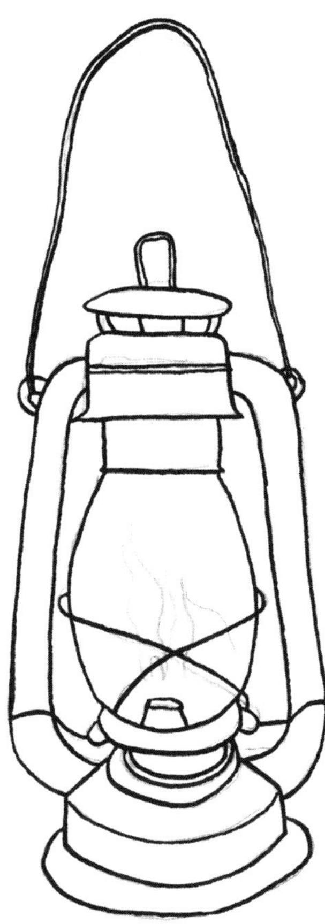

STEP 2

Follow your sketch and ink the outlines of the lamp, but don't ink the centre flame yet.

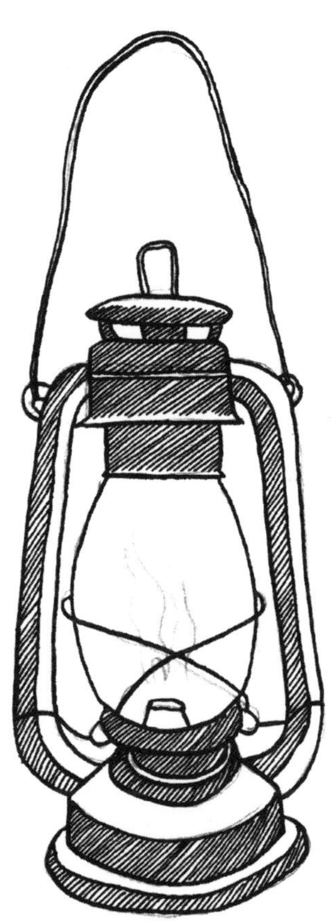

STEP 3

Use diagonal lines to shade the base, edges and top of the lamp.

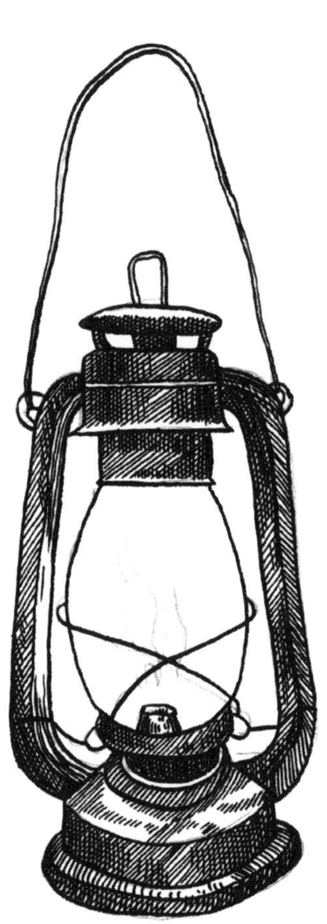

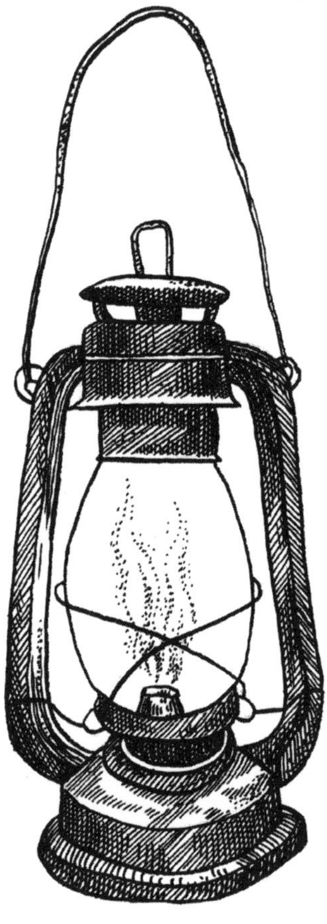

STEP 5

Map out your flame with dots and add a few more dots surrounding it for shadow and detail. Once the ink is completely dry, erase your pencil lines.

STEP 4

Next, use crosshatching to darken the shadows and give the lamp shape. You can keep your lines in a consistent direction for a tidier look, or use shorter strokes in various directions for a messier look.

Project 41

Teapot

A cup of tea is always a good idea – particularly when one is camping or drawing.

Sketch the shape of the teapot or trace the outline on page 237. Pick whatever pattern you like. Perhaps you have an old teapot you'd like to copy. I've gone with an old-fashioned floral design.

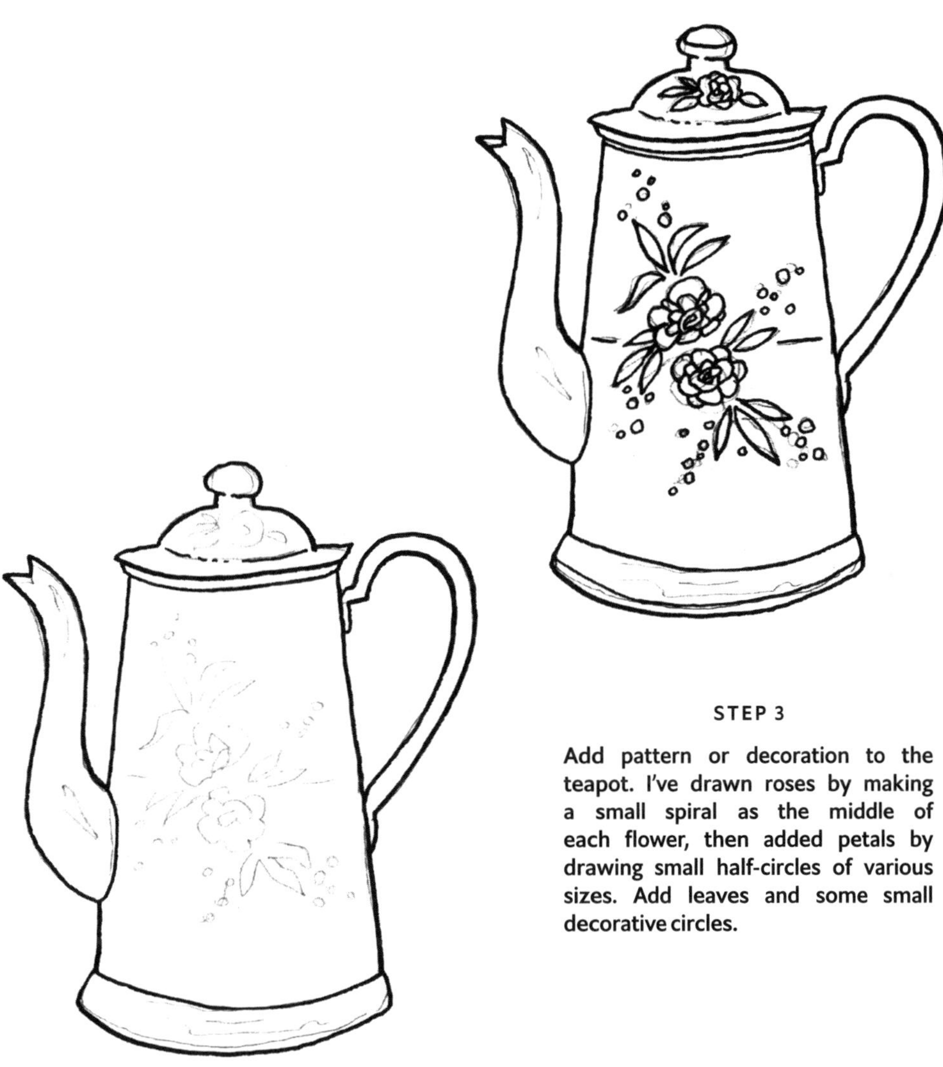

STEP 3

Add pattern or decoration to the teapot. I've drawn roses by making a small spiral as the middle of each flower, then added petals by drawing small half-circles of various sizes. Add leaves and some small decorative circles.

STEP 2

Ink the outline of the teapot.

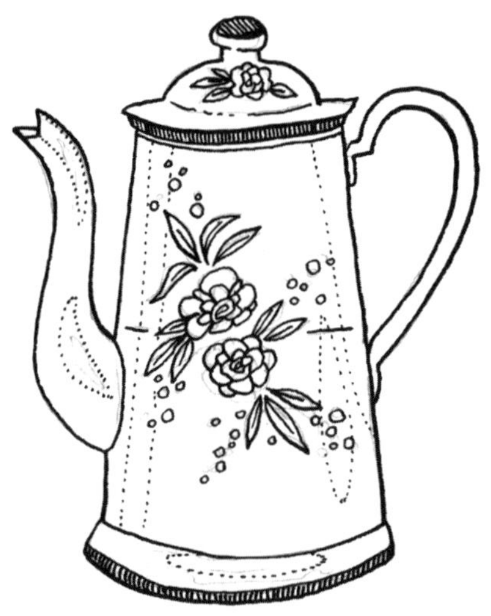

STEP 4

Add small decorative lines to the bottom of the teapot, the lid and its top. Add dots as guides to map out the placement of highlights and shaded areas.

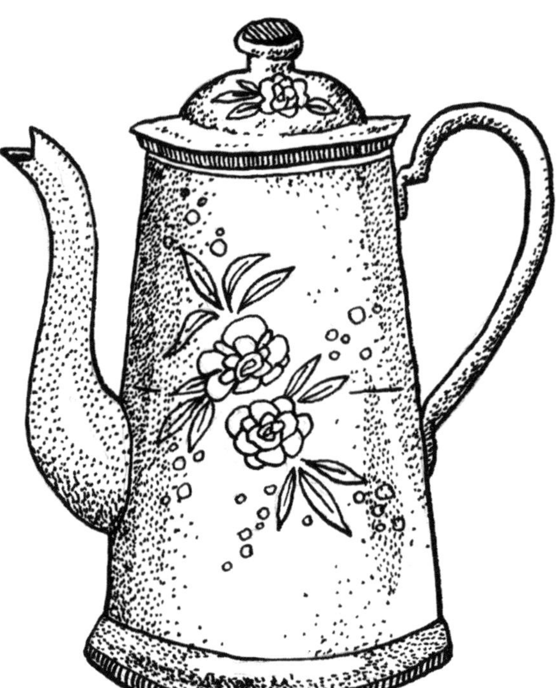

STEP 5

Use pointillism to shade the teapot. Once the ink is completely dry, rub out your pencil lines.

Project 42

Camera

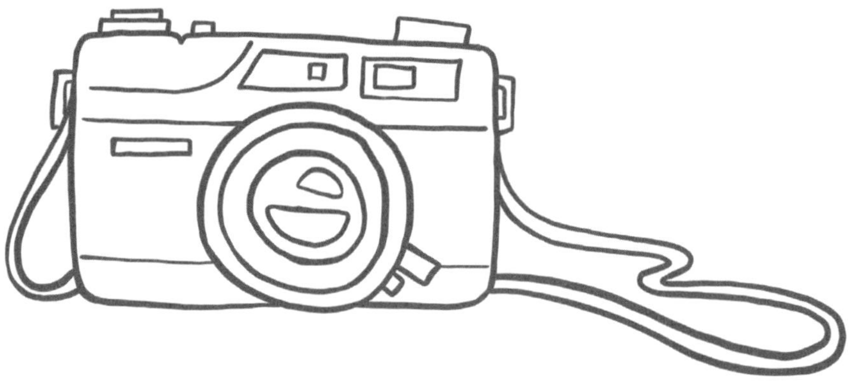

A camera is an essential tool for any nature enthusiast. Although I love the convenience of a phone camera, nothing beats a good digital or analogue camera for me – and they make a much more fun drawing project, too.

STEP 1

Sketch the outline of the camera, its features and strap, or trace the outline on page 238.

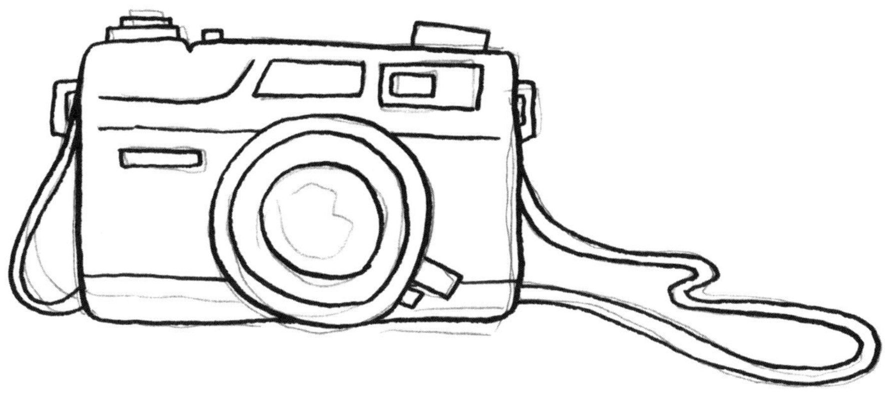

STEP 2

Following your sketch, ink the outline. I've left out the highlights on the lens, as I want to shade this later without leaving harsh lines.

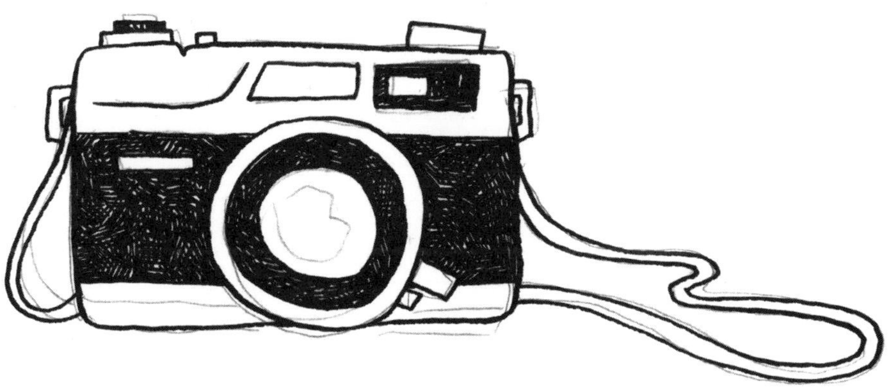

STEP 3

Use crosshatching or scratchy lines to colour in the camera's body. You can use solid black if you like, but I like to show a bit of texture and leave white spaces.

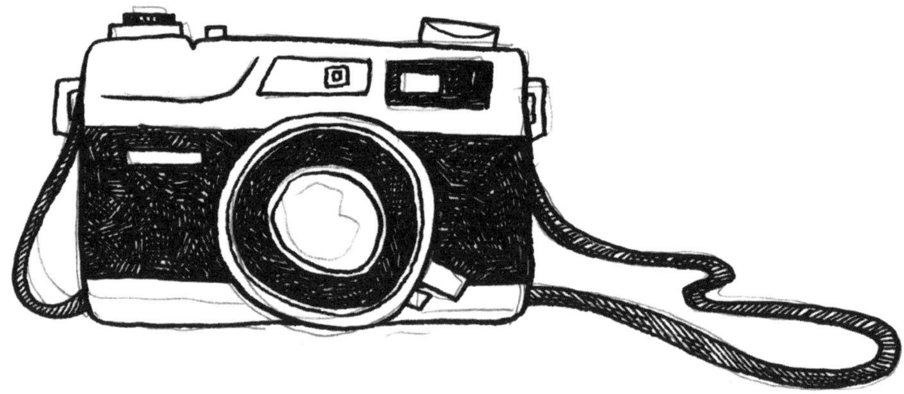

STEP 4

Add an additional small ring to the lens and a square within a square to the top centre button. Shade the strap using lines.

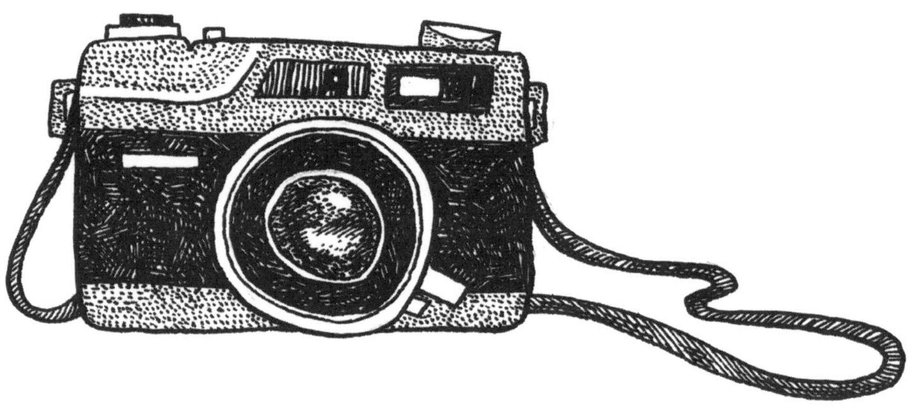

STEP 5

Using dots in an even pattern, shade the lighter grey areas. Make the viewfinder darker than the camera body surrounding it, and finally shade the lens, using a combination of dots and crosshatching. Use your sketch as a guide to mark the highlight, but don't be too precious – a gradient usually looks more natural than harsh lines. Once the ink is completely dry, rub out your pencil lines.

Project 43

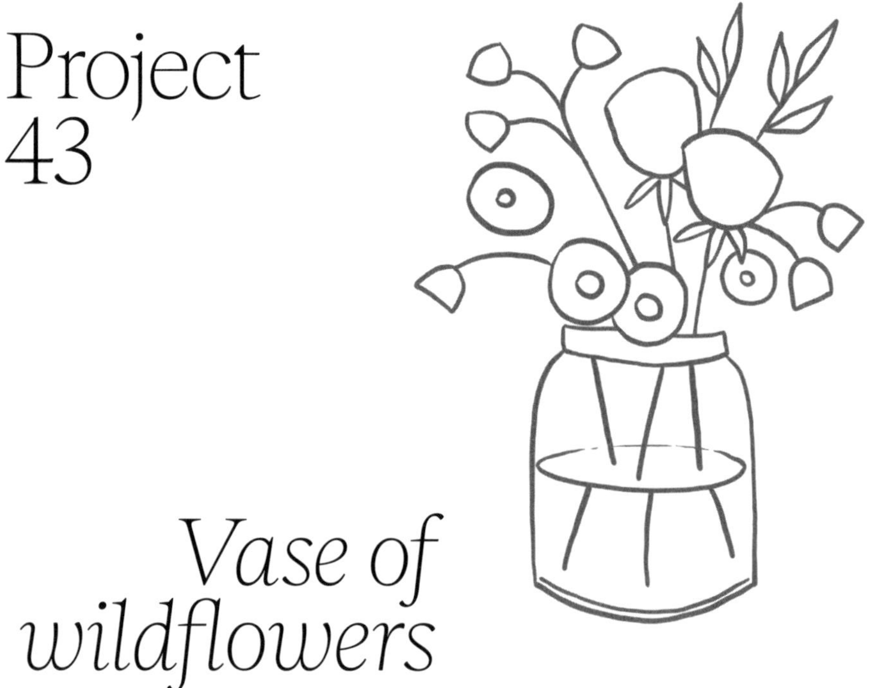

Vase of wildflowers

Flowers bring me a lot of joy. They are lovely to draw or paint, especially when I have a collection of different types from the hedgerows or garden.

STEP 1

Sketch the basic shape of your vase and flowers. I've gone for a mix of flowers, but feel free to make up your own bouquet! Alternatively, trace the outline on page 239.

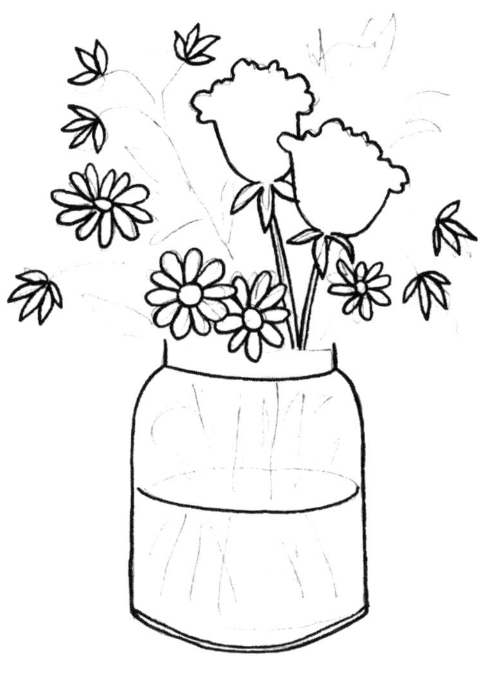

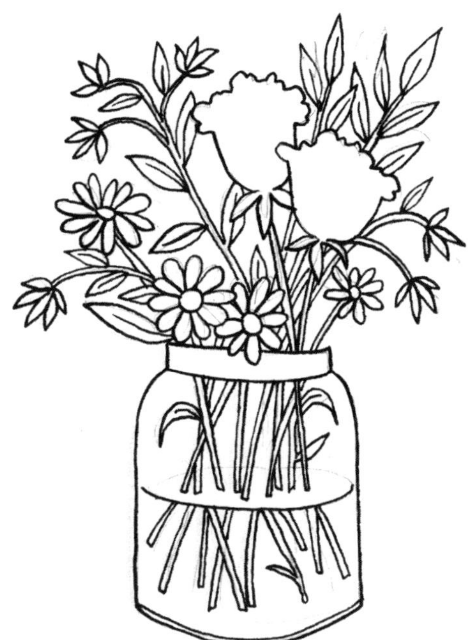

STEP 2

Ink the shape of the vase, leaving the top lines on the rim and water surface clear for now. Draw the daisies, cow parsley and small flowers.

STEP 3

Draw the top line of the vase underneath your daisies, and the leaves and stems for all your flowers. Inside the vase, make sure you leave a gap before the top line of the water and no gap in the bottom half. This will make it look as if the stems are piercing the water's surface.

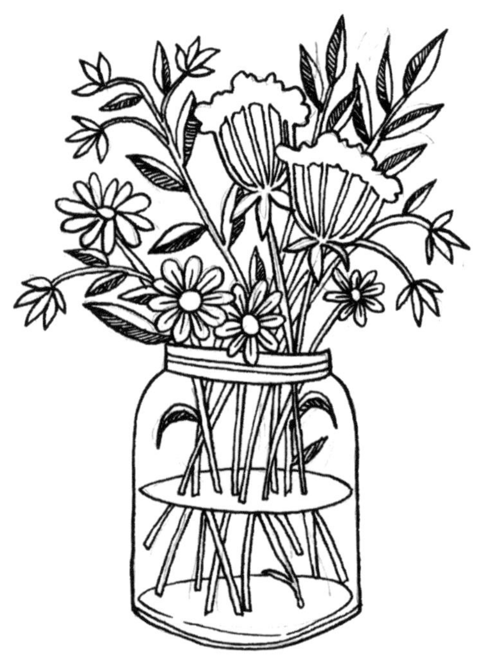

STEP 4

Add decorative lines to the neck of the vase, and add detail to the daisies' petals. Fill in half of each leaf with parallel lines to darken them. Cow parsley is made up of lots of thin stems, so I've drawn triangle-like shapes to make them look hollow.

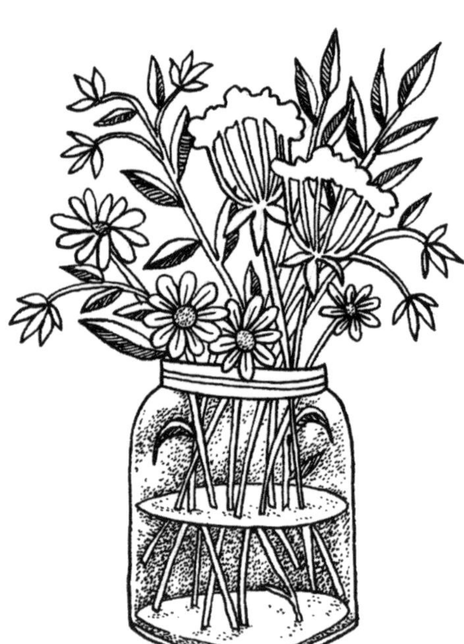

STEP 5

Fill in the gap behind the cow parsley with whatever foliage you can see through it. Add small dots to the centres of the daisies, and shade the vase with pointillism. The vase will look lighter on the water's surface and at the bottom, and darker behind the flower stems. Once the ink is completely dry, erase your pencil sketch.

Project 44

Tree bark boat

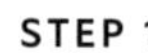

Carving little boats out of tree bark and making a small hole in the middle for a sail was one of my favourite activities as a kid in Norway. Racing them down the rivers and streams was great fun. I've gone for an oak leaf here, but feel free to pick a different one.

STEP 1

Sketch the shape of the boat, which is madeup of an uneven piece of bark, a leaf and a small stick holding up the sail. Alternatively, trace the outline on page 238.

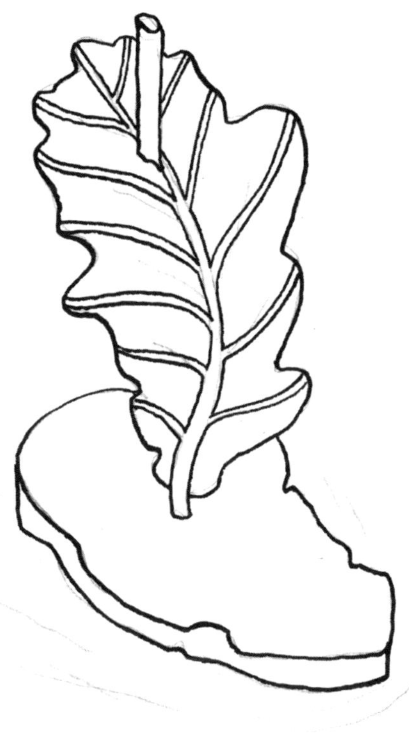

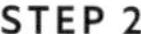

STEP 2

Ink the outline following your sketch, making sure to draw the pattern inside the leaf with double lines – it'll protect your white areas later.

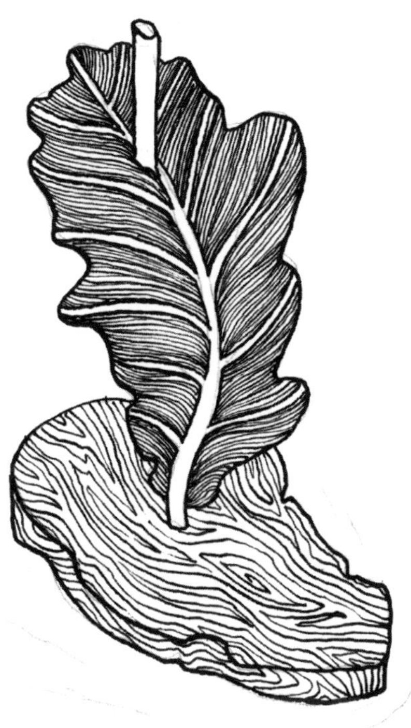

STEP 3

Draw thin, parallel, wavy lines to colour in the leaf and give it texture. Build wood grain on the bark by making wavy lines and hints at year rings. Take the ends of your lines right to the edge.

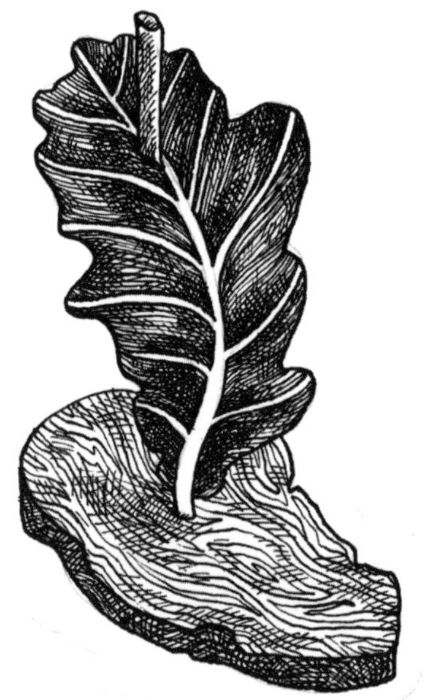

STEP 4

Use crosshatching to shade the leaf, boat and mast. Shade darkest along the middle and outside of the leaf. Shade the area below the mast, where the leaf creates a shadow on the bark, and on the edge of the bark that will meet the water.

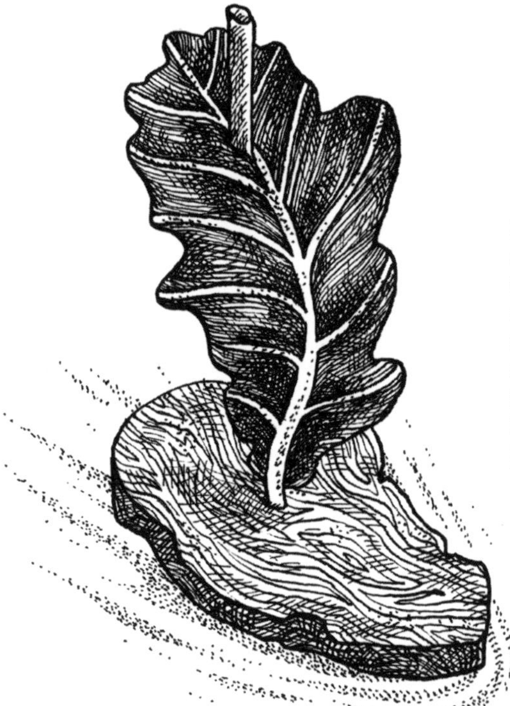

STEP 5

Use dots to shade the stem of the leaf. Add dots to create shadow underneath the boat to give the impression of water and speed. I like to make these up as I go, but it can also be helpful to use a pencil and map out where you want the movement to go first. Once the ink is completely dry, rub out your pencil lines.

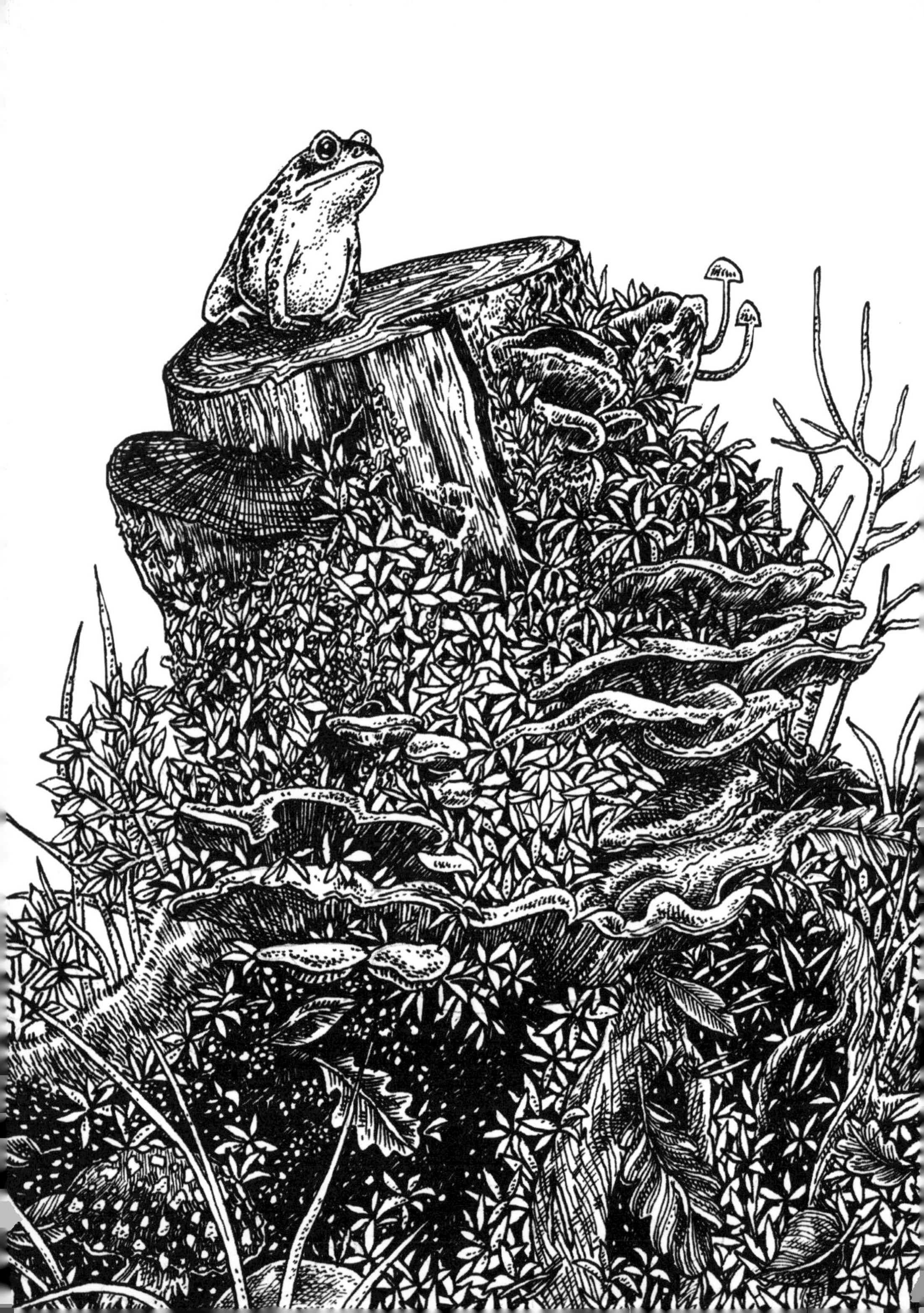

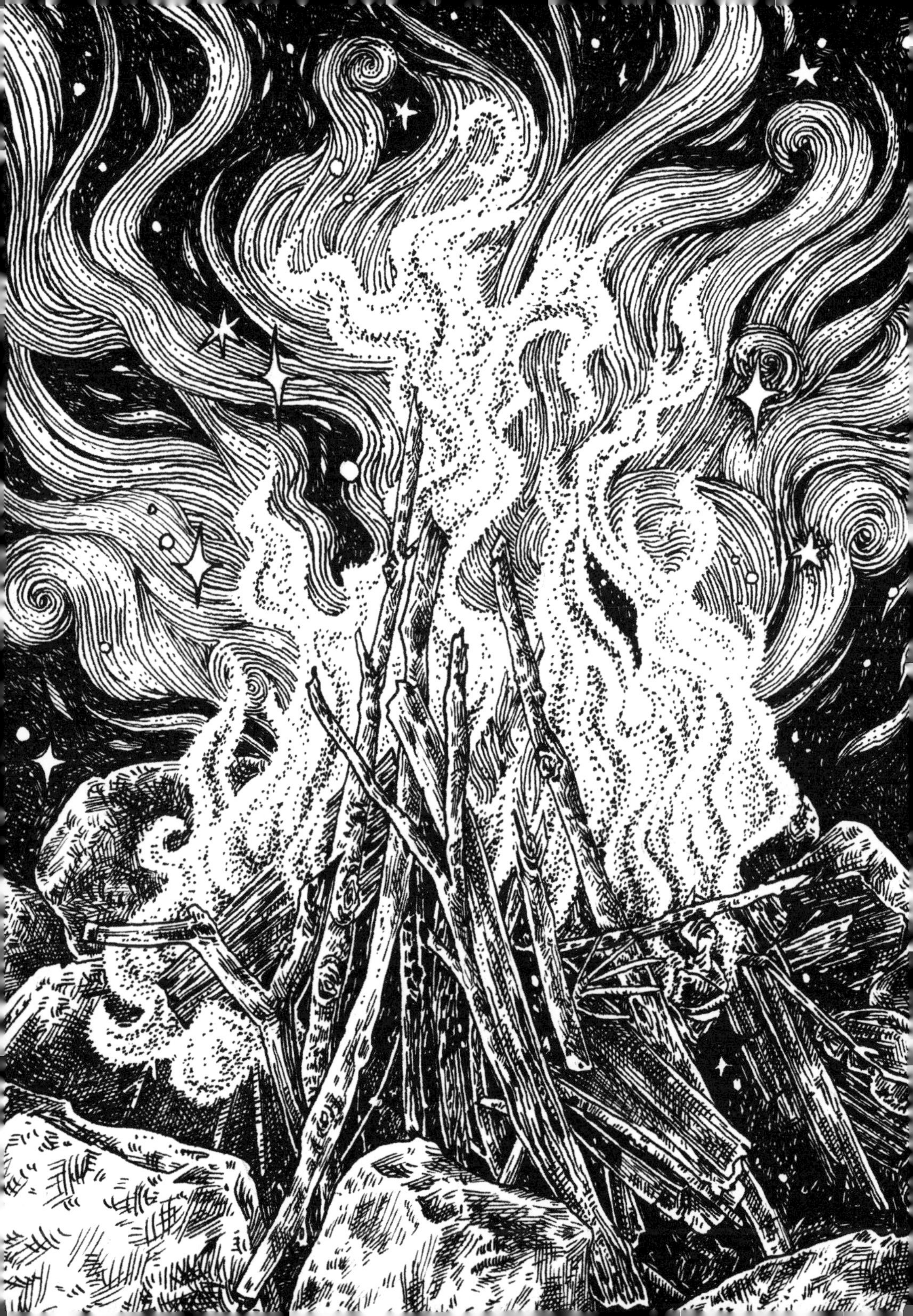

Project 45

Summer birch

Trees can be intimidating to draw as there is so much detail. As well as this, no tree looks the same. It helps to break your subject into simple shapes.

STEP 1

Sketch out the shape of your tree, or trace the outline on page 238.

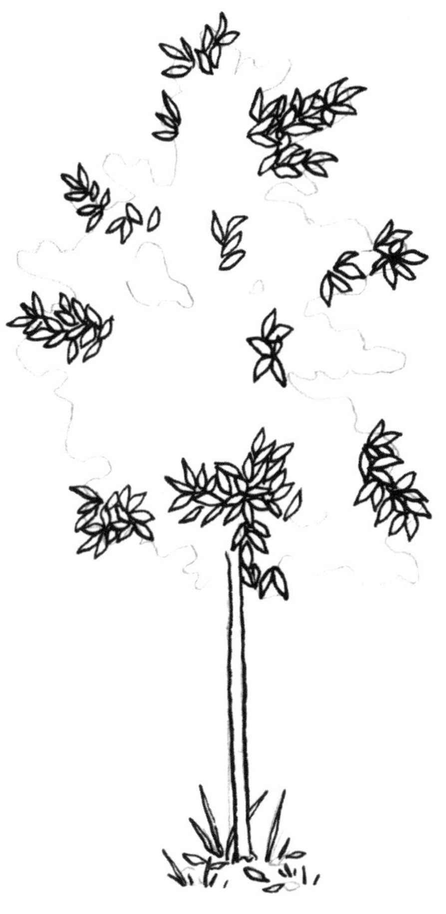

STEP 2

Ink the tree trunk as well as some grass and leaves on the ground. Start building the top of the tree by drawing small clusters of leaves in various directions.

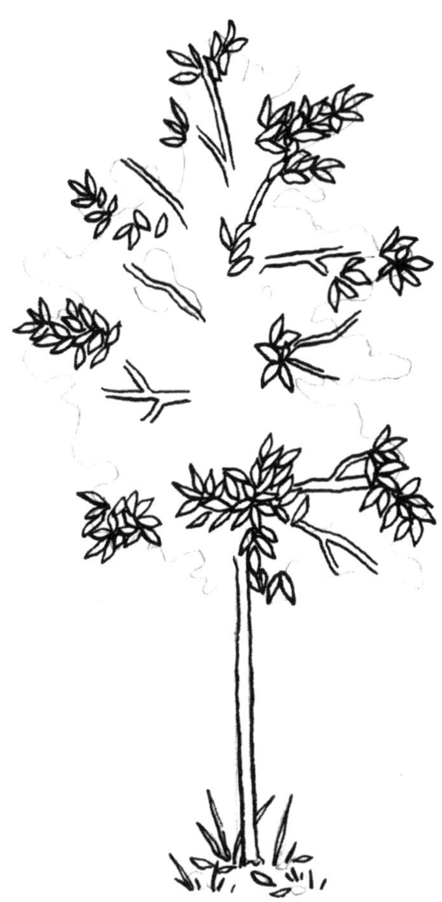

STEP 3

Add some small branches that will be poking out from the foliage. I've made them as random as possible, pointing away from the trunk, up towards the top, and down towards the ground.

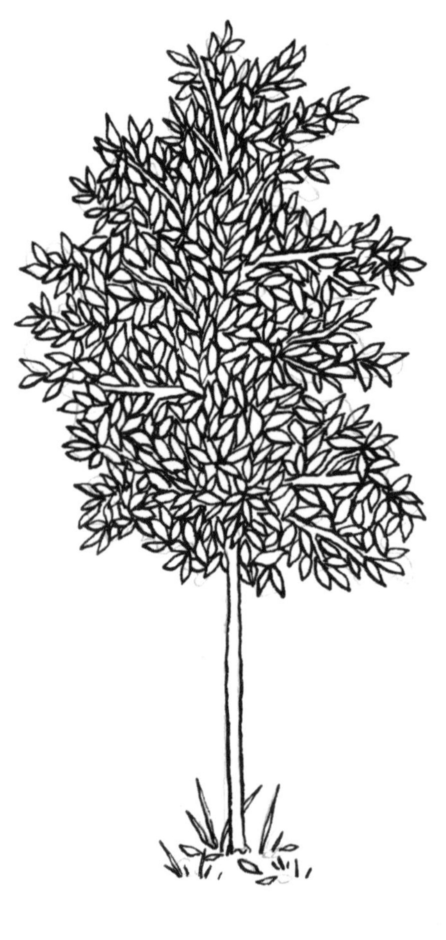

STEP 4

Fill in the rest of the tree shape with small leaves. Keep changing their direction to add variety.

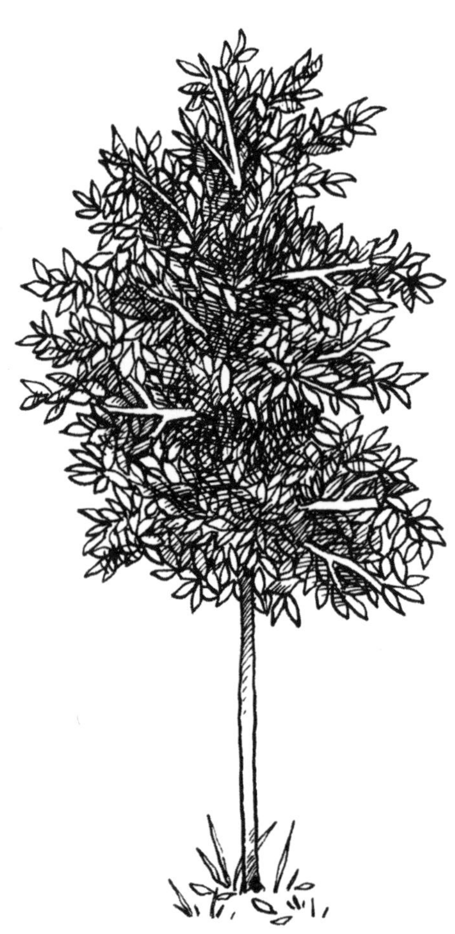

STEP 5

Use crosshatching to shade random sections of the tree, but be careful to keep the outer edges light. Add a little extra crosshatching to the top and bottom of the tree trunk. Finally, once the ink is completely dry, erase your pencil lines.

Project 46

Snowy pine

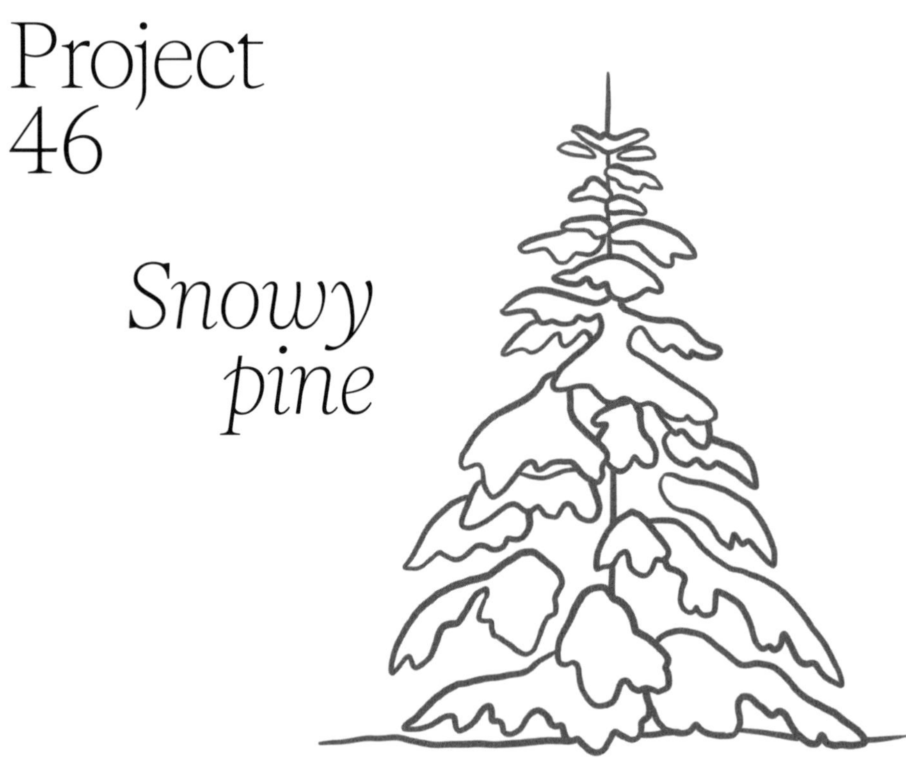

A snow-covered forest is one of the most magical places I know, and just as magical to draw. Everything is wrapped up or buried in crystalline white.

STEP 1

Sketch the shape of your snowy pine. Your tree will be thicker towards the bottom and, rather than individual branches, we see instead the blobs of snow covering them – smoother on top, and more rugged along the bottom. Alternatively, trace the outline on page 238.

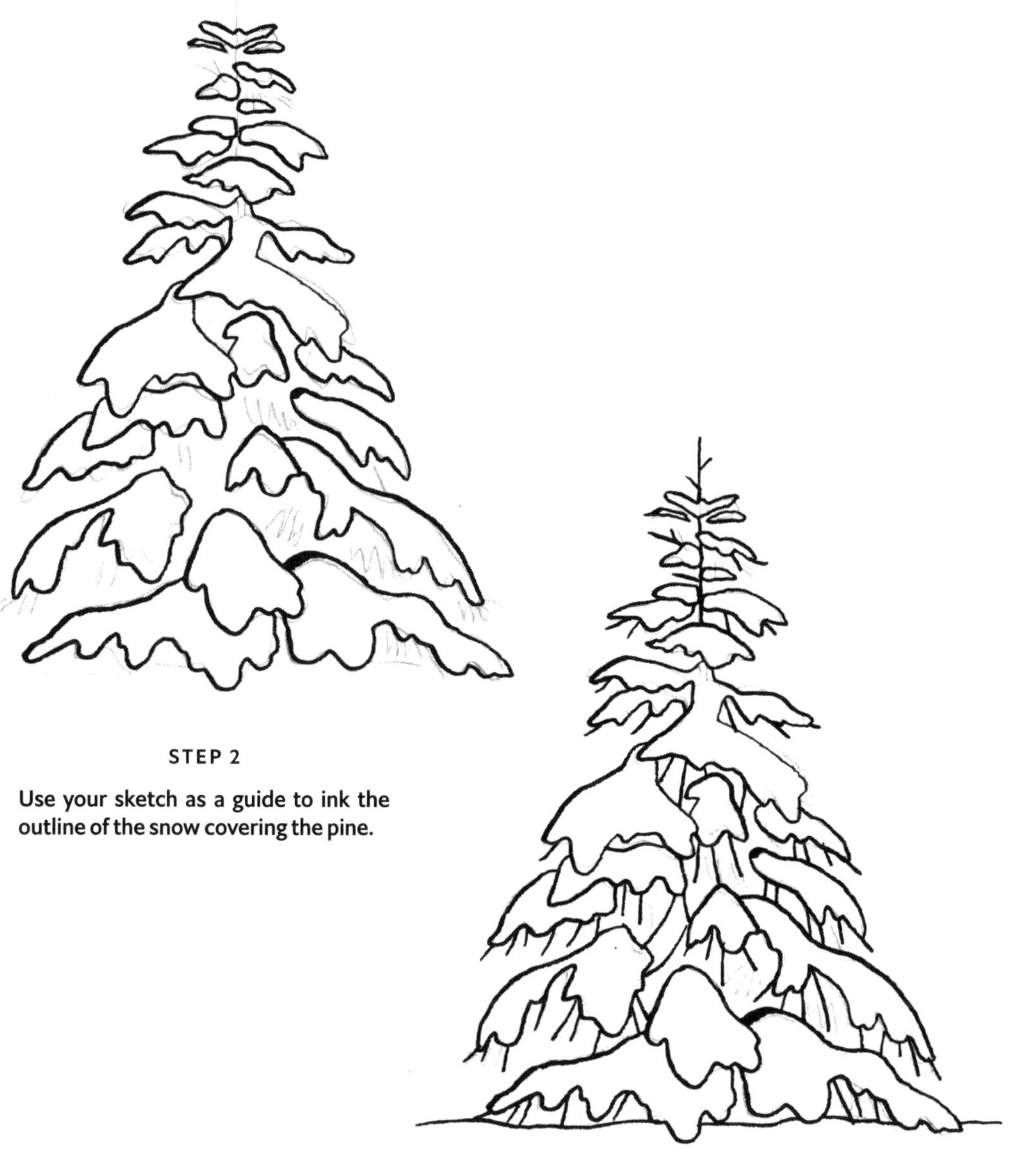

STEP 2

Use your sketch as a guide to ink the outline of the snow covering the pine.

STEP 3

Draw the branches behind the snow, straight along the tree trunk, and like forks poking out underneath the snow. Next, add an uneven, horizontal line for the snow on the ground.

STEP 4

Draw all the tiny individual pine needles at a downward angle along the branches.

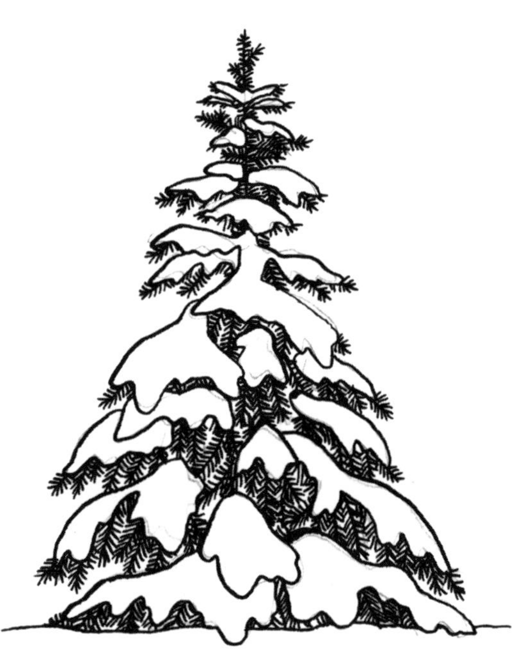

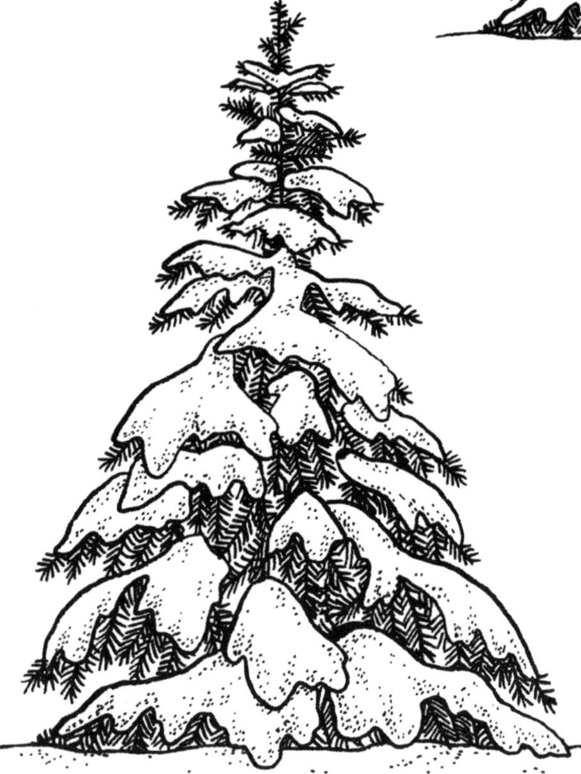

STEP 5

Shade the snow minimally with dots. Once the ink is completely dry, rub out your pencil lines.

Project 47

Small waterfall

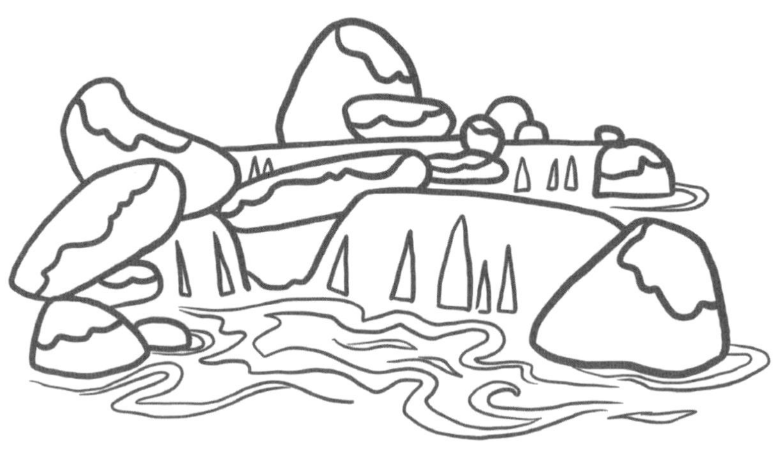

Few things are as universally calming as a little waterfall deep in the woods. Here we will use dots to capture the moving water.

STEP 1

Sketch your waterfall scene with big rocks and flowing water, or trace the outline on page 239.

STEP 2

Ink the outline of your rocks, and the top horizontal edge from where the water is flowing.

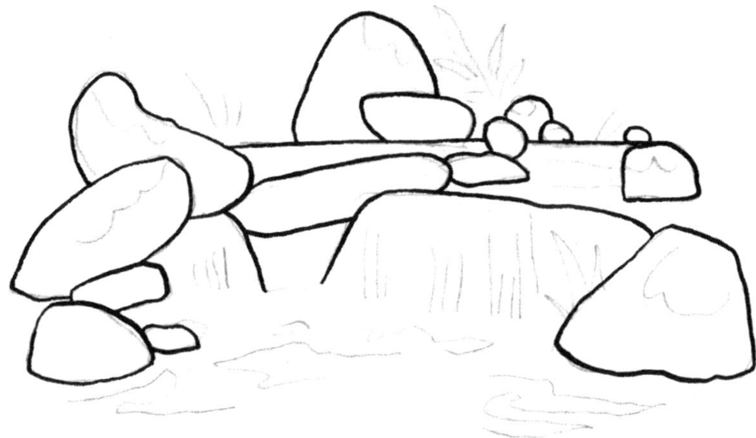

STEP 3

Map out the outer edge of the moss growing on the rocks, add some grass and foliage surrounding the scene, and add rounded triangles to the waterfall. These will be the darkest areas, showing the rock where there is no water falling.

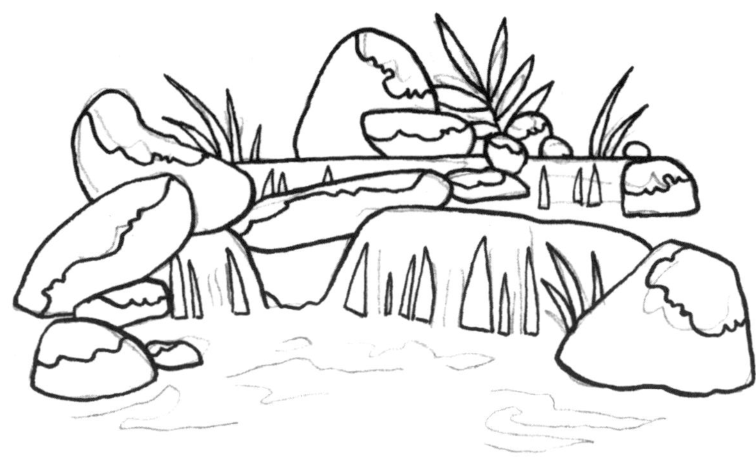

STEP 4

Fill in the rocky parts behind the waterfall and the parts of the surrounding rocks that are not covered in moss. Use dots to map out how the water flows – uneven, flowing lines add movement.

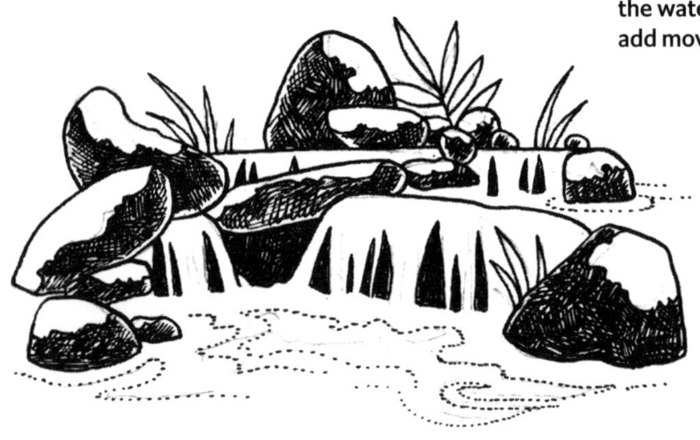

STEP 5

Use dots to shade the rocks and add detail to the moss. For the waterfall, add dots in horizontal lines to give the impression of fast-flowing water. Using your previous dots as a guide, shade thicker areas in the water. Once the ink is completely dry, erase your pencil lines.

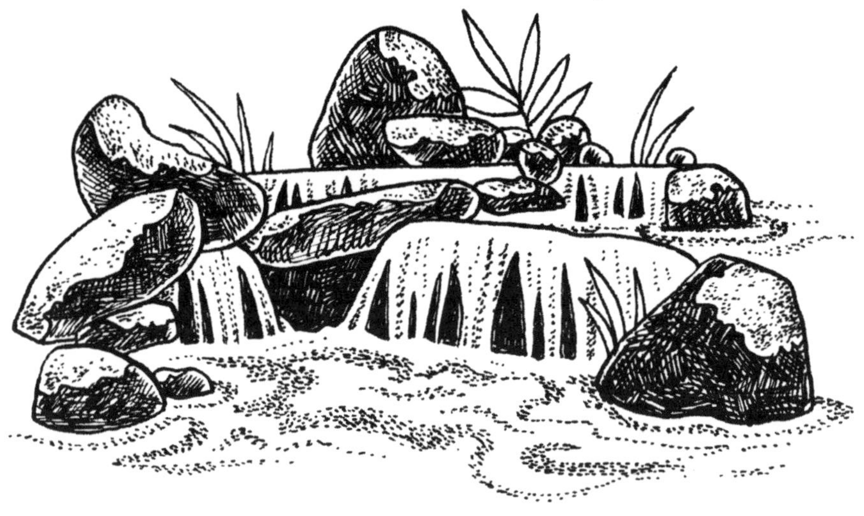

Project 48

Island house

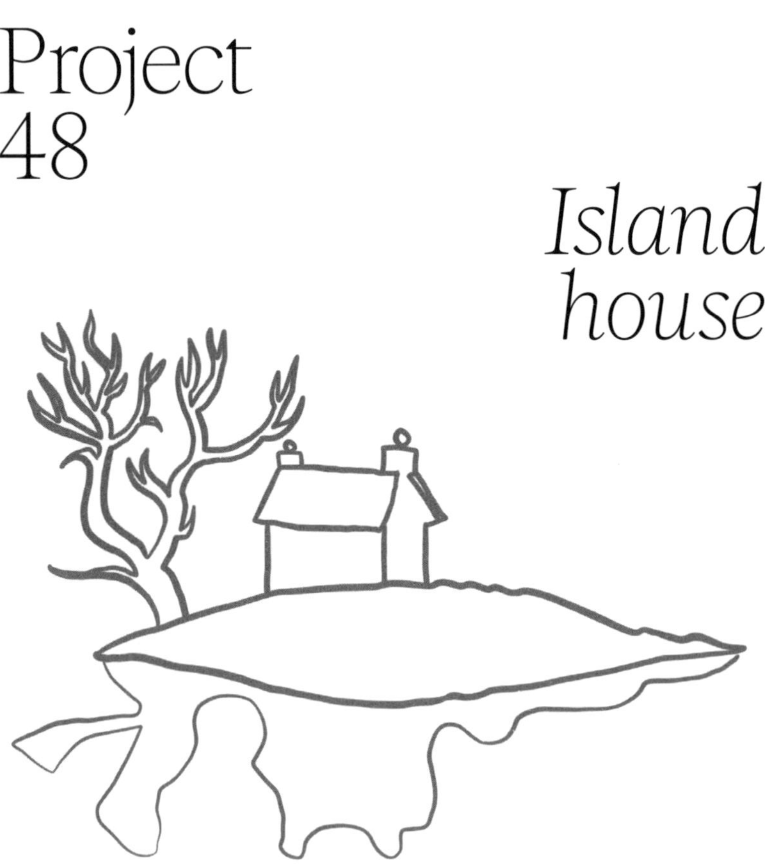

Who could live here? Let your imagination shape this drawing.

STEP 1

Sketch your tiny island with a house, tree and the rough shape of the island's reflection in the water. Alternatively, trace the outline on page 238.

STEP 2

Ink the outline of your island with an uneven line, to give the impression of a rugged and rocky landscape. Contrast it with straight lines on the house and curved lines to ink the shape of the tree and branches.

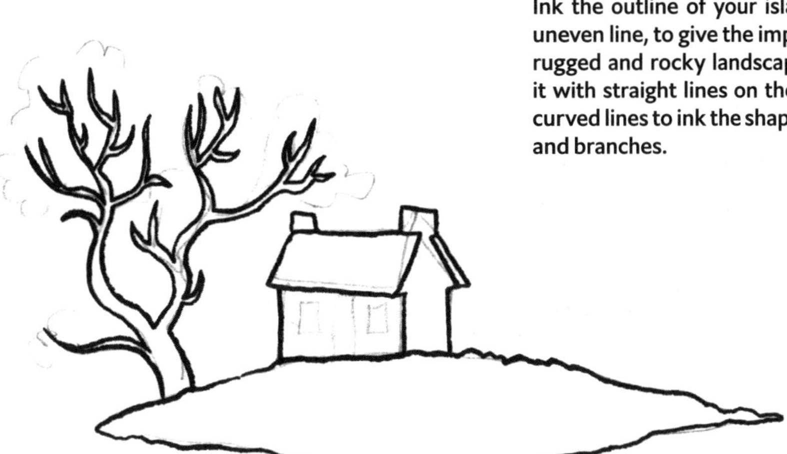

STEP 3

Add tiles to the roof by drawing small squares. Fill in the tree trunk and island with scratchy texture.

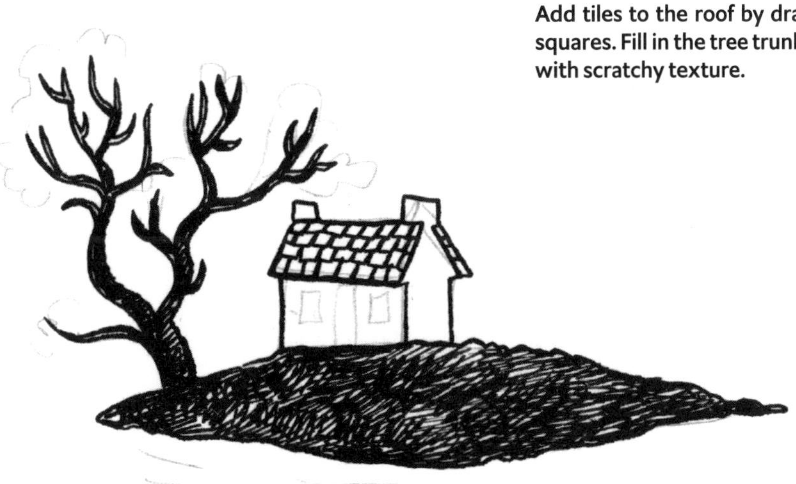

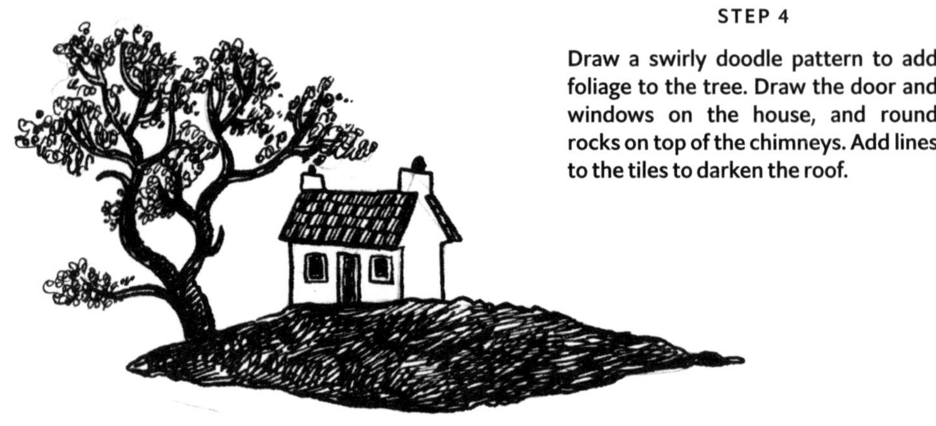

STEP 4

Draw a swirly doodle pattern to add foliage to the tree. Draw the door and windows on the house, and round rocks on top of the chimneys. Add lines to the tiles to darken the roof.

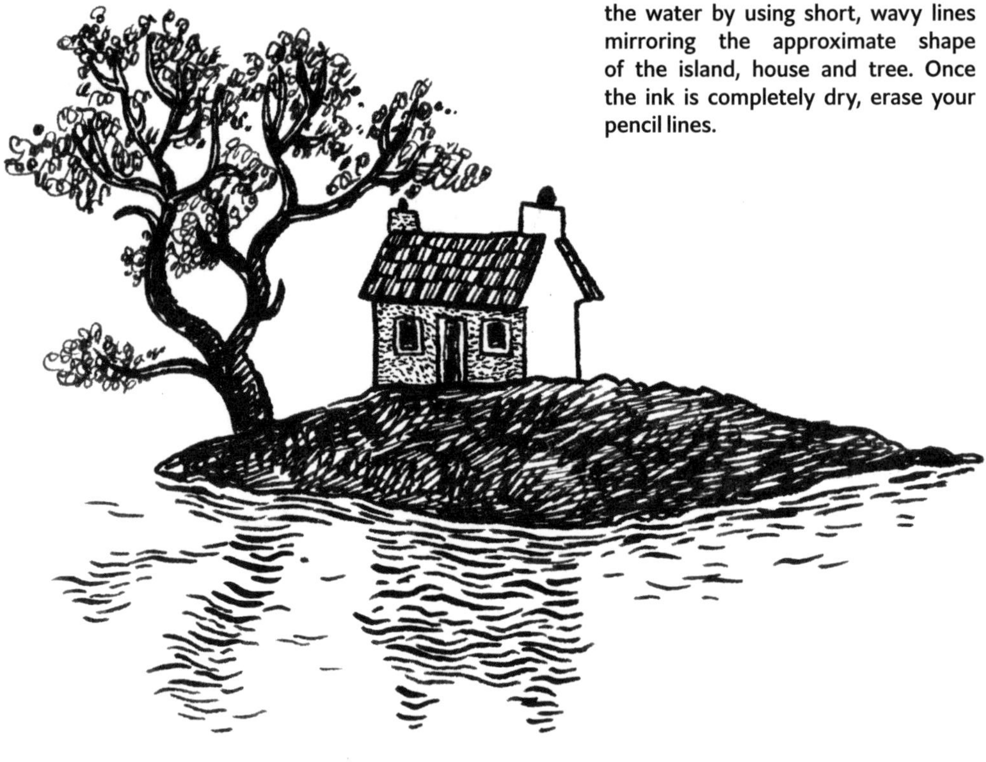

STEP 5

Add dots to one of the walls of the house, establishing the direction of the light. Add the shaded reflection in the water by using short, wavy lines mirroring the approximate shape of the island, house and tree. Once the ink is completely dry, erase your pencil lines.

Project 49

Ocean landscape

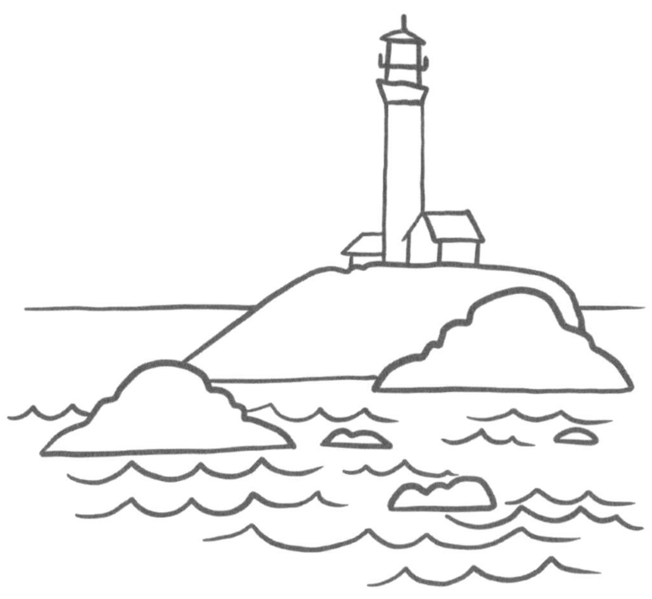

Use the techniques you've been practising to bring this dramatic lighthouse landscape to life.

STEP 1

Sketch your ocean landscape, or trace the outline on page 239. I've gone for a collection of small islands, as well as a lighthouse to add visual interest.

STEP 2

Ink the outline of your lighthouse, islands and horizon line. Take care to keep the bottom edges and horizon straight.

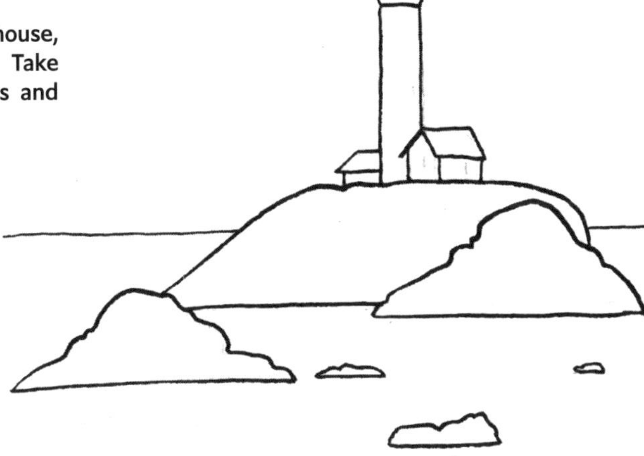

STEP 3

Fill in the islands with scratchy texture, fill in the roofs either in solid black or with the same scratchy texture, and use small lines to add detail to the lighthouse.

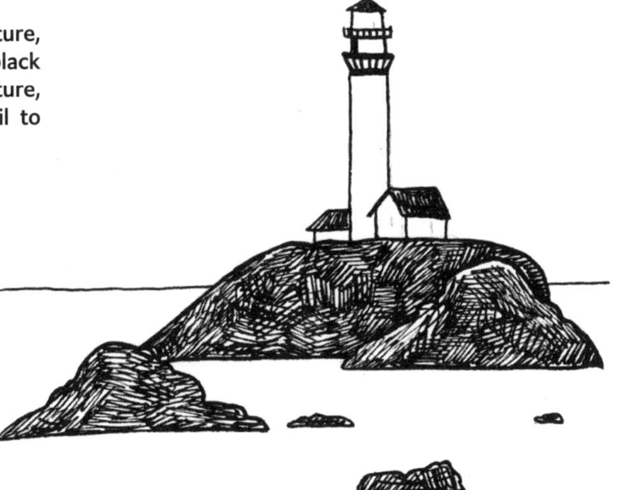

STEP 4

Add doors and windows to the buildings. Crosshatch the lowest areas of the rocks to darken them. Place dots to outline the shape of your waves, taller in the foreground, flatter closer to the horizon.

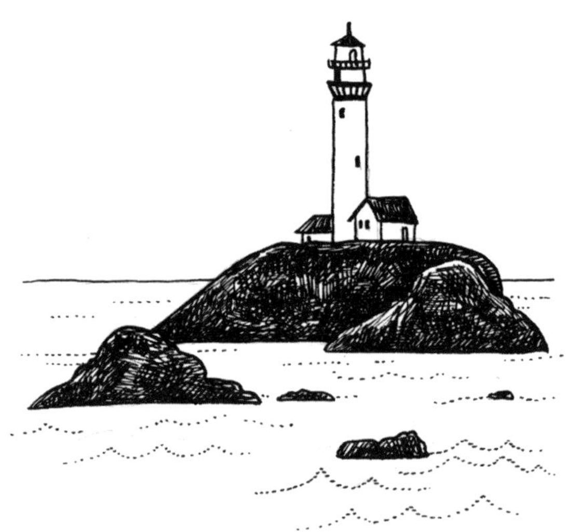

STEP 5

Use pointillism to shade the side of the lighthouse and the buildings next to it. When shading the waves, make the area behind your dotted guide the darkest, and add a little detail to the front afterwards. Once the ink is completely dry, erase your pencil lines.

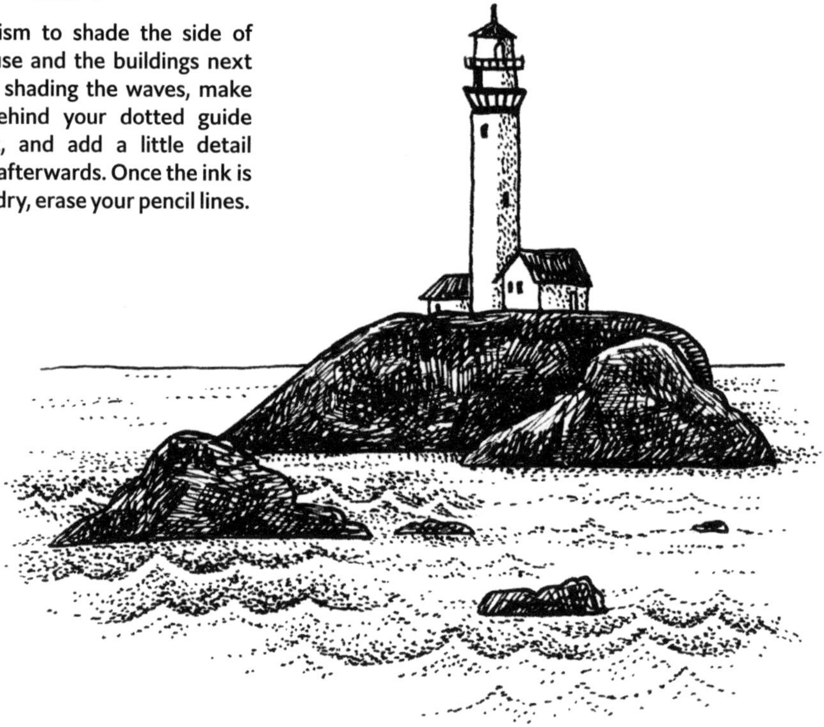

Project 50

Mountain landscape

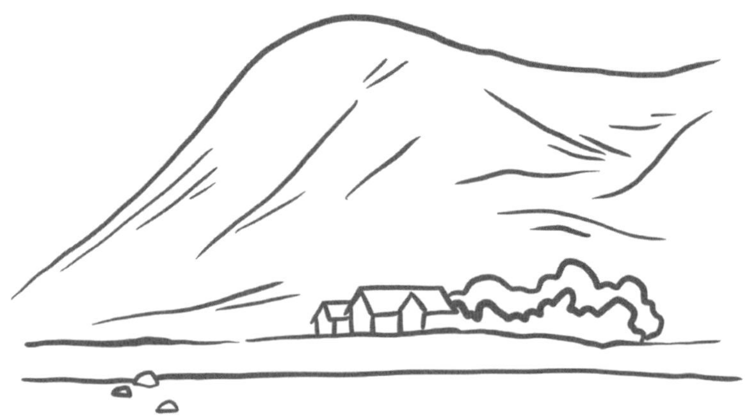

I avoided drawing landscapes for the longest time, thinking they were too complicated, or too big. However, a landscape drawing doesn't have to be complicated, and is made up of exactly the same elements as any other drawing.

STEP 1

Sketch your landscape scene. I've added a small house and a cluster of trees to give the impression of scale to the mountain. Alternatively, trace the outline on page 239.

STEP 2

Use your sketch as a guide to ink the
outlines of your landscape, and ink
the lines on the mountain to give it
some shape.

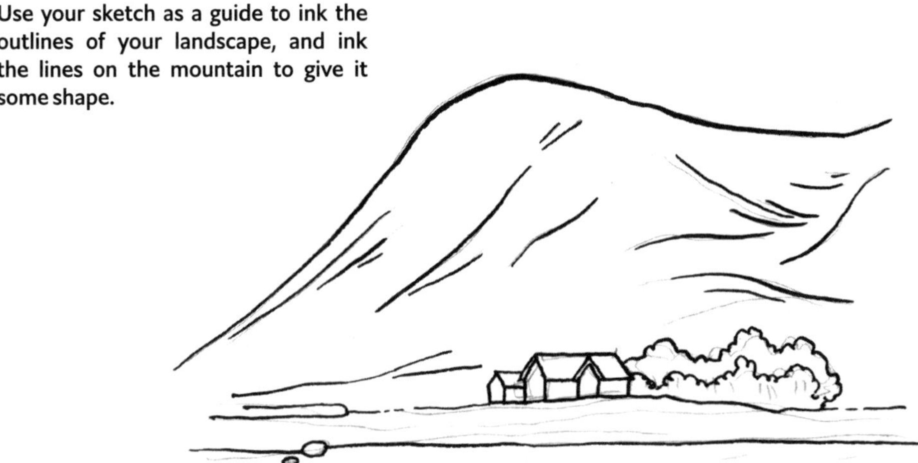

STEP 3

Add some more rocks to the water,
round on top and flat underneath. Use
short lines to shade the shoreline and
the undulations of the mountain.

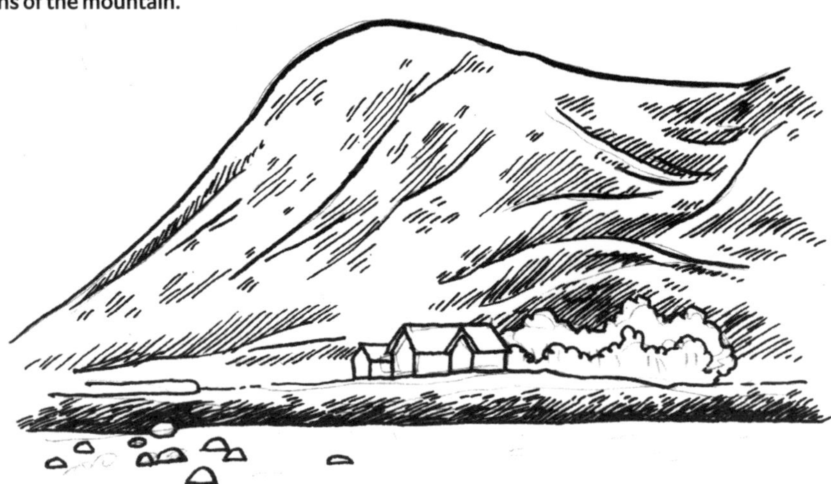

STEP 4

Fill in the roofs of the buildings and add windows and doors. Use scratchy texture to colour in the trees, but leave a highlight along the top edge to differentiate them from the background. Fill in the rocks in the lake, and use small lines to bring out the darkest areas of the mountain.

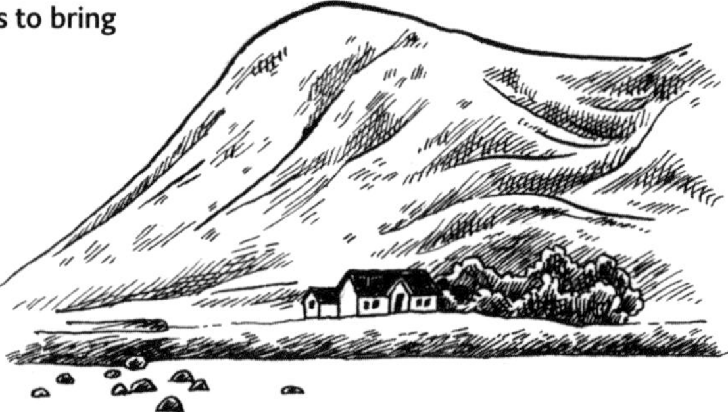

STEP 5

Add horizontal, short lines to the water, particularly underneath the rocks and along the waterline for shadow. Use dots to bring texture and detail to the mountain and the ground in front of the house. Once the ink is completely dry, erase your pencil lines.

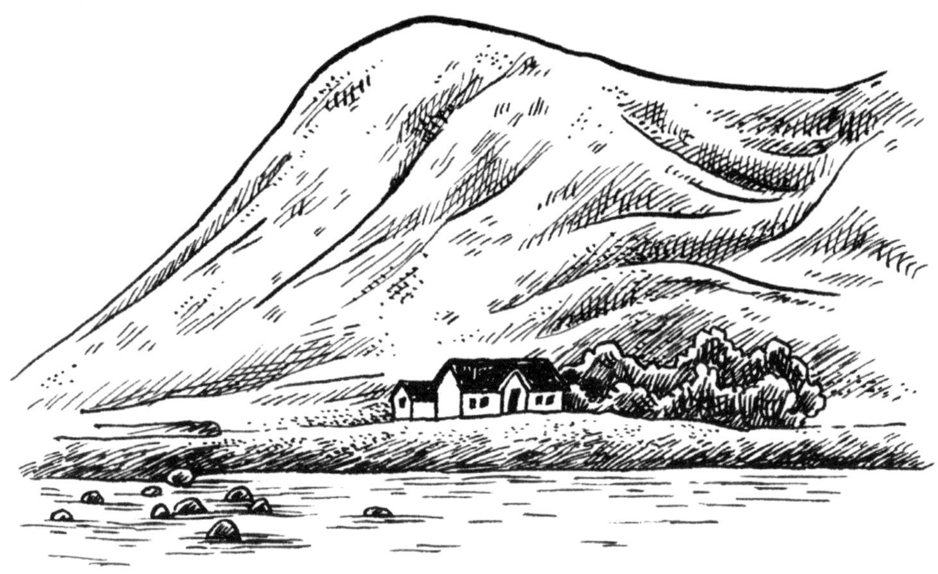

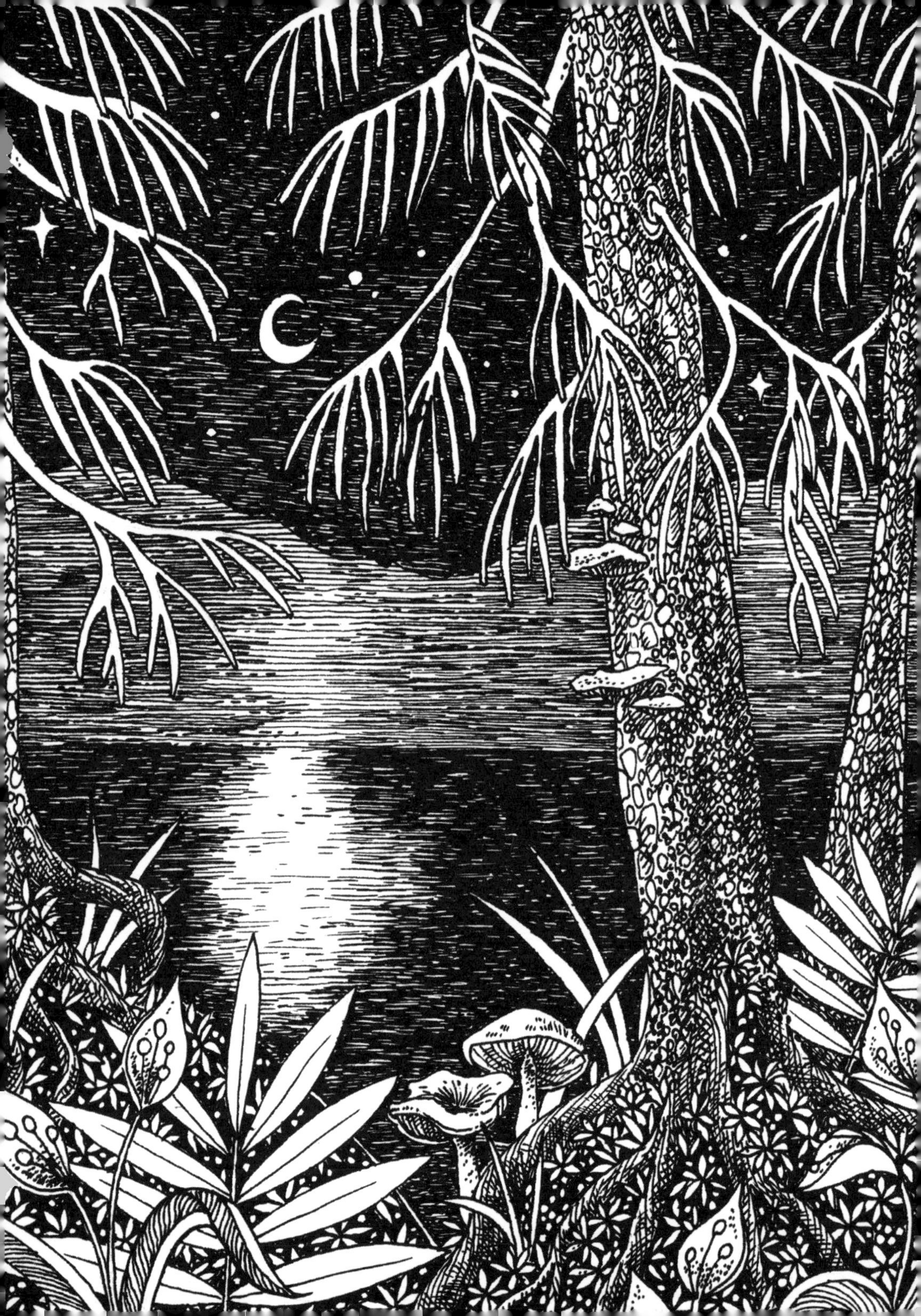

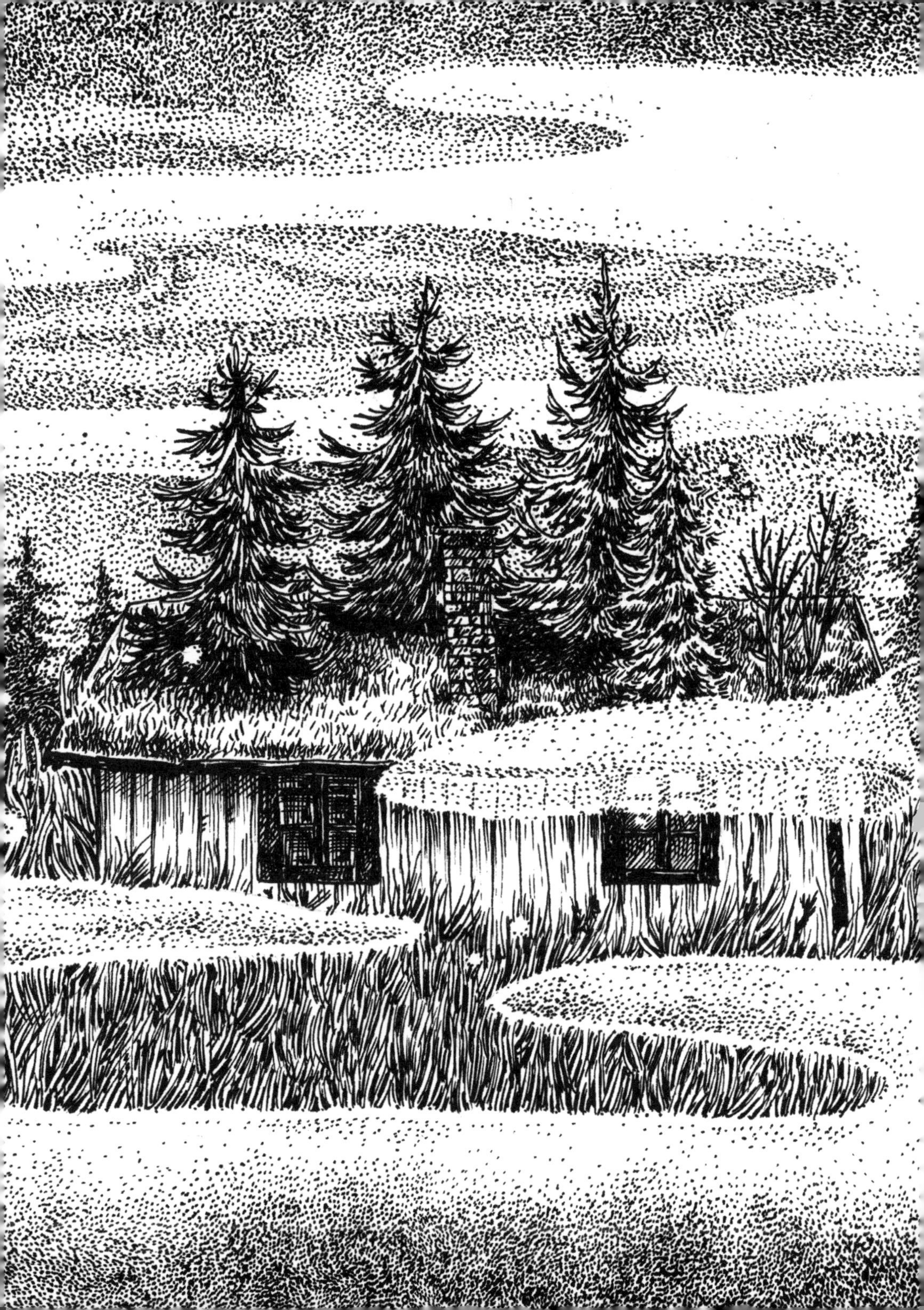

01.

02.

03.

04.

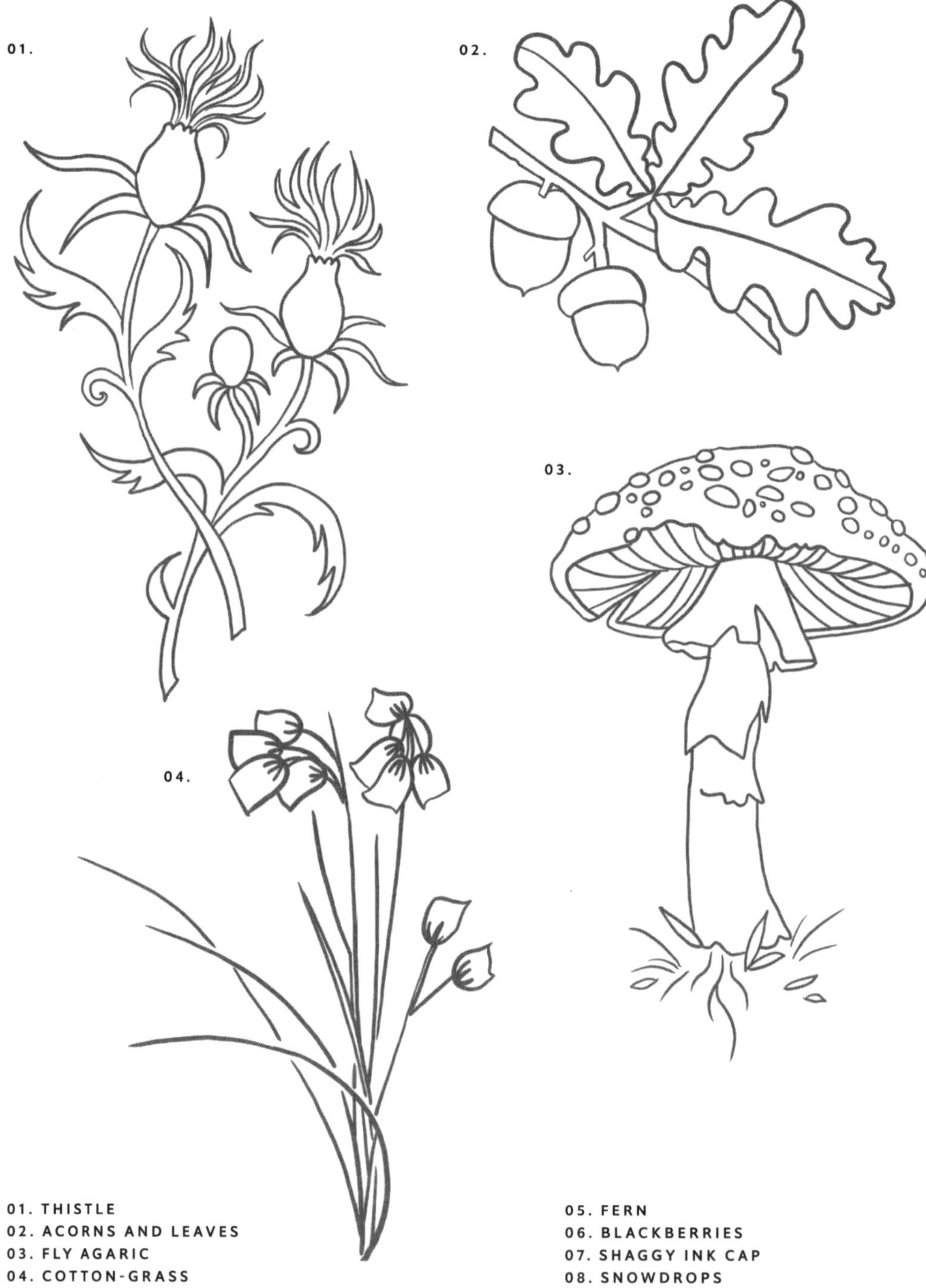

01. THISTLE
02. ACORNS AND LEAVES
03. FLY AGARIC
04. COTTON-GRASS

05. FERN
06. BLACKBERRIES
07. SHAGGY INK CAP
08. SNOWDROPS

05.

06.

07.

08.

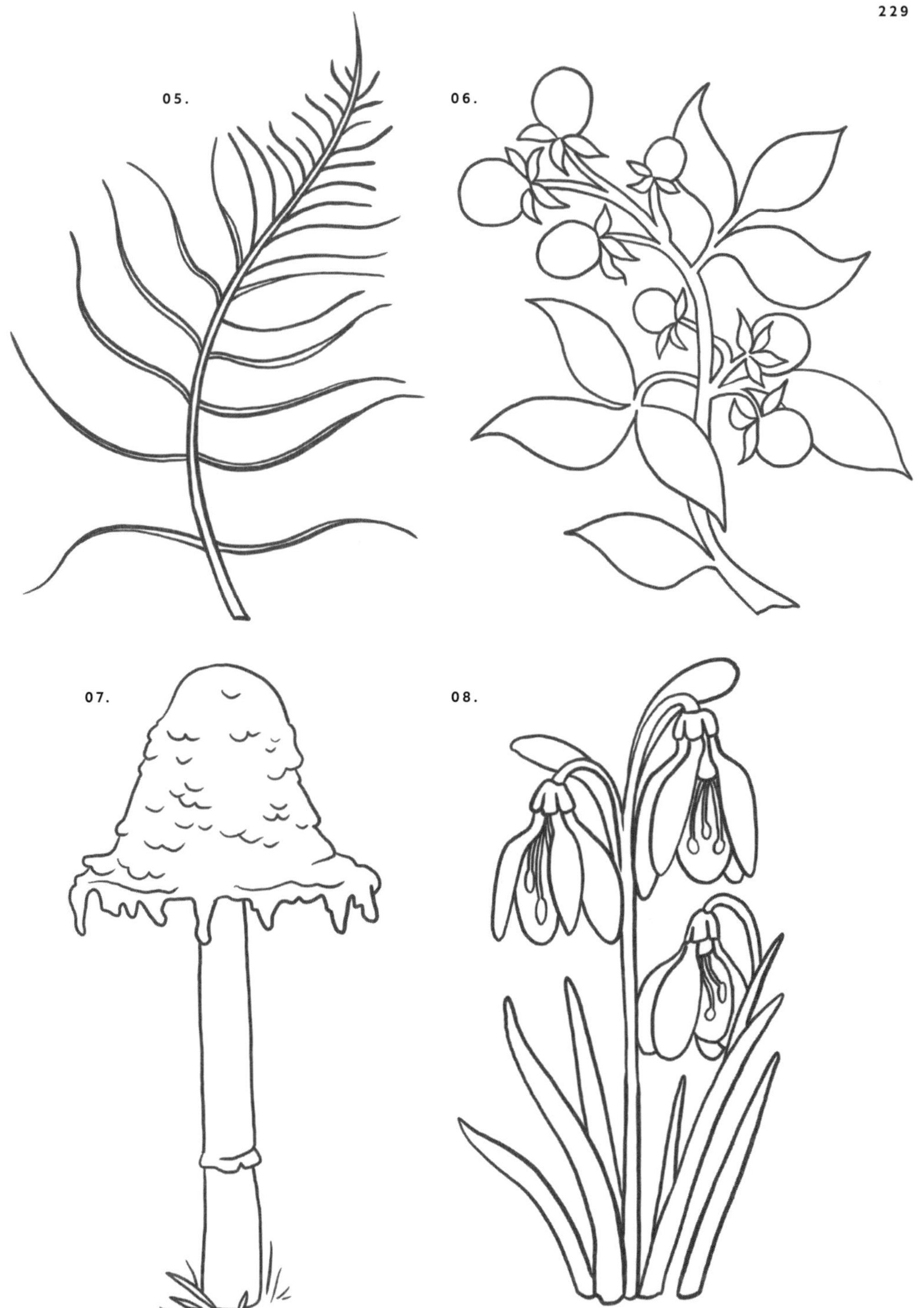

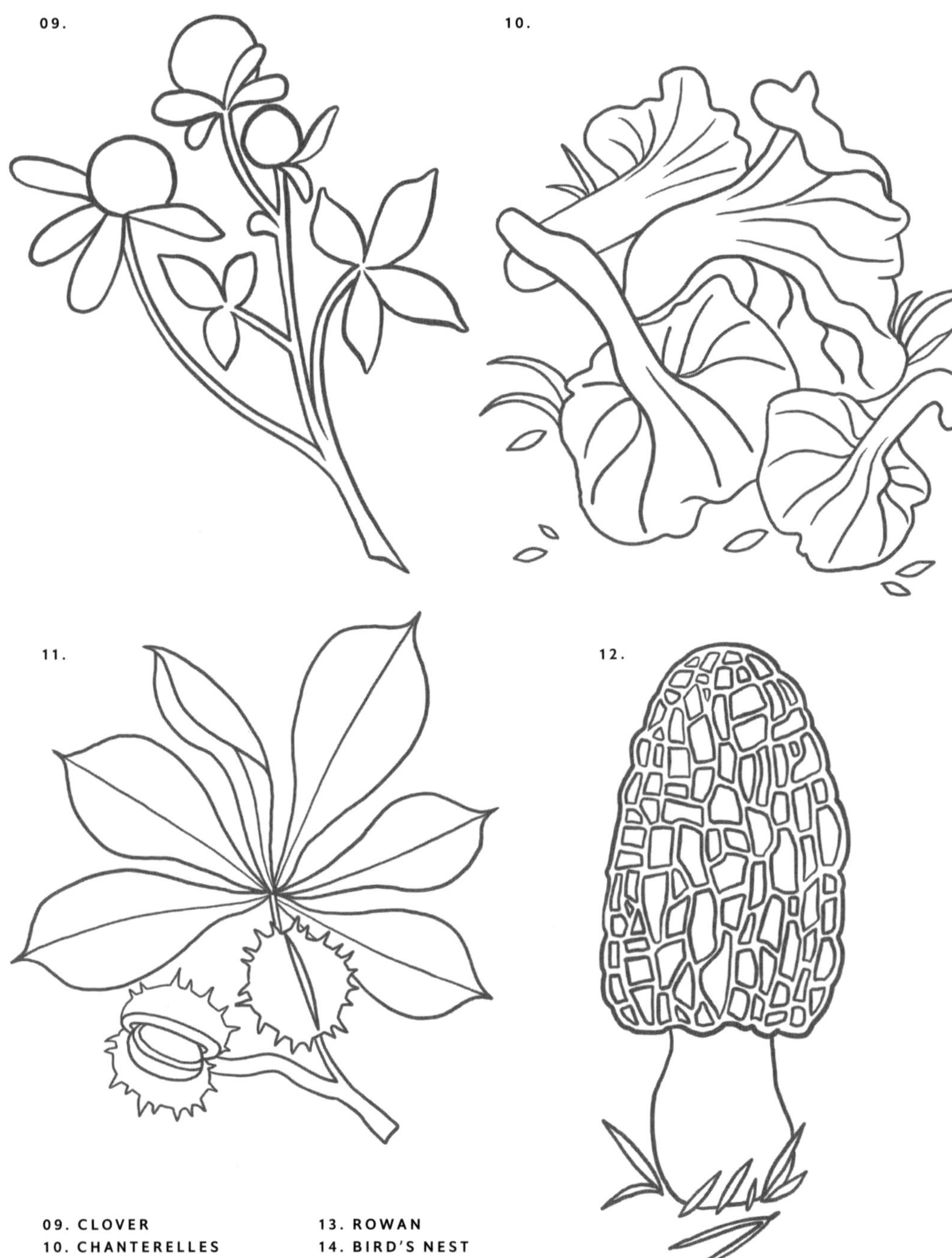

09. CLOVER
10. CHANTERELLES
11. HORSE CHESTNUT
12. MOREL

13. ROWAN
14. BIRD'S NEST
15. FEATHER
16. MUSHROOM BASKET

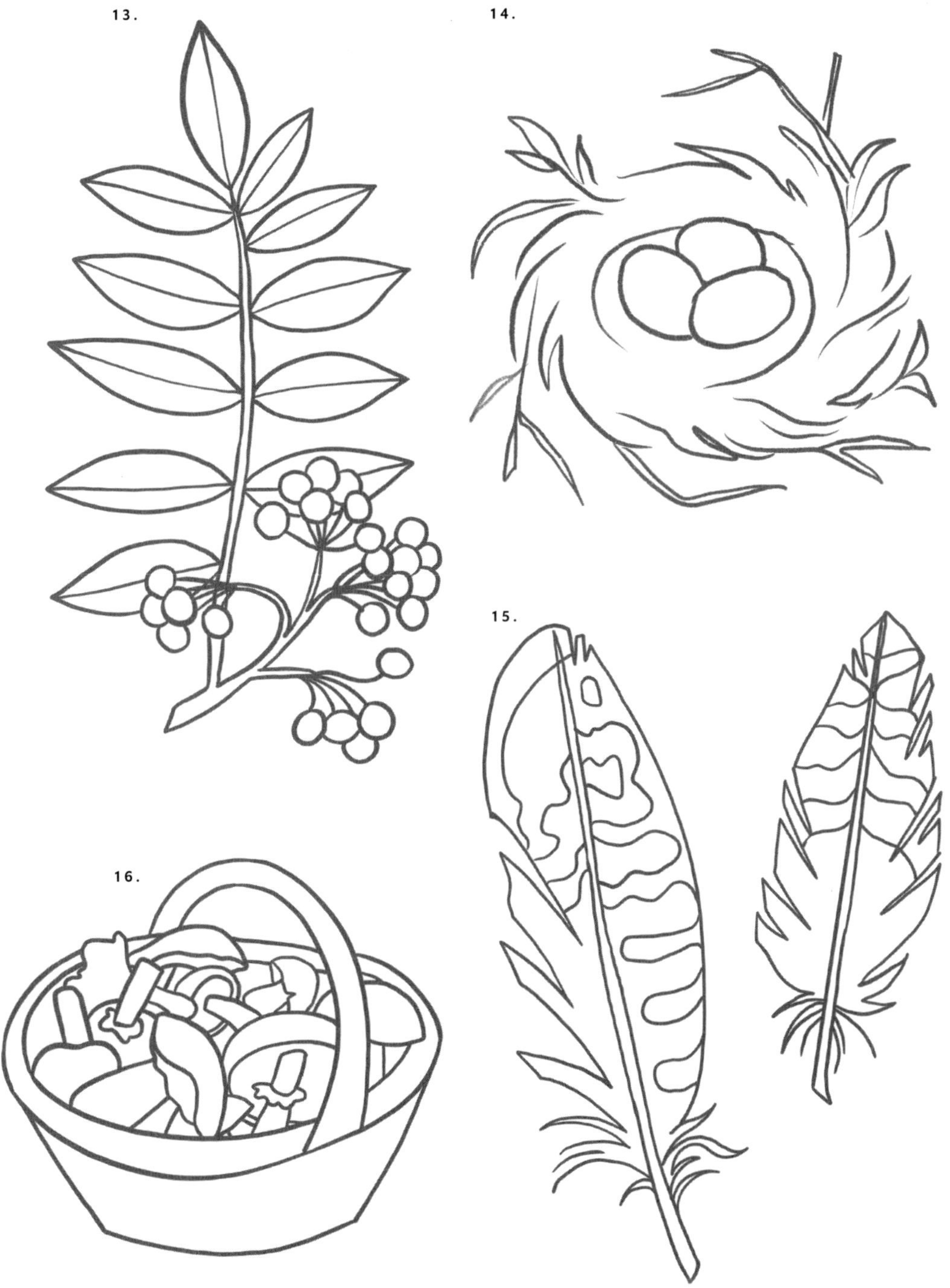
13.
14.
15.
16.

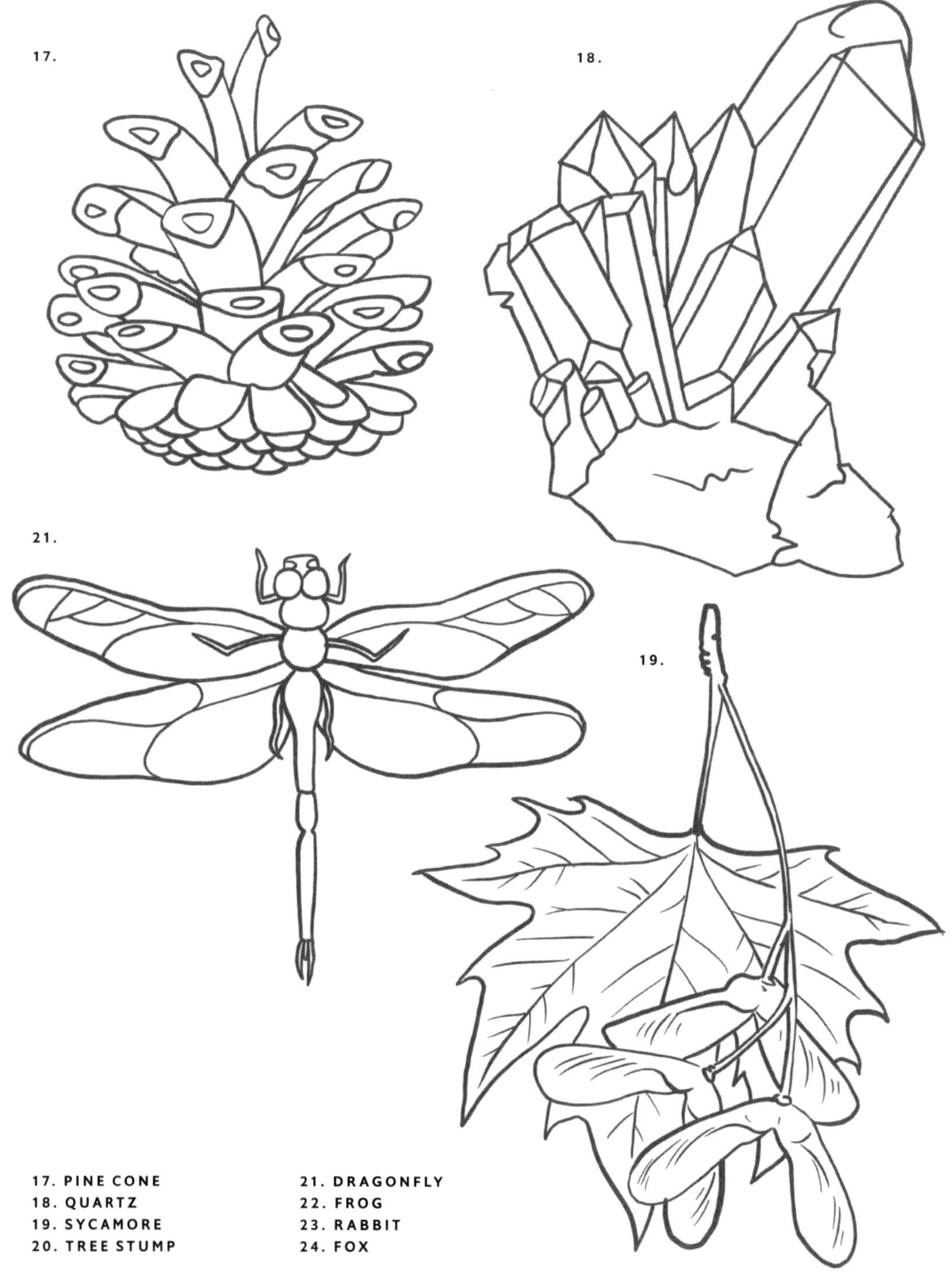

17. PINE CONE
18. QUARTZ
19. SYCAMORE
20. TREE STUMP

21. DRAGONFLY
22. FROG
23. RABBIT
24. FOX

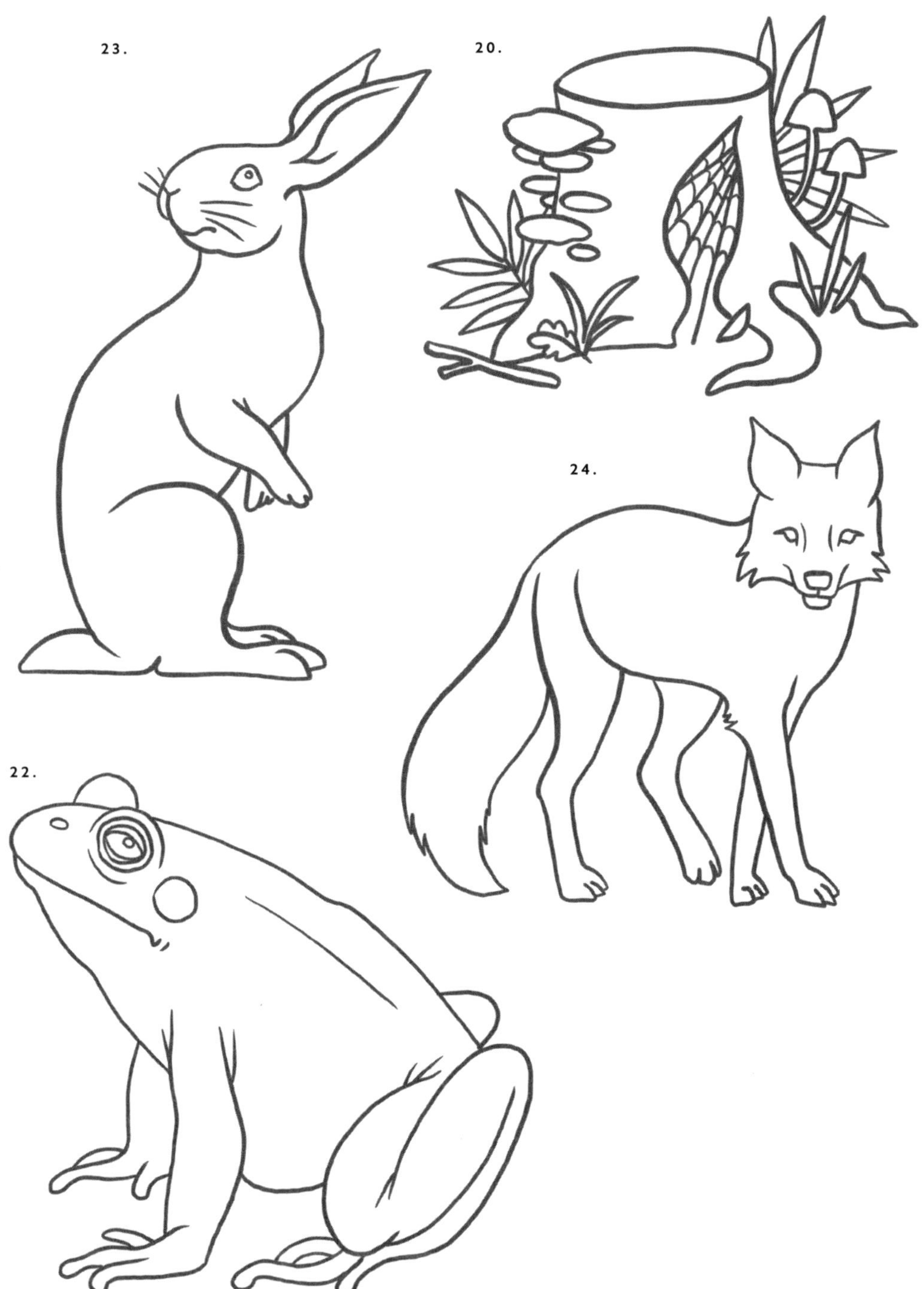
23.
20.
24.
22.

234

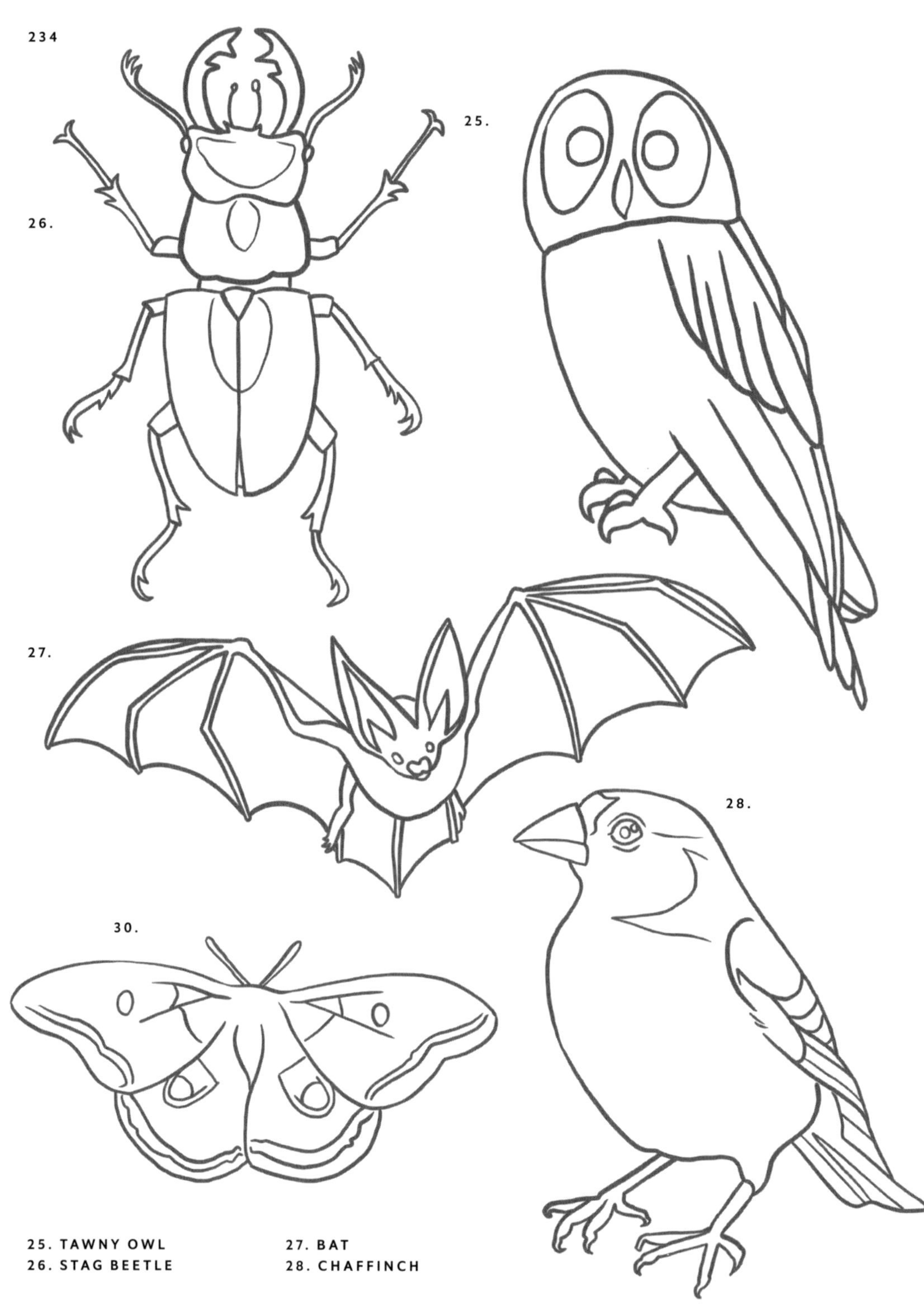

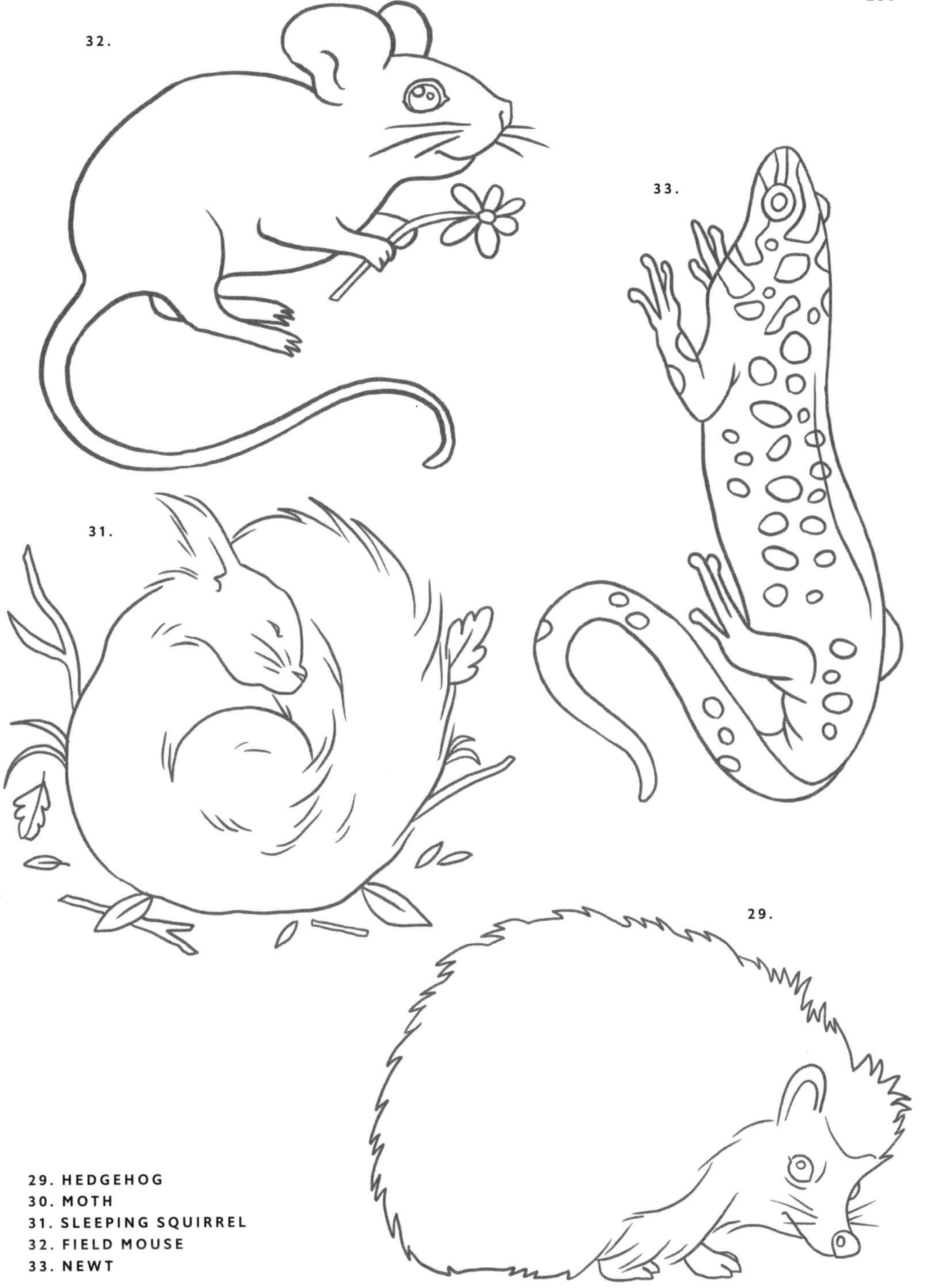

32.
33.
31.
29.
29. HEDGEHOG
30. MOTH
31. SLEEPING SQUIRREL
32. FIELD MOUSE
33. NEWT

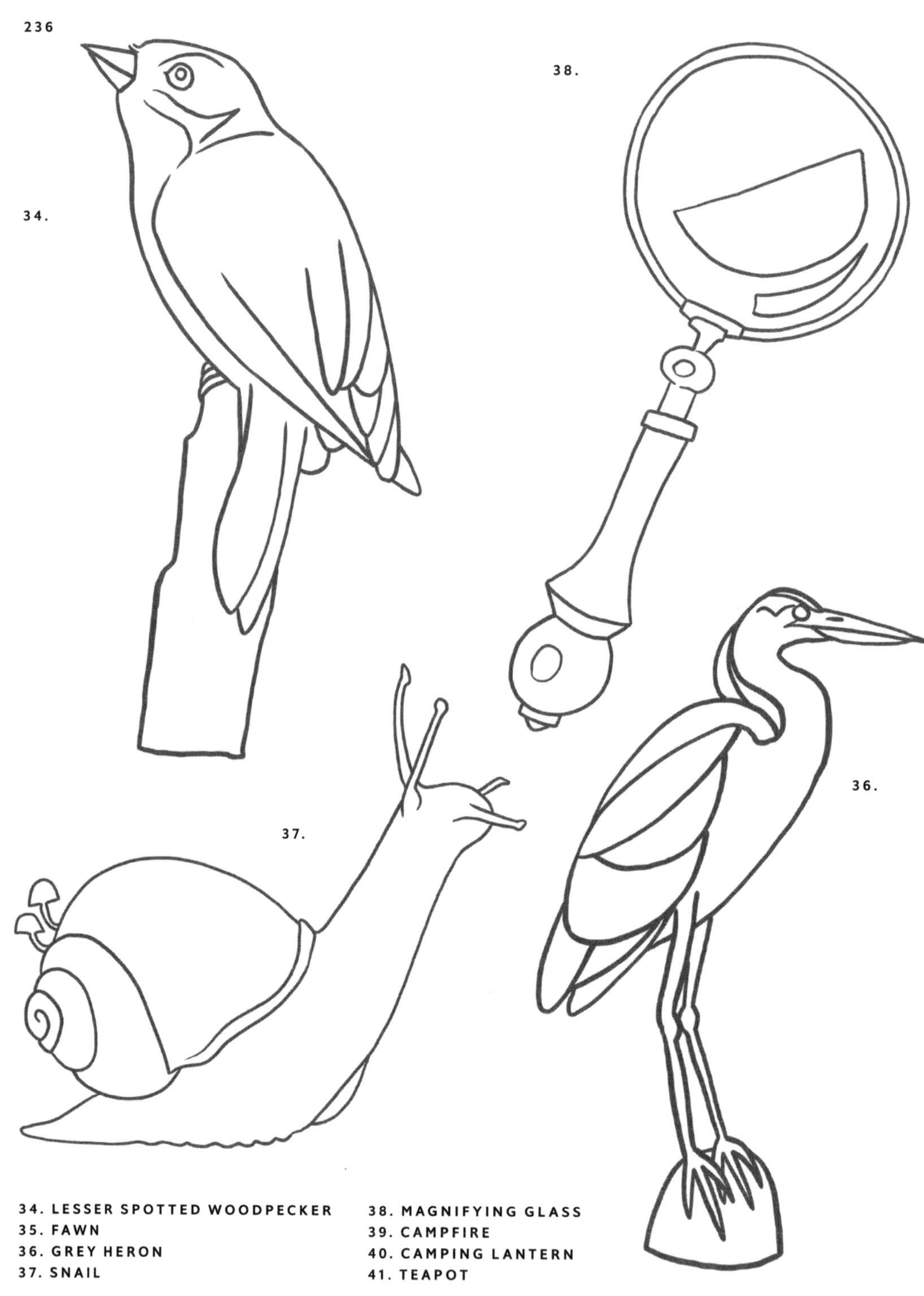

34. LESSER SPOTTED WOODPECKER
35. FAWN
36. GREY HERON
37. SNAIL

38. MAGNIFYING GLASS
39. CAMPFIRE
40. CAMPING LANTERN
41. TEAPOT

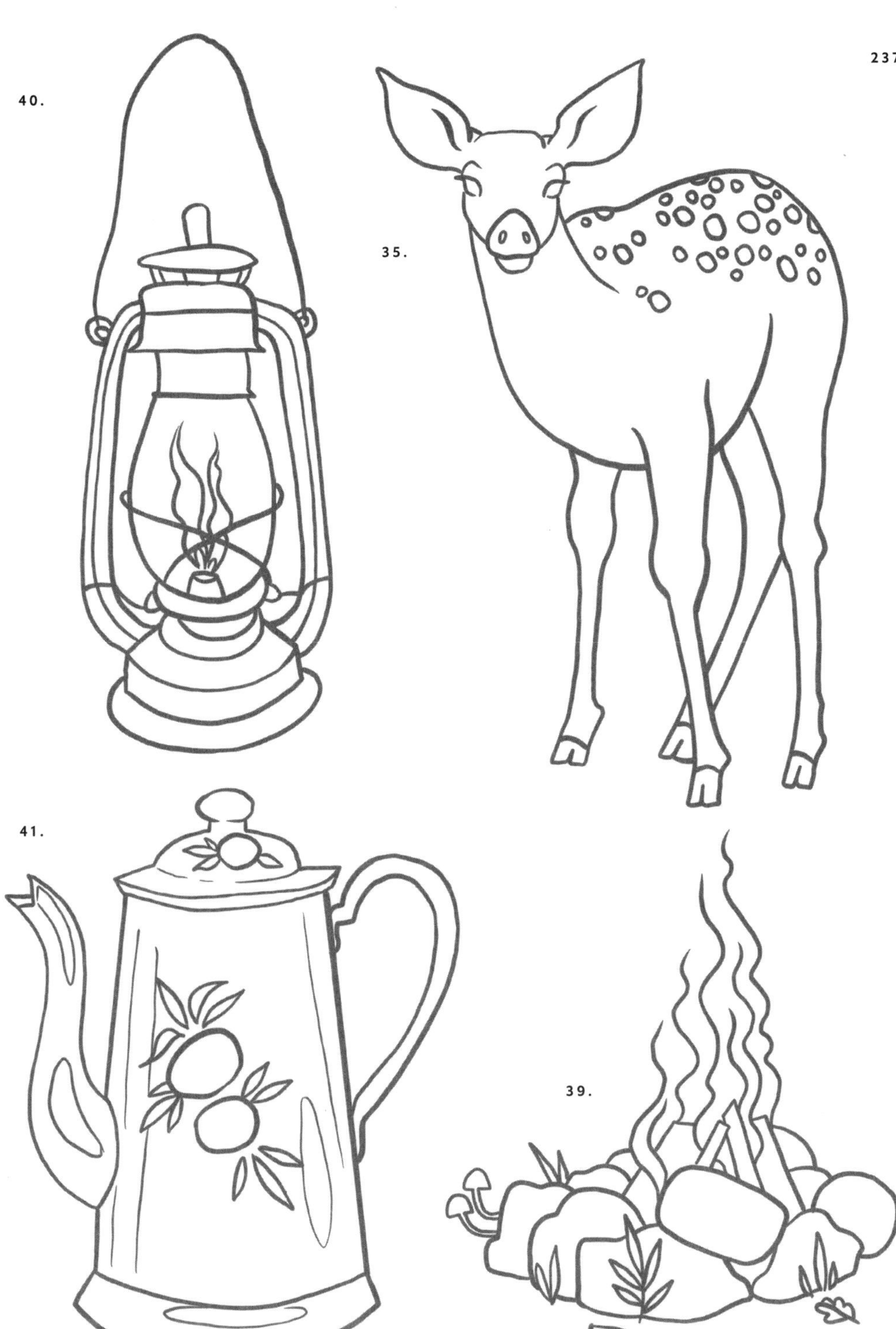
40.
35.
41.
39.

42.

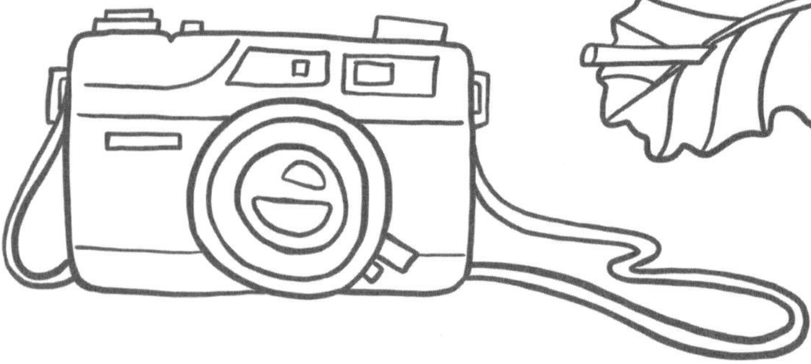

44.

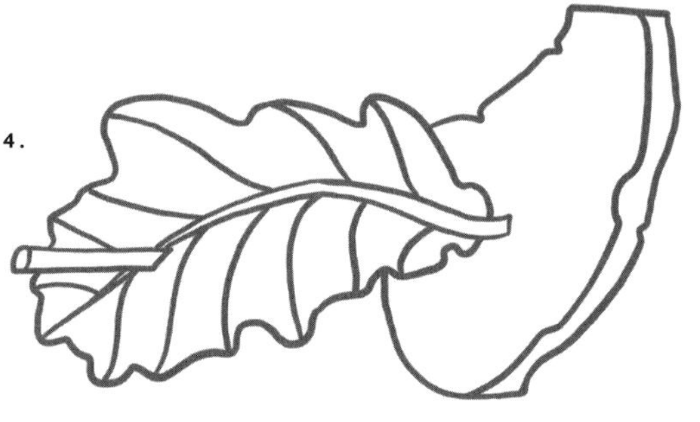

45.

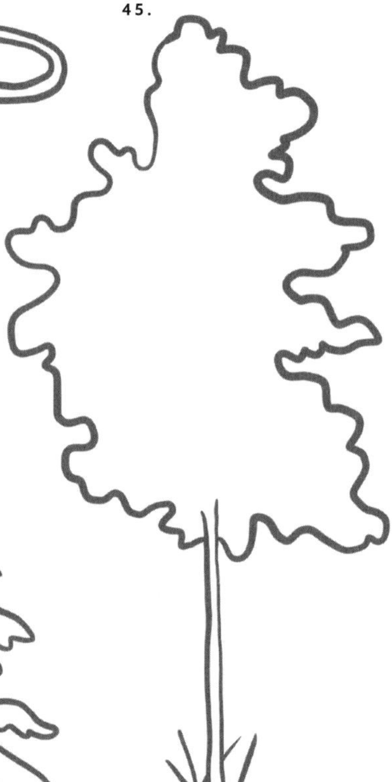

48.

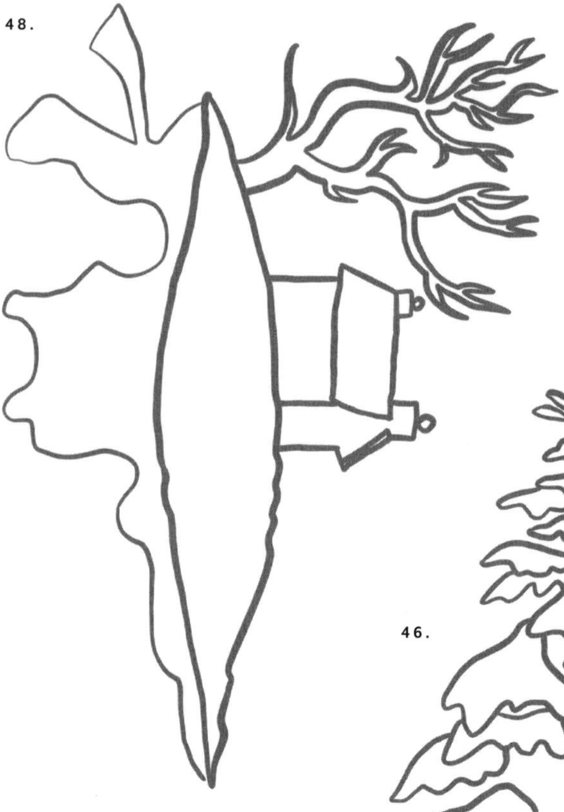

46.

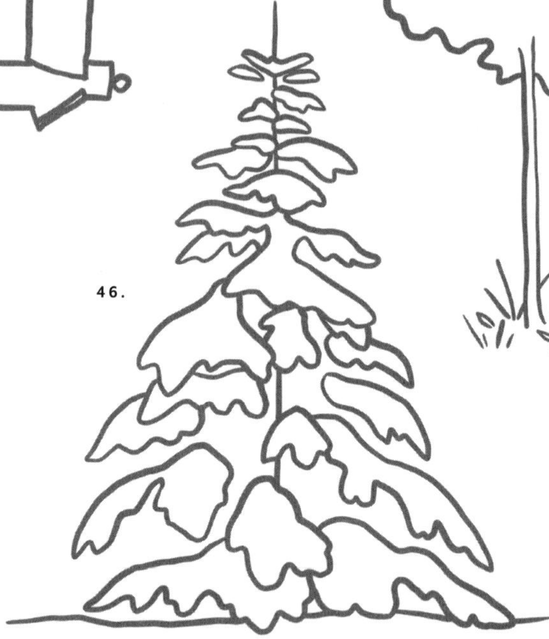

42. CAMERA
43. VASE OF WILDFLOWERS
44. TREE BARK BOAT
45. SUMMER BIRCH

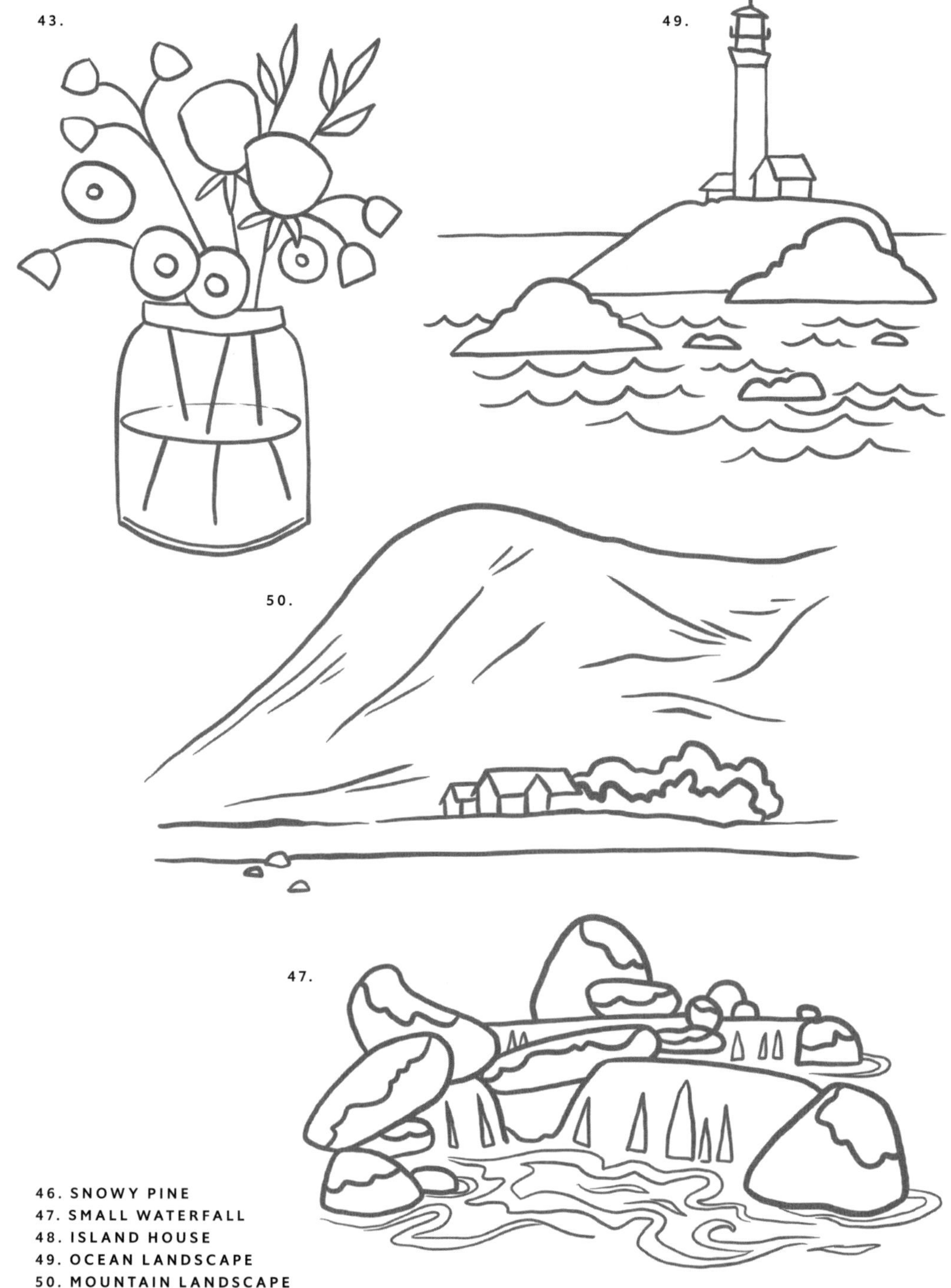

43.

49.

50.

47.

46. SNOWY PINE
47. SMALL WATERFALL
48. ISLAND HOUSE
49. OCEAN LANDSCAPE
50. MOUNTAIN LANDSCAPE